CHASING SHADOWS

Confronting Juvenile Violence in America

Gordon A. Crews, Ph.D.

Jacksonville State University
Jacksonville, Alabama

Reid H. Montgomery, Jr., Ph.D.

University of South Carolina
Columbia, South Carolina

Upper Saddle River, New Jersey 07458

Library of Congress Cataloging-in-Publication Data

Crews, Gordon A.
    Chasing shadows : confronting juvenile violence in America / Gordon A. Crews, Reid
  H. Montgomery, Jr.
       p. cm.
    Includes bibliographical references and index.
    ISBN 0-13-084784-4
     1. Juvenile delinquency--United States. 2. Violence in children--United States. 3.
  Juvenile delinquency--Prevention--United States. I. Montgomery, Reid H. II. Title.

HV9104.C733 2000
364.36'0973--dc21   00-041651

Senior Acquisitions Editor: Kim Davies
Associate Editor: Marion Gottlieb
Production Editor: Naomi Sysak
Production Liaison: Adele M. Kupchik
Director of Manufacturing and Production: Bruce Johnson
Managing Editor: Mary Carnis
Manufacturing Buyer: Ed O'Dougherty
Art Director: Marianne Frasco
Senior Design Coordinator: Miguel Ortiz
Marketing Manager: Chris Ruel
Marketing Assistant: Joe Toohey
Editorial Assistant: Lisa Schwartz
Cover Designer: Wanta España
Cover Photograph: Gordon A. Crews
Composition and Interior Design: Naomi Sysak
Printer/Binder: R.R. Donnelley, Harrisonburg, VA
Cover Printer: Phoenix

Prentice-Hall International (UK) Limited, London
Prentice-Hall of Australia Pty. Limited, Sydney
Prentice-Hall Canada Inc., Toronto
Prentice-Hall Hispanoamericana, S.A., Mexico
Prentice-Hall of India Private Limited, New Delhi
Prentice-Hall of Japan, Inc., Tokyo
Prentice-Hall Singapore Pte. Ltd.
Editora Prentice-Hall do Brasil, Ltda., Rio de Janeiro

10 9 8 7 6 5 4 3 2 1

ISBN: 0-13-084784-4

CONTENTS

3

From Gum Chewing to Gun Toting: School Violence   45

4

From Trick or Treat to Sacrifice or Suicide: Occult and Satanic Practices   73

5

From Lack of Discipline to Lack of Conscience: Theories of Juvenile Violence

6

From Family, Church, and School to Police, Courts, and Corrections: Possible Solutions

7

Dusk Before the Dawn or Thunder before the Storm? A Look at the Future

VOICES FROM THE PAST...

These children that come at you with knives, they are your children, you taught them. I didn't teach them….I am whatever you make me, but what you want is a fiend; you want a sadistic fiend, because that is what you are.

Charles Manson, at his trial in 1970

Society has always, traditionally, tried to find scapegoats for its problems. Well, here I am.

Marilyn Manson, October 1996

No one, especially children, just becomes a murderer. Something had to happen to push them to that point.

Luke Woodham, 16, Pearl Mississippi High School shooter,
during an interview on why the shooting had occurred, 1997

DEDICATION

To my family: my wife, Pamela Player Crews; my son, Garrison Allen Crews; and my daughter, Samantha Leigh Crews

G. A. C.

To my parents: Dr. and Mrs. Reid H. Montgomery, Sr., who always encouraged me to strive for the best in my work and life.

R. H. M., Jr.

FOREWORD

As the year 2000 marked the beginning of a new millennium, juvenile violence
was (and is) the criminal justice issue foremost in the minds of the American
people—with good reason. In recent years the nation has been saturated with
news accounts describing in graphic detail unimaginable acts of juvenile violence
occurring in our schools and our communities. The violent acts and the media
coverage have focused the nation's attention on this critical issue, triggering various
national, state, and local responses. Why is this violence happening? Do these
violent behaviors have a pattern? Is the growing attention and widespread concern
with juvenile violence deserved? What can we do to prevent juvenile violence?
These are complex questions for which the nation continues to seek answers.

The horrific incidents that the media have brought into our homes to witness
almost instantaneously and seemingly firsthand include the following.

- In October 1997, 17-year-old Luke Woodham was arrested for killing two
  classmates and wounding seven others following a shooting spree at Pearl
  High School in Hattiesburg, Mississippi. Earlier that day Woodham had
  brutally beaten and stabbed his mother to death.

- In March 1998, 13-year-old Mitchell Johnson and 11-year-old Andrew
  Golden were arrested following a sniper attack into the schoolyard of
  Westside Middle School in Jonesboro, Arkansas, killing four young girls
  and a teacher.

- In May 1998, Kipland Kinkle, a 15-year-old student at Thurston High
  School in Springfield, Oregon, was arrested following the killing of his parents
  and the shooting deaths of two of his classmates. One of them, Jake Ryder,
  was shot in his chest and hand as he and three students subdued Kinkle.

- In January 1999, a Carrolton, Georgia student was killed and her boyfriend
  was wounded in a shooting with a .22 caliber pistol at Central High
  School. The shootings seem to have been an attempted murder-suicide or
  double suicide.

- In April 1999, the nation struggled to understand why Eric Harris, age 18, and Dylan Klebold, age 17, gunned down 12 students and a teacher at Columbine High School in Littleton, Colorado, and then killed themselves. The two, dressed in black trench coats and wearing masks, had planned their acts well. They made copies of school keys, constructed and planted numerous bombs, and kept a detailed diary.

- That same year, at Heritage High School in Conyers, Georgia, T. J. Solomon shot and wounded six fellow students and was in the process of committing suicide before being stopped by an assistant principal.

These and other tragic incidents of juvenile violence have captured the nation's attention. The reasons that Americans are so concerned with issues of youth violence are easy to understand: The nation's youth and their future remain foremost in the hearts and minds of their parents and families. The question of whether public concerns are justified or exaggerated is somewhat more difficult to answer. The answer requires that we better understand the nature and extent of youth violence. The most difficult issue by far is *what should be done*, as matters of public policy as well as personal and community involvement, to combat and prevent juvenile violence.

Americans have ample reasons to be concerned about juvenile violence. First and foremost, American youths represent the adults and leaders of tomorrow. As such they are our most important legacy and the keys to our future. Today's youth comprise the generation that will be responsible for the future needs of the nation: national defense, economic prosperity and social welfare, democratic principles, freedoms, and liberties, and overall quality of life. The desire to combat and prevent violence among youth also stems from a host of personal, religious, and humanitarian reasons.

Students and scholars of public opinion differ on the question of whether the current level of attention being given to juvenile violence is deserved. Is the attention too much attention or not enough? Generally, this debate does not represent disagreement regarding the importance of juvenile violence as a public safety priority for the nation and its communities. Instead, the arguments frequently assert that available research and accurate data do not support national perceptions or various government responses. Critics of media coverage and government responses sometimes argue that, although youth violence is indeed an important national, state, and community concern, the public should not panic or embrace quick and simple solutions when the media portray shocking incidents of juvenile violence.

When issues of perceived importance and government responsibility, such as public safety, gain national attention through media coverage of sensational incidents, the demand for government action follows. In recent years, the widely reported incidents of school and juvenile violence have sparked an array of responses at national, state and local levels. In response, most state legislatures, governors, and attorneys general have launched special initiatives to combat juvenile violence. In addition, nongovernmental organizations—churches, businesses, and civic associations—have taken actions to combat and prevent youth violence. Increasingly, the initiatives of nongovernmental groups and individuals are having positive impacts and offering new opportunities that are helping families and communities to respond effectively to violent youth behaviors.

At the national level, efforts aimed at combating and preventing juvenile violence include controversial proposals by President Bill Clinton, his administration, and the U.S. Congress. These proposals often originate with, or have support from, various national organizations and interest groups.

As the new millennium approached during the 106th Congress, both the Senate and the House held numerous hearings on topics of juvenile violence. Participants in these hearings included scholars and authorities on juvenile violence, law-enforcement officials with front-line experience, and families and friends who had experienced tragedies firsthand. Other participants and witnesses included students, teachers, school administrators, counselors, and psychologists. In addition, the President, Vice President, and administration officials visited the sites of school violence and spoke with community officials. Both the Congress and the President recommended initiatives to respond to juvenile and school violence. In his final State of the Union address, President Clinton recognized an invited parent of a student killed at Columbine High School as an act of symbolic concern while unveiling his latest gun control proposal.

While the responses to juvenile and school violence that the Congress and the President (who represent opposing political parties) have offered have some elements in common, they also have stark differences that make national juvenile justice policies and initiatives problematic. The most contentious and visible issue separating the major political parties and their candidates is that of gun control. This is where symbolism and opinions often receive greater attention and have more influence than accurate data or rigorous research. For example, the beneficial results of targeted programs to apprehend and prosecute gun-law violators with criminal records for violent crimes have been documented in evaluations of programs such as Project Exile, first implemented in Richmond, Virginia. Advocates favoring more stringent gun-control laws were slow to accept Project Exile because it emphasized enforcement of existing gun laws. More recently, however, other jurisdictions across the nation have adopted this approach, even mustering support from interest groups with opposing gun control positions.

Although Clinton administration officials were slow to endorse the Project Exile approach to gun control, the President's final State of the Union Address recommended funding for more federal resources to support initiatives such as this. President Clinton received more attention, however, for his proposed new restrictions on gun purchases. President Clinton's Secretary for Housing and Urban Development added to the gun-control controversy by attempting to involve his agency in litigation against gun manufacturers.

In all likelihood, issues of the government's responses to juvenile violence, albeit through surrogate issues such as gun control, will remain a topic in

Presidential, Congressional, state, and local elections. Accordingly, legislative and programmatic initiatives and reforms will continue at national, state, and local levels. For example, some government officials advocate mandating new technologies to prevent weapon discharges by unauthorized users. Beyond reforming gun laws, government officials have announced other types of programs and initiatives, such as improvements to the U.S. Department of Education's Safe and Drug-Free Schools program to combat school violence. Certainly, a plethora of national, state, and local initiatives will continue to emerge in an attempt to combat and prevent youth violence.

In sum, juvenile violence is a salient and complex topic and policy issue that continues to confront and perplex our nation, states and communities. Consequently, we have continuing obligations to learn as much as possible about this topic and to pursue government and nongovernment initiatives that are effective. Even though elected officials and legislative bodies at all levels will continue to propose new laws and programs to fix perceived deficiencies, meaningful solutions will remain elusive. The limitations of government in shaping human behaviors, especially among youth, are obvious. All who work with youth and all who can influence our youth must learn as much as possible about the nature and dynamics of youth violence. Greater knowledge can empower groups and individuals to make meaningful contributions that will result in real differences. This book contributes to the effort by providing new and valuable insights upon which meaningful approaches to juvenile crime and violence can be developed and applied in communities across the United States.

Dr. Stephen D. Dillingham, *Special Counsel*
U.S. House of Representatives
Subcommittee on Criminal Justice, Drug Policy, and Human Resources
Washington, DC

PREFACE

- *Chasing:* to follow quickly or persistently in order to catch.
- *Shadows:* the dark images made by a body intercepting the existing light rays.

Many colleagues have asked me why I wanted to entitle this book *Chasing Shadows*. Most have no idea what the title is supposed to convey. The answer is simple: I believe that "chasing shadows" is what we do most of the time when we are trying to deal with juvenile delinquency.

This unusual analogy came to me one afternoon while watching my children play at the beach. They were trying to jump on each other's shadow while protecting their own shadow at the same time. One child could be standing right next to the other but, depending on their position in relation to the sun, may not have been able to reach the other's shadow. It was as though they were oblivious to the close proximity to each other, focusing only on what they were seeking—the other's shadow.

I think we often approach the problems of juvenile delinquency and violence in the same manner. This is especially true as we try to understand its causes and manifestations. Often the *shadow* is what we chase, instead of what is blocking the light. Let us take a moment to examine a few of these possible shadows.

Shadows

the Internet	availability of guns
violent or horror movies	Hollywood and the entertainment industry
Marilyn Manson concerts	gangsta' rap music
violent video games	National Rifle Association conventions
hate-group Web pages	availability of alcohol and other drugs

These are all nice fat targets at which we can shoot. But if we sit down and really think about it, is not this sort of like blaming paper for bad poetry? Instead, why do we often miss that which is blocking the light?

Blocking the Light

boredom	dysfunctional families
alienation	lack of proper role-models
pessimism	lack of parental involvement
abandonment	deteriorating neighborhoods and communities
powerlessness	low educational achievement

We must continue to look for strategies to prevent further massacres in schools and to stem the tide of juvenile violence in the United States. This is not to suggest that we are doing nothing at present. But let us take a more realistic approach to the problem. We probably will *never* be able to curtail the availability of guns and drugs, nor can we control the myriad of exposures the average child will have. Maybe, then, we should attack the areas we *can* impact.

With concentrated, practical, community-based efforts, we might be able to have a positive influence in many of these areas. Can we possibly impact *alienation and pessimism* in many youth? Might we work with families and communities to fight *boredom* and the feeling of *powerlessness* in many youth? Can we provide *positive role models* and work in our schools for *educational achievement*?

Are these the types of questions we should focus on, or should we continue to throw darts at a violence-obsessed U.S. culture? Maybe by attacking these root causes of juvenile misconduct, we can shine a little more light on what is really going on.

With this in mind, we have written this text to address many of these "shadows" and to offer helpful information to readers about this pressing problem. We hope that by examining these areas of juvenile violence, the reader will confront many of the misconceptions and stereotypes of the past.

Chapter 1 begins the text with a brief discussion of some of the issues involved in examining juvenile violence. This chapter examines some of the existing information on the extent of juvenile violence and its many characteristics.

Chapter 2 consists of a possibly unconventional approach to the examination of gangs and group juvenile violence. It explores the various ways by which group activities influence juvenile delinquency.

Chapter 3 gives an overview of the myriad of problems involved in school violence. The increasing number of school shootings in the 1990s serves as a backdrop to a discussion of this form of juvenile violence.

Chapter 4 offers an examination of a topic that has not received the proper academic examination it deserves: occult and satanic involvement by youth. This chapter gives a solid review of the many and complex issues related to the connection between this type of involvement and juvenile violence.

Chapter 5 presents a well-rounded review of the many possible causes of juvenile violence. The discussion includes traditional versus contemporary theories of the causes of juvenile violence.

Chapter 6 offers various points of view in suggesting solutions to juvenile violence. The discussion is complemented by numerous examples of efforts that have been shown to work.

Chapter 7 brings the book to a close by offering ideas for future efforts. It does not simply reexamine material presented in the preceding chapters. Instead, it examines various topics that readers need to continue exploring. We hope, in this chapter, as in the entire text, to leave readers with a thirst to pursue for themselves the topics presented in this text.

Gordon A. Crews, Ph.D.
January 1, 2000

ACKNOWLEDGMENTS

The authors would like to acknowledge each of the following:

Dr. Steven Dillingham and Mr. Jeffrey Tipton for their priceless contributions to this work.

Dr. David Kleckley, Dr. Bob Heckel, Dr. Steve Katsikas, Mr. Burt Hayner, Dr. Don Thomas, Dr. Bob Evans, Dr. Debbi Robinson, and Dr. Sid Hopkins, for allowing us the opportunity to gain from their vast knowledge in the area of juvenile violence.

Dr. Bill Meehan, Dr. W. David Watts, and Dr. J. Earl Wade of Jacksonville State University for their trust and confidence.

Dr. Bob Evans, Dr. Debbi Robinson, and the Sociology, Anthropology, and Criminal Justice Department at Valdosta State University, for their support, encouragement, and assistance.

Ms. Kim Davies, Mr. Neil Marquardt, and Ms. Carol Hill, at Prentice Hall, without whom this work would not have been possible.

We would also like to extend our thanks and appreciation to the following reviewers for their many helpful critiques of the manuscript: Dorothy L. Berger-Fuller, Lord Fairfax Community College, Middletown, VA; Melton E. Beane, Tidewater Community College, Virginia Beach, VA; and Roger J. R. Levesque, Indiana University.

Ms. Lane Harper for her support and encouragement during the rough times.

A very special acknowledgment to Dr. Charles Gibbs (1949-2000), a colleague and beloved friend, for years of advice and insight—we will miss you.

And, last but not least, our loved ones, Ms. Jane Cauthen, Gordon and Joyce Crews, and Paul and Jean Player for being there when we needed them.

chapter 1

FROM DENNIS THE MENACE TO BART SIMPSON

An Overview of Juvenile Violence in America

The typical adolescent spends 3.5 hours of the day totally alone. Children spend 11 fewer hours with parents each week, compared to the 1960s. There has been a 721% increase in the number of minutes the local evening news spent covering homicide between 1993 and 1996. By the end of [the] elementary school experience…[children] will have seen 8,000 murders in all media. There has been a 300% increase in the number of teen suicides since the 1960s. There has been a 1000% increase in the number of children diagnosed as suffering from "depression" since the 1950s.

What Can the Schools Do?, 1999

School-Associated Violent Deaths
1992–1993 = 55
1993–1994 = 51
1994–1995 = 20
1995–1996 = 35
1996–1997 = 25
1997–1998 = 40

National School Safety Center, 1999

If I die, feel no pity, bury my body in the gangsta' city. Place two shotguns at my feet, place two pitchforks at my chest, and tell King Hoover I did my best.

A *Crip* prayer

Bandido hasta yo morir (Outlaw till I die).

A *Latin Kings'* saying

INTRODUCTION

Juvenile delinquency dates back to the beginning of recorded history. There have been many changes over the centuries in the types of delinquent behavior encountered, how much of it was present, what were believed to be the *causes*, and what people of the time thought should be done to control the problem.

Parents realize early that, from their child's first moment out of their sight, they cannot offer their child absolute protection at all times. This becomes painfully true on the first day of school for a son or daughter. It is almost as if the child suddenly disappears into an unknown world of cliques, gangs, competitive sports, fantasy, and adolescent emotional uproar.

Parents in general try to keep track of whom their children are "hanging out" with. In the past, most thought this was enough. With the increase in the number of school shootings and violent juvenile attacks, however, this alone does not seem to be enough. Much more is needed. What does this mean? Can parents be expected to keep up with their child's friends, enemies, contacts, and all of the alienated loners who are lurking around their child's schools?

This chapter offers a brief overview of many of the issues involved in understanding juvenile violence in America. First, we need to know the extent of the problem.

Extent of Juvenile Violence

One point of major contention in any examination of juvenile violence is the basic question: What is the extent of the problem? This would seem like an easy question to answer, but it is not. It often depends upon where one looks for the answers. The focus for this chapter—and the entire book—is to examine juvenile *violence*, not just crime or delinquency in general.

Where We Get Our Information

We get our information relating to juvenile violence from arrest statistics, the media, and self-report surveys, polls, and reports. What can we learn from these?

Arrest Statistics   The examination of arrest statistics is not sufficient to reveal the prevalence or seriousness of juvenile violence. The actual prevalence might be overestimated, on the one hand, if, as some contend, a small minority of repeat offenders is responsible for a highly disproportionate share of juvenile offenses. On the other hand, the statistics may underestimate the problem because, as others point out, most offenses do not come to police attention, and of those that do, few lead to an arrest.

Even data on gender, class, and ethic differences in arrests are open to question. Boys are four times more likely to be arrested than girls. Adolescents of lower socioeconomic status (SES) are almost twice as likely to be arrested as middle-class adolescents. Black and Latino youth are about twice as likely to be arrested as Whites.

It has been consistently shown that, at least in some jurisdictions, the police are more inclined to arrest teenagers of lower socioeconomic status or dark skin than middle-class or light-skinned teens, and the police similarly are more inclined to arrest boys than girls. Moreover, arrest statistics are subject to marked variation from place to place and time to time, probably more because of the changing politics and policies of law enforcement than changes in adolescent behavior (Berger, 1994).

Media   The media comprise a major venue for the dissemination of information relating to juvenile violence. Unfortunately, this is the *only* source of information for many Americans, who do not investigate what is going on in the world beyond the nightly TV news or the morning newspaper. But do these venues give accurate information? Do they really provide the reader with an unbiased presentation of the facts?

Most people who rely only on the daily newspaper read mainly the headlines, and often only those that catch their attention. Because of time constraints and people's schedules, many do not have time to sit down and read the paper from front to back. Do headlines give a proper review of the event? The answer is obviously no. The purpose of headlines is to catch the readers' eye, to draw them into buying the paper.

Another phenomenon is the growing number of people who receive most, if not all, of their information from the daily "talk shows." Many jokes have been made about talk shows and the people who watch them daily without fail. More frightening, these programs have become a major source of information. It would be interesting to know how many people in the United States use talk shows as their only source of information on current events.

If these two observations have any credibility, what information are the readers and watchers receiving about juvenile violence in America? What view of this problem might they have? Most probably would get a negative and frightening view of what is going on pertaining to juvenile violence across the country. Headlines are going to pull out the "attention grabber," and talk shows are going to pick topics that draw viewers. Sadly, what catches Americans' attention is most often the negative or violent. So is this fear about juvenile violence really such a mystery?

Self-Report Surveys, National Polls, and National Reports   Other sources of information on the extent of juvenile violence are self-report srveys, national polls, and federal reports. These sources yield an interesting and mixed picture of what is occurring in juvenile violence in America.

In a CCN Gallup Poll of Teenagers (1999), 33% of those polled believed that a tragedy on the scale of the Columbine High School shooting on April 20, 1999 could occur at their school. Half thought that this incident had given ideas to troubled students at their school, and 20% said they had actually heard someone express that they had these ideas. When asked what they thought is responsible for the amount of juvenile violence, 75% considered the Internet a factor, 67% named parents as responsible, and 66% said television and music are to blame for recent increases in this type of violence. Another 56% named violent video games as primarily responsible.

Since 1989, the National Crime Victimization Survey has gathered information pertaining specifically to school violence in the United States through its *School Crime Supplement*. In the first 10 years of this data collection, it has offered evidence that juvenile victimization in schools has steadily declined. All property and personal victimization has declined as well.

These decreases, ironically, may be a result somewhat of some increases that also were found: 94% of schools across the country have developed zero-tolerance policies; 84% have developed low-level security programs; and 78% have in place formal school violence prevention programs. About 3% of schools have instituted school uniform requirements.

Another positive sign is the reported general decrease in drug use by American youth between 1982 and 1999. Alcohol use remains high, but some evidence shows that this usage has decreased as well.

PATTERNS OF VIOLENCE

The seven most recent major school shooting incidents in the United States are synopsized below. This information might be used to answer a few of the questions commonly asked about the causes of the violence.

Question 1: Is the problem a result of big schools and large student populations?

Location	School Population	Number Killed/Wounded
Moses Lake, Washington	600	3/1
Pearl, Mississippi	1000	2/7
West Paducah, Kentucky	600	3/5
Jonesboro, Arkansas	250	5/10
Springfield, Oregon	1400	2/20
Littleton, Colorado	1900	13/23
Conyers, Georgia	1300	0/6

Many researchers and educational reformers are beginning to promote smaller schools (those with 250 or fewer students) across the United States. They believe that lower student populations will remedy much of the alienation that students often feel when they are placed into college-size schools. Schools in major cities typically have student populations of 2,000 to 4,000.

Two major benefits of smaller school populations are obvious.

1. Smaller schools allow students and teachers to know one another and interact more closely.

2. Smaller schools are less crowded, and competition for participation in extracurricular activities such as band, athletics, or student organizations is less of a factor in the daily lives of students. Interaction with teachers and involvement in activities are the primary ways students express and define themselves.

The above data provide some evidence of the impact of larger school populations. It is interesting, though, that the only school that met the 250-student threshold (Jonesboro, Arkansas) had the second highest death rate. The explanation probably lies in the manner in which the school shooting occurred—students filing out during a false fire alarm into a "killing field." This is probably true also for the largest student population (Littleton, Colorado) having the largest death rate (13)—the amount of firepower the students used in the assault.

Question 2: What impact might bullying or teasing have on this violence?

Location	Reported Reason for Violence
Moses Lake, Washington	Teased/Bullied
Pearl, Mississippi	Teased/Bullied
West Paducah, Kentucky	Teased/Bullied
Jonesboro, Arkansas	Teased/Bullied
Springfield, Oregon	Outcast/Expelled
Littleton, Colorado	Teased/Bullied
Conyers, Georgia	Teased/Bullied

The story behind each of the above incidents is an old one—the outcasts against the popular students. The problem is that these outcasts, or children on the margins of society, have begun to fight back. This has taken on the form of violent attacks. By examining the seven events listed above, the lives of approximately 107 people were completely destroyed or impacted, apparently because of the teasing, bullying, and alienation of nine youths.

Adolescents always have been cruel to other adolescents. Children seem to begin in preschool separating themselves from other children. Adolescents, particularly, are psychologically fragile and react deeply to mistreatment from other adolescents. In decades past these bullied children most often disappeared into the backdrop of a school or neighborhood. The 1990s found these types of students coming together to establish their own groups or cliques—often becoming part of marginal groups susceptible to initiating violent behavior. This susceptibility is based on the growing belief that violent assaults are paybacks for the abuse the perpetrators have received for no other reason than being different.

Question 3: What is the possible influence of music or violent video games?

Location	Reported Interests
Moses Lake, Washington	Violent movies and books
Pearl, Mississippi	Marilyn Manson (music)
West Paducah, Kentucky	Doom, Quake (video games)
Jonesboro, Arkansas	Mortal Kombat (video game)/Tupac Shakur (music)
Springfield, Oregon	Marilyn Manson (music)
Littleton, Colorado	Marilyn Manson (music)
Conyers, Georgia	Mortal Kombat (video game)/Tupac Shakur (music)

Many people want to blame the increase in juvenile violence on popular culture. Examples like those listed above seem to fuel this belief. Adults look at what adolescents are watching and listening to, and it is not difficult to understand why they would identify violent music, movies, or video games as a primary cause of juvenile violence.

In a realistic examination of the problem a variation of an old adage immediately comes to mind: "Movies and music don't kill people; people kill people." To blame these external factors for the violence is too simplistic.

Research has found that prolonged exposure to violent movies and music *can* desensitize children to violence. This also can lead to a lack of respect for life in some children. But does that exposure alone cause incidents like those listed?

Question 4: What about the availability of guns?

Location	Source of Weapons
Moses Lake, Washington	Home
Pearl, Mississippi	Home
West Paducah, Kentucky	Stolen from neighbor's home
Jonesboro, Arkansas	Stolen from relative's home
Springfield, Oregon	Presents from father/home
Littleton, Colorado	Purchased by friends
Conyers, Georgia	Home

The availability of guns is drawing more and more debate. Many believe that this is the primary reason the United States is experiencing these types of shootings. Some researchers are referring to a growing "American gun culture." Others are trying to pinpoint it further by stating that it is a "Southern gun culture." Again, the question is whether the availability of guns is what *causes* the problems of juvenile violence. Or is this something that exacerbates the problem?

Looking at the above list, these juveniles clearly had access to guns. Of the seven cases listed, four consisted of weapons readily available in the students' own homes. In two other cases, the juveniles stole weapons from a relative's or neighbor's home. In one incident, Littleton, Colorado, the juveniles obtained their weapons from external sources and received them from friends.

Are these examples enough to justify the belief that the availability of guns *causes* the problems? It is probably fair to say that the firepower (high-powered rifles, semiautomatics, and explosives) available did allow those committing the violence to do more damage. But does not this overall argument lose some momentum when considering the number of homes that have weapons but do not prompt any type of violence?

Question 5: Is the family situation the problem?

Location	Reported Family Situation
Moses Lake, Washington	Suicidal mother, divorce in progress
Pearl, Mississippi	Father left when child was age 11
West Paducah, Kentucky	Both parents at home
Jonesboro, Arkansas	One child—parents divorced; one child—both parents at home
Springfield, Oregon	Both parents in home
Littleton, Colorado	Both sets of parents in home
Conyers, Georgia	Mother and stepfather at home

Dysfunctional families are an oft-cited cause of negative juvenile behavior. This topic is discussed at length later in this text. It is interesting—albeit frightening, maybe—to see the new trend that has emerged. Two-parent, affluent, White, suburban homes are producing violent juvenile murders. More than half of the juveniles involved in the above incidents came from affluent homes and communities. Therefore, many of the stereotypes or common beliefs of the past must be reevaluated in the light of what is being seen increasingly.

What does all of this mean? Probably that things are changing—maybe *evolving* is a better term. The ways in which some adolescents' problems are being manifested in their behavior are increasingly different from decades past. One thing is interesting though: The root causes of alienation, boredom, and abuse have not changed—only their outcomes.

WHY ARE JUVENILES VIOLENT THEN?

The numerous causes of juvenile violence will be discussed in detail in Chapter 5. We will mention this topic briefly here to set the stage for subsequent chapters.

What becomes readily apparent is that this extremely complex question has no one answer. Many believe that they can identify one cause for this violence and press for America to place all of its efforts to address that single area. The problem is that, for every child who is involved in or a victim of this one cause and does become involved in violent behavior, two similar children do not. If it were the sole cause, would not it lead all who experience it to similar violent behavior? Most of what people identify are factors that interact with a myriad of other influences to cause a certain type of behavior to become apparent.

A growing body of research is rediscovering that the roots of violence in children continue to involve both nature and nurture. Many researchers are offering the position that experiences actually rewire the brain (modifying cognitive processes). Keeping in mind that a child's brain is more malleable than an adult's brain, it is not difficult to understand the importance of the first 3 to 5 years of a child's life. Children who experience verbal and physical abuse or neglect during these years are more likely to have problems in the future. These negative experiences rewire a child's brain, impacting how they feel about and adjust to their world and that of others.

Mistreatment of children is the cornerstone of future negative behavior. This mistreatment manifests itself in different ways in different children. Some children demonstrate abuse by becoming impulsively aggressive. Others become "shell-shocked" and are constantly on "hair-trigger alert." Many continue to be victims until they reach a point at which they can take no more abuse, and they strike out violently. A growing number—possibly the most frightening—consists of those who become unresponsive to anything. These are the children with antisocial personalities. They have no empathy for anyone or anything. Maybe this is the new breed that popular media has repeatedly warned America about.

The final piece comes when these children then become involved in additional risk factors—drug or alcohol use, gang involvement, or association with violent peers. This combination sets the stage for future juvenile violence.

THE RELATIONSHIP BETWEEN SELF-CONCEPT AND DELINQUENCY

Attempts to establish the relationship between self-concept and delinquency are too many to cite. The most consistent conclusion has been that delinquent youths have a significantly lower self-concept than nondelinquents. Some theorists and researchers are convinced that a low-self-concept (LSC) makes youths susceptible to delinquent behavior, and one popular myth would have us believe that delinquent behavior is the consequence of low-self-concept. A popular theory that evolved during the 1960s and 1970s was that those with a LSC were most likely to associate with delinquent types because they so desperately wanted to feel worthy as individuals. By engaging in delinquent behavior, they felt worth and a sense of belonging. Thus, LSC led them to adopt a deviant lifestyle and to form associations with delinquents and delinquent groups.

This same explanation has been used many times to explain why gang members tend to develop an unshakable loyalty to the gang and its criminal and often violent activities. To briefly illustrate these points, consider two theoretical perspectives that seem to guide much of the research on self-concept.

1. The self-theory of deviance (Stephen and Stephen, 1990), which suggests that the fundamental motivating aspect of human behavior rests in protecting and maintaining positive images of self. In this view, delinquent behavior is regarded either as a product of LSC or as a "self-enhancing" mechanism through which the youthful offender judges "self" by standards other than those of the middle class, "straight" society (Kaplan, Martin, and Johnson, 1986).

2. Labeling theory, which postulates that formally adjudicating youths delinquent and their subsequent involvement in the justice system tend to result in acceptance of the stigma and adoption of a concordant deviant lifestyle (Lemert, 1951; Fitts and Hammer, 1969; Lund and Salary, 1980).

Another popular belief of the same period (1960s and 1970s) was that delinquents derive positive reinforcement from others who are similarly prone and, as a consequence of being accepted and feeling worthy, their abnormally LSC improved.

Still, the research and theoretical explanations raised more questions than they answered.

Early Studies

In 1980, Dr. Robert C. Evans and his research team embarked on a series of self-concept studies in an attempt to clarify some of the confusing and frequently opposing views concerning the relationship of LSC and delinquency. First they attempted to determine if delinquent youths' self-concepts were lower or if previously reported findings were anomalies. All of their studies, each of which involved a larger sample of delinquent subjects than the previous one, clearly demonstrated that imprisoned youthful offenders had not only a lower self-concept than nonoffenders but such an abnormally LSC as to be classified as pathological in many cases.

The findings of one of the early studies, for example, indicated that a sample of incarcerated delinquent males had a mean self-concept score significantly below the lowest normal range for nondelinquents—in fact so low as to be severely abnormal. Even more disturbing was that their female counterparts had even lower scores. And, though the males' mean self-concept tended to improve slightly (albeit not statistically significant) during their incarceration, the females' perceptions of self remained abnormally low.

Some of the implications of these initial studies were that male offenders may receive positive reinforcement from their delinquent counterparts, resulting in a slight improvement in their self-perception, but that female offenders did not seem to gain the same reinforcement from close association with other female offenders. The studies tended also to refute the notion that delinquents derive significant reinforcement from other delinquents, as the perceptions of

Dr. Robert Evans, Professor of Criminal Justice and Director of Graduate Criminal Justice Studies at Valdosta State University, Valdosta, Georgia

self did not improve significantly during the period of closest association with other delinquents.

Subsequent studies of imprisoned youthful offenders consistently confirmed the earlier findings that the mean self-concept scores of male and female delinquents were abnormally lower than nonoffenders of the same ages and that offenders' self-concept remained unchanged throughout their incarceration. One consistent observation not previously reported was that the self-perception of females continued to be significantly lower than that of their male counterparts, which suggests that delinquency and the consequences that result have a greater negative effect on females than on males.

Still, several intriguing questions remained concerning the relationship of LSC and deviant behaviors. For instance, could it be that a low-self-concept is the result of social disapproval and the stigmatization imposed on delinquent youths as a result of their behaviors, or is it that the stigma of being labeled delinquent damages an otherwise healthy self-concept? Also, is self-concept associated with factors such as race, parental marital status, and culture?

Delinquency and Culture

In an attempt to gain some insight into the foregoing questions, the same instrument was used to measure the self-concept of imprisoned youthful offenders in the United Kingdom, as well as the United States. First, it was conclusively discovered that LSC is not a culture-bound phenomenon. Youthful offenders in the United States and the United Kingdom were found to have mean self-concept scores significantly below the norm for nonoffenders. Although both groups had abnormally LSC scores, the U.S. subjects scored significantly lower than their British counterparts. On one of the scales comprising the total positive self-concept, *Family*, the U.K. subjects scored well within the normal range—which accounted for much of their overall higher positive self-concept.

Upon close examination of the two groups, it was found that more than two-thirds of the U.S. young offenders neither knew their fathers nor knew their whereabouts, and the vast majority of the subjects had come from one-parent homes. In contrast, more than 90% of the U.K. subjects had come from intact two-family homes. This finding tends to confirm the strong influence of the family in terms of developing a healthy self-esteem.

Cross-cultural analyses revealed no significant differences in self-concept according to race; however, it was confirmed that, among the nearly 1,000 subjects of these studies, Black youthful offenders had significantly lower mean self-concept scores than White youthful offenders. The same findings were observed among female subjects.

The cross-cultural studies seemed to clarify some of the questions concerning the relationship of LSC and delinquency. One factor that became self-evident as a result of the series of studies was that a significantly lower self-concept in delinquents is not a cultural phenomenon; it is equally likely to occur in delinquent groups in comparable cultural sample groups.

Further, when self-concept scores were analyzed while controlling for age, although younger offenders tended to have the lowest mean self-concept scores, the differences by age were statistically insignificant. This finding suggests that a low self concept most likely is formed early in life, probably before youths become delinquent. If this explanation is accurate, delinquency is not the result of LSC. Still, the extent to which LSC contributes to delinquency, if at all, remains uncertain. It may be reasoned that if youths consider themselves unworthy, they may seek relationships in which they are made to feel worthy, and these relationships may be formed most often with those who feel similarly about themselves.

Finally, immersion in the justice system does not seem to have a significant effect on self-concept, a finding that seems to dismiss the notion that the justice system and close association of delinquents are what contribute to an unhealthy perception of self. Although this is not entirely conclusive, LSC seems to form early in life from factors associated with intimate relationships early in life—not from environmental influences or associations to which youth are exposed during adolescence.

Changing the Physical Environment

On February 2, 2000, we conducted an interview with Dr. Deborah Mitchell Robinson, Assistant Professor of Criminal Justice, Valdosta, Georgia. Dr. Robinson has conducted extensive research in the areas of crime prevention and victimology and published the findings in both areas.

Dr. Deborah Mitchell Robinson, Associate Professor of Criminal Justice at Valdosta State University, Valdosta, Georgia. She was interviewed concerning school violence and the use of CPTED to reduce violence on campus on June 8, 2000 in Valdosta, Georgia

Question: Dr. Robinson, what is your background with regard to crime prevention and school violence?

Answer: I have conducted research in the areas of crime prevention, specifically CPTED, and victimology, with several studies examining victimization and CPTED on school campuses.

Question: What exactly is CPTED?

Answer: Crime Prevention Through Environmental Design (CPTED) is a concept developed by C. Ray Jeffery in his 1971 and 1977 books of the same name. The basic premise of the concept is that by decreasing the number of targets available for victimization, crime will decrease. In other words, if there are no targets, there will be no crime.

Question: What do you mean by "targets"?

Answer: By targets, I mean anything or anyone who is in a position to be victimized.

Question: How is CPTED related to "targets"?

Answer: CPTED proposes that changing the physical environment in which targets are found will naturally decrease the amount of victimization or criminal activities.

Question: What do you mean by changing the physical environment?

Answer: Most crime prevention programs focus on the offender and how to prevent the offender from committing crimes. CPTED focuses on the physical environment to decrease the opportunity for crime—thus, no need to focus on the offender. The physical environment can promote or discourage criminal activity. Many aspects of the physical environment which can be examined using the CPTED analysis.

For example, lighting, pedestrian traffic, shrubbery, and building layout can be examined with regard to the availability of targets. Lighting plays a major role in the availability of targets in any given area. The darker an area, the better a potential offender can hide and surprise an unsuspecting target. Lighting pathways, buildings, and areas between buildings is another issue of lighting. For example, focusing light from the ground up to light the outside of a building provides a pleasing or aesthetic sense to the building.

That same lighting, however, can pose a hazard to an individual exiting the building. Putting lights in the ground to shine on a building blinds exiting individuals to what is waiting in the dark surrounding the building. CPTED proposes putting lights at the top of buildings to shine down, thus illuminating the land around the building, eliminating the possibility of hiding places, and thereby decreasing targets. The same is true for shrubbery. Higher and denser areas of shrubbery provide excellent hiding places for offenders.

Pedestrian traffic can influence target availability by providing what Jane Jacobs termed "eyes on the street." She proposed that having many individuals milling about on the street would provide many eyes to see criminal activity. Many researchers have identified that a major concern of certain offenders, particularly burglars and robbers, is being seen. More individuals present on the street will increase visibility, naturally decreasing the availability of targets and, thus, decreasing criminal activity.

Building layout is another major aspect of CPTED. Buildings should be designed and built with the physical environment in the forefront, both inside and outside. Within the building, lighting should be prominent and dark hallways and rooms should be at a minimum. Outside the building, parking lots should be positioned in such a way that all automobiles are visible, with lighting bright and shrubbery at a minimum.

Through my research on CPTED and placements of criminal activity within school settings, it is evident that the physical environment currently is one in which beauty and aesthetics take a primary role over safety.

Question: How can CPTED be applied to juvenile violence in public primary and secondary schools?

Answer: By applying the concepts of CPTED in the design and structure of public schools, targets will decrease and criminal activity will decrease. Classrooms can be structured in such a way, by changing the physical layout, to promote a constant visible presence of those in the classroom. Parking lots can be designed to ensure that all automobiles are visible to those in the school buildings and lighting is such that there exists no dark areas in which criminal activity can occur. Individuals can be placed in areas to monitor the comings and goings of students and school personnel, to ensure that only individuals with a legitimate interest in the school and/or grounds are permitted.

Shrubbery and trees on the school grounds should be trimmed and kept at a minimum. The bottom line for schools is to create an atmosphere in which learning can take place while providing a physically secure area. The schools do not need electric fences around them like a prison, but the physical environment should be developed to act as an electric fence to those with no legitimate interests in the school. As for those with legitimate interests in the school—namely the students—the physical layout of the school buildings and grounds should reflect and promote constant surveillance of the students.

School boards and administrators have made some strides in crime prevention in their schools. Most of their focus, however, has been on security measures to deter criminal activity—for example, electronic surveillance in the form of cameras within and outside school buildings. Schools across the country are increasingly using metal detectors and other electronic and human devices to monitor weapons coming into the school buildings. Schools are also increasing the presence of police officers in the form of School Resource Officers who are present on school grounds any time school is in session. All of these measures are effective to a certain extent.

> But these measures do not address a major CPTED issue—namely, the number of potential targets. Cameras are a positive step but cannot help students escape a potentially dangerous situation if there are not enough, or improperly placed, safety or exit points within the schools. School boards and administrators need to focus on the physical environment of the schools. This will not eliminate all criminal activity on school campuses, but it will decrease the number of potential targets, thus decreasing criminal activity.
>
> **Question:** Any final comments on school violence and CPTED?
>
> **Answer:** It's a sad reality that learning is no longer the major function of primary and secondary schools. Too many schools have had to trade an emphasis on learning for an emphasis on keeping kids safe from themselves for eight hours a day. Although CPTED is not the ultimate and only answer to school violence, it is a positive and much-unrecognized component of school safety.

CONCLUSION

The bottom line seems to be that children must be helped and guided through the wide range of social ups and downs. These begin the first day of school and continue throughout the child's various developmental stages.

In the early grades, children learn how to make friends and the rules of *fair play*. In the middle grades, issues of being self-conscious and trial-and-error efforts to feel comfortable in their bodies and environment emerge. By the high school years, young people are developing their identity and establishing plans for the future.

For parents, the responsibility is to help children and adolescents establish a moral compass as to what is right and what is wrong. This also involves giving children the ability to generalize what is right or wrong to situations that their parents could not even imagine.

How can parents do that? In addressing the issues discussed in the following chapters, this information, we hope, will help in answering this question. At least the discussion should provide food for thought as to the direction in which America should move in the twenty-first century.

chapter 2

FROM SOUTH CENTRAL TO NEXTDOOR

Gang and Group Violence

Don't refuse to think about the grim remedy of a civil war—because the alternative is far grimmer and far bloodier. The fate that Mr. Clinton and the Jewish bosses have planned for us is infinitely worse than any civil war could possibly be. Civil war is thinkable, civil war is plannable—when the alternative is extinction.

> Dr. William Pierce, Director of National Vanguard Books
> and Chairman of the Patriotic National Alliance, July 7, 1999

Blood = Blood love overcomes our depressions.

> The meaning of the word *Blood*

Crip = Crown Royal International Posse

> The meaning of the word *Crip*

If a child thinks he's a Crip, he's a Crip.

> Steve Nawojczyk, National Gang Expert

INTRODUCTION

Are gangs a relatively new phenomenon, or have they simply been given more consideration in recent times? The fact is that youth gangs have existed for centuries. What actually constitutes a gang varies from one to another. Before discussing their daily functioning, purpose, and overall impact on society, we must have a working definition of what constitutes a gang. Once these characteristics have been identified, proper intervention programs—such as anti-gang task forces and community programs–can be developed. An understanding of the facets of such an organization, no matter how loosely constructed they may be, can be gained only by looking first at the origins of this subculture.

A BRIEF OVERVIEW OF GANGS IN THE UNITED STATES

Youth gangs actually might have appeared first in Europe or Mexico. No one is absolutely sure when or why gangs eventually emerged in the United States. The first record of their appearance in America could have been as early as 1783, as the American Revolution ended. Some believe that gangs might have emerged spontaneously from adolescent playgroups or as collective responses to urban conditions in the country. They also may have grown out of the difficulties that Mexican youths encountered with their social and cultural adjustment to the American way of life under extremely poor conditions in the Southwest (Office of Juvenile Justice and Delinquency Prevention, 1998).

Immigration patterns, economic conditions, and increased violence have been identified as contributing factors to continued gang interest in American youth (Albanese, 1996). These factors might emerge out of the lack of order in a youth's life, which gang membership helps to restore. Gangs' organization, identifiable leadership, territorial identification, continuous association, and specific purpose have historically distinguished youth gangs from other groups. Functioning as a socializing institution for their members when other societal institutions have failed, gangs have evolved in many cases not so much as an issue of status but, rather, survivability.

Youth gangs in the nineteenth century often were associated—as they are in modern times—with second and sometimes later generation male adolescent and young adult immigrant groups, or *in-migrant groups* (groups that move to a new part of the country). These groups were clustered most often in low-income neighborhoods of expanding or declining industrial or postindustrial urban centers (Spergel, 1995).

The origins of youth gangs also can be traced farther back in time to the Emancipation Proclamation of 1865, signed by President Abraham Lincoln, freeing Blacks from slavery. During this time, many newly freed slaves migrated to the North, mainly to large cities, in search of employment and the start of a new life. Upon arriving at these northern cities, which were inhabited mainly by White people, many newly freed slaves met with great resistance. With no formal education or chance of finding gainful employment, they grouped together, living in close proximity to one another mainly to ensure their survival as a people.

Black people were not the only ones who were oppressed and living under harsh conditions. Italians, Irish, and others also were fighting for the survivability of their people and were tucked in pockets in the major cities of the North.

The conditions that many minority and underprivileged youths have experienced from the beginning of mass immigration movements in the United States have provided conditions that have spawned youth gangs. Prior to the year 2000, the United States has had four distinct periods of gang growth and peak activity: the late 1800s, 1920s, 1960s, and the 1990s (Office of Juvenile Justice and Delinquency Prevention, 1998). Gang proliferation in the United States has been unstable and is continuing to rise and fall with the changing conditions of the environment.

Youth gangs are most likely to develop as a result of problems in local communities or societies that are undergoing extensive change and, often, deteriorating. During this change, social institutions are weak and unstable, and organizations tend to be poorly integrated and in conflict with each other. As a result of this disorder, gangs become a viable option for the youth and membership because they restore order and structure in the youth's life. According to Spergel (1995), contemporary youth gangs are found primarily in lower class, slum, ghetto, and working-class communities. What is not clear is whether class, poverty, culture, race or ethnicity, or social change primarily account for gang problems.

The recent and renewed interest in youth gangs can be attributed to many factors. First, the heightened sense of awareness about gangs in the United States can be attributed to the recent upswing in violent incidents. Another possible reason is that fear of crime is increasing again.

Fear of gang victimization is very real to those who live in large cities. While fear of victimization is on the increase, though, crimes of a violent nature committed by juveniles actually have begun to decline. For example, arrests for juvenile violent crimes began to increase in the mid-1980s, reaching a peak in 1994. In 1997, for the third year in a row, violent crimes committed by youths declined (3 % in 1995, 6 % in 1996, and 4 % in 1997) (Snyder, 1999).

Western culture often has romanticized actual and fictional gangs that were criminal or otherwise socially threatening. Examples include Robin Hood's band of merry men and numerous Wild West outlaws, most notably the Jesse James gang. Attitudes toward gangs have changed over time—almost without exception for the worse. This is not solely the result of increases in the number or size of gangs or the extent or seriousness of their delinquency. Rather, interest in gangs has been explained as a result of four interrelated factors (Miller and Rush, 1996):

1. Dominant ideology
2. Advances in methodology
3. Applicability of popular social theory to gang issues
4. General sociopolitical conditions.

Although many theories have been suggested to explain the origin of youth gangs in the United States, no single cause can adequately explain the youth gang phenomenon. One study on youth gangs that is often referenced in regard to the origin of youth gangs is Fredrick Thrasher's 1927 landmark study. After studying more than 1,300 gangs with a total membership of 25,000, he found that most gangs were small (6 to 20 members) and formed spontaneously in poor and socially disorganized neighborhoods. Rather than having a criminal purpose, he discovered, most gangs were formed to fulfill a youthful need for play and adventure that sometimes led to acts of delinquency. Continued conflict with authorities helped to solidify these emerging gangs (Albanese, 1996). In modern times, many law enforcement officials are reluctant to identify a troublesome group as a gang because this provides undue notoriety and confirms their structure and existence.

GROUP VIOLENCE AND DELINQUENT BEHAVIOR

Why do youths engage in group criminality or violence? This question has several possible answers, but one area that should be discussed is what differentiates group violence from gang violence. *Group violence* can be defined as the spontaneous, criminal, destructive act of two or more people that have loose, little, or no affiliation with each other. *Gang violence* is defined as behavior which is perpetuated by a group of individuals who have a purpose, common identity, and a history together. Unlike group violence, gang violence is most often planned and calculated.

What drives individuals to spontaneously erupt into violence? One possible answer may be that youths want to belong so much that they are willing to participate in criminal acts. Wanting to belong to the "in" group and struggling to fit in or prove their worthiness, the youth gets caught up in the activity with no real understanding of the cause-and-effect aspects of the situation.

Another possible answer is the need for mere affiliation with the group. For example, if one member of a group of friends assaults a patron at a night club and the other friends join in the assault, the thinking of the joining party might be, "Why not join in? The guy must have deserved it." Another example of group violence is the riots. Riots arise many times from the concept of mob mentality. People frequently are stimulated by the aggressive nature of others and thank that because so many people are involved, they will not be singled out and punished. Juveniles that become involved in group violence many times are aware of the consequences but disregard them and decide to participate because of the perceived leniency of the Juvenile Court. The benefits of belonging, status, comaraderie, and excitement outweigh the possible punishments that may or may not be imposed.

Another characteristic of youth that may be a characteristic of group violence as well is *compulsiveness*. Youths who have not cognitively developed the ability to weigh rewards versus punishments or pleasure versus pain tend to be more spontaneous in their thinking and decisions. Not being able or refusing to see the possible end results of their actions, youths, thus, are more susceptible to group violence.

Over time, group violence (or spontaneous violence) has proved itself to be more dangerous than any organized group or gang. Its spontaneous nature makes the prediction of future incidents difficult at best. The most startling characteristic of group violence is that it does not flourish more in one age group, ethnicity, or geographic location. Group violence has erupted at universities, social celebrations, and street corners.

Examples of Gang and Group Violence

- *April 22, 1996:* Troy Dion Price, a 17-year-old Burtonsville, Virginia, 11th grader, was shot and killed by twins Kevin and Kelvin Powell, age 17. This happened one week after a witnessed argument between the three. One of the twins walked up to Price on a street corner, grabbed him, and shot him once in the chest.

- *October 1, 1997:* In Pearl, Mississippi, Luke Woodham, age 16, was accused of killing his mother, then going to school and shooting nine students, two of whom died, including the boy's ex-girlfriend. Authorities later accused six friends of conspiracy, stating that the suspects were part of a group that dabbled in Satanism.

- *March 24, 1998:* Mitchell Johnson, 13, and Andrew Golden, 11, opened fire with rifles on classmates and teachers when they came out of the school during a false fire alarm set off by the shooters at Westside Middle School, Jonesboro, Arkansas. Four girls and a teacher were killed, and 11 people were wounded.

- *November 23, 1998:* In Virginia Beach, Virginia, Robert Durant, 16, stabbed the father of a rival gang member to death. Durant had gone to the home of Benjamin Parks, Jr., to confront his son. During an ensuing fight between the youths in the yard, Parks was stabbed trying to protect his son.

- *April 20, 1999:* Eric Harris, 18, and Dylan Klebold, 17, entered Columbine High School in Littleton, Colorado, carrying a handgun, a rifle, two shotguns, and various explosives. One teacher and 12 students were killed, and 23 others were wounded. Both students committed suicide after the attack.

- *May 16, 1999:* Four boys were charged with plotting a shooting at their middle school similar to the April rampage at Colorado's Columbine High School. Justin Schnepp and Jedaiah Zinzo, both 14, were charged as adults with conspiracy to commit murder for allegedly planning to kill classmates at their 560-student Holland Woods Middle School. The two others, ages 12 and 13, were charged as juveniles with the same crime. The teens reportedly planned to "top the death toll" of Columbine. The four were arrested after a 14-year-old-girl overhead them talking about an elaborate killing spree.

- *May 28, 1999:* Two 16-year-old Portsmouth, Virginia, middle-school students were convicted of threatening to bomb their school. These threats reportedly were in response to the Columbine High School incident the preceding month.

- *June 15, 1999:* In Suffolk, Virginia, a 15-year-old boy was charged with two counts of making bomb threats to local elementary schools. Three other boys, a 13-year-old and two 15-year-olds, were charged with conspiracy in the incidents.
- *June 22, 1999:* Quincy Eugene Ward, 19, was shot once in the head and killed during a party in Suffolk, Virginia. A crowd at the party reportedly had been violent toward Ward earlier in the evening, and many were standing within 4 to 5 feet of him at the time of the shooting. None of these individuals said they could give a description of the shooter, nor had they seen the actual act.

Origins of the Bloods and Crips

In the late 1960s, much of the United States was in turmoil. Many young men were in Vietnam, and many others were involved with the civil rights movement. Many youths joined organizations such as the Black Panthers that spoke out against the government. Some left to find more radical alternatives to this type of group membership. Raymond Washington (then 15) and Stanley Williams from Los Angeles decided to organize a group to preserve the Panther aura. They called it the Baby Avenues, named after an established gang known as the Avenue Boys, which served sometimes as a quasi-political group. Later the Baby Avenues came to be known as the Avenue Crips, later shortened to the modern-day term Crips (Alonso, 1997).

Prior to 1970, Los Angeles did not have many Crip gangs, but by the later part of 1971, the Avalon Garden Crips and the Inglewood Crips joined forces with the other Crip-affiliated groups. The Crip gangs began to fuse and eventually took over non-Crip territories. Although this migration expanded into non-Crip territories, other gangs such as the Piru Street Boys, Bishops, Athens Park Boys, and the Denver Lanes began to associate with the Crips prior to 1972. During this territorial migration period, the Crips became known as the Piru Street Crips. The Piru and Crip gangs got along for a short time, but in the mid-1970s, the Crips from Compton and the Pirus had a conflict that ended the friendship between the two groups (Ray, 1999).

After the conflict, the Pirus separated and created a new alliance with the Bishops, Athens Boys and the Denver Lanes. With this new alliance, the group discontinued wearing the Crips' trademark blue and adopted the opposite color, red, to signify its organization, the Bloods. In the late 1990s, there were more than 100,000 Bloods and Crips in Los Angeles County alone, and authorities could only approximate the extent to which they existed in other parts of the country (Ray, 1999).

Racial Make-Up of the Bloods
Black
Hispanic
Greek
Chinese
White

Members of the gang must "Blood-in." This means they must spill someone's blood or their own. Recruits can achieve this in various ways: fights, rapes, slashing, robberies, assaults against law enforcement, or group sex for female initiates. Regardless of the method, blood must be spilt.

Skinhead and Neo-Nazi Subculture

The concept of hate and how it relates to criminal activity is an evolving concept that has crept into America's reality. Hatred by itself is not necessarily criminal, but when some types of crime (such as assault, vandalism, and theft) can be shown legally to have been motivated by hate against a specified group, the punitive hate crime mechanism becomes active (Czajkoski, 1992). Therefore, the concepts of hate and crime have been brought together to define offenses that focus on race, religion, ethnicity, gender, or the victim's sexual orientation.

The skinhead movement in the United States was patterned after the groups of working-class London youths in the late 1960s and early 1970s who blamed many of the problems in England on the influx of Blacks and other minorities. Since the late 1980s, White gangs continued to be dominated by a diverse group of lower- and middle-class youths whose members, according to the police and media, frequently engage in intimidating or violent activities. Skinheads perhaps have been the most violent of these gangs. Often identifying with the Neo-Nazis and Ku Klux Klan organizations, skinheads, like most other hate groups, express hatred for homosexuals, Jews, Blacks, Asians, and most other immigrant groups. Their racism seems to be tied to a belief that American society has been declining as a result of the increase in numbers of minority and non-White ethnic groups (Regoli and Hewitt, 1997).

National Alliance

The National Alliance is a White supremacist group located throughout the United States (Anti-Defamation League, 1998). This group thrives off of the hate it has for minorities and has spoken publicly about a pure White race for the new millennium. The National Alliance has three components that clearly add fuel to the hate this group feels for minorities: militant membership, exploitation of the Internet, and bonds with other hate groups.

In 1999, the militant membership of the National Alliance consisted of 16 active groups from coast to coast with an estimated membership of 1,000. After a weekly, half-hour radio broadcast, a transcription of the show could be found at the National Alliance Web page for interested parties who could not or did not have the opportunity to listen to the show. In addition, 21 telephone hotlines served as regional National Alliance propoganda centers (Anti-Defamation League, 1998).

The National Alliance also has made a vast effort to bond with other groups like itself. In the past, the National Alliance provided a speaking venue for David Duke, a former Klan leader and founder of the National Association for the Advancement of White People, and for David Irving, the well-known British denier of the Holocaust. All over the world, the National Alliance claims to have relationships with other pro-White, anti-minority groups; these countries include Holland, France, Great Britain, and Germany (Anti-Defamation League, 1998).

The National Alliance developed the following goals (National Alliance Web Page, 2000):

- A totally White living space
- A total Aryan society
- Replacement of government officials with a more responsible government
- A new educational system that teaches Aryan principles
- An economic policy based on racial principles.

Knights of Freedom

The Knights of Freedom, formed in the mid-1990s, has received considerable attention from the media and stirred much controversy in the Southeastern part of the United States. Davis Wolfgang Hawke, a 20-year-old junior at Wofford College in Spartanburg, South Carolina, claimed that he founded the organization to defend the rights of White people, and that he considers the Jewish race the primary enemy in his fight to purify the White race. According to an interview published in the University of South Carolina school newspaper *Gamecock* (Student Nazis, 1999), Hawke's ultimate goal is elimination of the Jewish race as an entity, to be accomplished by not letting the Jewish people breed.

Although the Knights of Freedom has existed only since 1996 and the following of youths pledging allegiance to this group is small, Hawke has traveled to colleges, when invited, to promote this organization. The Knights of Freedom, Hawke says, presents people with an alternative viewpoint to counteract the liberal Jewish media viewpoint. Hawke explains that all he is trying to do is to give people a different interpretation of history and how that different interpretation applies to present-day America.

Aryan Nations Youth Corps (ANYC)

The Aryan Nations, also known as Call to the Nation, established in the 1960s, has been an influential group. In 1999, its founder, Pastor Richard G. Butler, headed the Aryan Nations. Although Butler led this organization, the most danger to the youth of the United States was not coming from the top. Instead, Pastor Mike Teague, staff leader at the headquarters of the Aryan Nations, created an organization targeting youths who had ideas and beliefs like those of older Aryans and wanted to learn the ways of the "brotherhood."

According to Teague (1999) the purpose of the Aryan Nations Youth Corps (ANYC) was to get the message of Yahweh/God to all the White, Aryan youths of America. This message, Teague explained, was intended to regenerate all Aryan youths to their God-ordained mission: the education and survival of Our Glorious

Aryan Race. In Teague's message to youth, he explained that interested parties would be paired with an adult in their town if an Aryan Nation organization existed there. By this pairing, the youths would be guided and taught the ways of the Aryan people, to prepare them as the next generation of leaders.

The ANYC consists of young White Aryan people dedicated to the preservation and building of a racially pure homeland. A recruitment article for the Aryan Nation seeks youths who will carry on in the finest tradition of the White Aryan youth worldwide (Teague, 1999). Membership in this Youth Corps is the gateway to the future for the Aryan Nation group. Leaders of the group want youths with the same belief system as the current members and also the following (Aryan Nations Home Page, 1999):

- White Aryan youth of good character
- Between the ages of 14 and 20 years
- Belief in the principles, Biblical truths, and Life Laws of the Heavenly Father
- Belief in the Victory Plan laid out by Pastor Butler, leader of the Aryan Nations.

Currently thousands of hate groups share the beliefs that have been discussed. Some of these groups are highly organized, and others are loosely tied to one another. The more prominent hate groups are outlined as follows.

Current Racially Based Controversial Groups

14: 14 words—shorthand for an expression popularized by White supremacist David Lane: "We must secure the existence of our people and a future for White children."

Jewish Defense League: An anti-Arab group led by Irv Rubin.

Ku Klux Klan: Group espousing race purification; the blood drop on its symbol exemplifies this.

National Alliance: Neo-Nazi organization based in West Virginia.

Nation of Islam: An anti-White religion; teaches that Whites are the devil created by an evil experiment.

Posse Comitatus: Christian identity organization preaching that Jews are literally "children of Satan."

White Aryan Resistance: Racist skinhead organization based in California and led by Tom and John Metzger.

TECHNOLOGY, SOCIETY, THE MEDIA, AND HATE GROUPS

A growing number of youths seem to be susceptible to the influences of gangs and other deviant subcultures. The technological growth of the United States has drastically impacted middle- and upper-class families across the country. From large cities to small farming towns, children continue to be influenced by technology. For example, introduction of the *information superhighway* has made research and exploration available with the click of a button. Not only has the introduction of computer technology made information easier to obtain, but it also has made it easier to disseminate.

Although most people use the Internet as a means of entertainment and as a way of keeping in touch with friends and relatives, it increasingly has been used to recruit individuals of all ages into groups that promote violence. An example of this use is the White supremacist group known as the *National Alliance*. This organization has its own Web page that can be accessed easily. This Web page is easy to find, and it gives users links to access from the National Alliance home page. Although some of these groups are located in foreign countries they can be tapped into from the privacy of one's home. These organizations include the Holocaust Revisionists, the Aryan Nation, the Euro-American Students Union, the National Socialist German Workers Party/American Order, and the World Church of the Creator.

Thus, the Internet and advancing technology can be viewed as a possible threat to the overall safety of communities. Some people also see the entertainment industry as playing a vital role in attracting youths who are alienated from their peers. In the dramatic movie *Higher Learning*, by John Singleton, a Neo-Nazi group on a college campus recruits a young man from a small town. This young man, later identified as Remmy, is an outcast who does not fit in with the mainstream population at that college. With no friends and far away from home, Remmy is recruited by the Neo-Nazi group and is taught the ideology behind the organization. This ideology pushes Remmy to go on a shooting spree to prove his loyalty to the group and show his commitment to the White supremacist cause.

This scenario is not unusual in modern America. More and more youths are similar to this fictional character. The environment that school-aged youths are exposed to is competitive, not only academically but also socially. Youths traditionally have determined which clothes are acceptable to wear, what music is considered "cool," and who are the "in" crowd. Youths who fall outside the parameters of what is deemed socially acceptable are labeled in negative ways and left with few alternatives to meet their social needs. Some follow the path into deviant subcultures as a means toward belonging and acceptance.

SATANIC GROUPS

When discussing the subculture of Satanism, many images immediately appear. People view images of burning pentagrams, human and animal sacrifices, and other manifestations of the dark side of society. Some, or all, of these images are true for Satanic groups throughout American history. Satanism encompasses many different belief systems and practices. Most notable of the Satanic groups are those that fall under what is known as *religious* Satanism, which includes the recognition of Satan, either as a deity or as a principle. Followers usually are serious adults, although increasing numbers of teenagers are involved. The three main traditions or religious Satanic groups are the Church of Satan, the Temple of Set, and the Church of Satanic Liberation (Religious Tolerance.com, 2000).

Of these, the Church of Satan is believed to have the largest group of Satanic worshippers. According to U.S. Department of the Army pamphlet #165–13, an estimated 10,000 to 20,000 members were active in the church in the late 1970s. As the twenty-first century begins, an approximate number of members involved with the church is impossible to know, for the Church of Satan does not release its membership totals.

Anton Szandor LaVey founded the Church of Satan on April 30, 1966. The group headed by LaVey was the first aboveground organization in history openly dedicated to acceptance of what this groups calls man's true nature, that of a carnal beast (LaVey, 1969, 1972, 1989).

At the core of the Church of Satan are the Nine Satanic Statements, written by Anton LaVey. It is immediately obvious why this belief system might be appealing to juveniles who are interested in alternative groups. Satan represents (Religious Tolerance Web page, 2000):

1. Indulgence, not abstinence
2. Vital existence, not spiritual pipe dreams
3. Undefiled wisdom, not hypocritical self-deceit
4. Kindness to those deserving of it, not love wasted on ingrates
5. Vengeance, not turning the other cheek
6. Responsibility to the responsible instead of concern for psychic vampires
7. Man as just another animal—the most vicious of all
8. Gratification of all one's desires
9. The best friend the Christian Church has had, as he has kept it in business for centuries.

These are at the core of the Church of Satan and included in the teachings of LaVey. Although the teachings of the Church of Satan seem to be nonviolent, these nine Satanic statements and ritual practices seem to contradict the message that recruiters are sending to inquisitive youths searching for their identity and place in mainstream society.

GOTHIC SUBCULTURE

Are Gothic members violent? The truth is that the vast majority of members of the Gothic movement are not criminal. The media have much to do with the portrayal of a violent Goth movement. The criminal activity that the media exploits generally includes ritual sacrifices and heavy drug use. Skeptics of the Goth movement need to understand that Goths encompass a variety of types of young people. Some are music followers; others live a vampire lifestyle; and still others are interested in vampirism, witchcraft, Satanism, and Pagan beliefs (Are Gothics Gangs? web page, 2000).

The date of origin of the Gothic movement is usually placed in the late 1970s. During this time, the song "Bela Lugosi's Dead" by Bauhaus was released. Many young fans took it as the inspiration for the budding Gothic subculture. The song had a certain mystery that listeners quickly latched onto.

The first generation of the Gothic movement emerged in the United Kingdom in the late 1970s and early 1980s as a splinter group from the punk movement of the same period. At the time, these groups were not considered Gothic and, to date, no one is sure where the name Goth or Gothic came from.

The Gothic movement more recently entered American culture and encountered great controversy. Some people believe the Goths are inherently evil and comprise a delinquent, violent group. Again, though, there are many different types of Gothic groups. Two of the main ones are the *Vampire Goths* and the *Punk Goths*.

Vampire Goths

Goths in general are attracted to the dark side of life. Some, but not all, Goths are attracted to the vampire subculture. Unlike the movies and pop culture of past years, vampirism is associated not with demons and the devil but, instead, is symbolic of what humanity wishes it could be: fearless, immortal, indulgent, and powerful. Many youths are attracted to the Vampire Goth subculture when they reach a time in their lives when they feel powerless. For some, association with the subculture renews their sense of balance and personal power in the world.

Another trademark of the vampire world is the drinking of blood. Although not all Vampire Goths drink blood, many do. The Web site "What is Gothic" (2000) explains that true Gothics are not violent and only revel in the lifestyle. Though drinking another's blood may seem violent, Goths drink only from willing participants and from themselves, they say.

Punk Gothics

The other main subgroup of Gothics consists of *Punk Gothics*. These youths primarily follow the fashion of the punk rock culture. Many Gothics dress and live a dark existence much like the bands they listen to. Examples of popular Goth bands include Marilyn Manson, The Banshees, Sisters of Mercy, The Cure, Southern Death Cult, Bauhaus, Alice Cooper, and The Mission.

Even though this group of Gothics is primarily music-motivated, it does share some beliefs and clothing styles with other Gothics. Some of the popular fashions of the Gothic culture are black lipstick, fishnet hose for females, pale skin, eye shadow, painted fingernails (usually black), white theatrical face paint, theatrical cloaks and capes, dyed hair (red, purple, green, pink), T-shirts depicting the individual's favorite band or make of car, and gas station attendant work shirts.

Although *Punk Goths* are not on the surface a violent delinquent group, one element of their existence is disturbing: Since its inception, many Goths have used drugs regularly. Some Goths are more involved than others with illicit drugs. Although being a Goth has no prerequisites for drug use, Satanic beliefs, or Paganism, many Goths practice these beliefs and engage in this behavior.

GANG STRUCTURE AND YOUTH BACKGROUND

Gangs typically have a recognizable inner structure that can be broken down into three categories or levels of gang member involvement (Williams, 1992):

1. *Wannabees* are considered to be the least involved. They're peripheral figures that are not a direct part of the gang, though they talk and act the role of a gang member.

2. *Associates* are at the middle of the hierarchy of involvement. They are basically followers and represent the vast majority of gang members. Associates of a gang are the foot soldiers. They jump in and out of gang activity and are not privy to the gang's strategies, plans, and intelligence.

3. *Hardcore members* of the organization are at the top of the hierarchy. These gang members are the leaders, directing and perpetuating the gang's actions. They plan and manage the gang's day-to-day activities and form its inner clique.

Another way of classifying gang members is age-related. The ages of gang members vary greatly, and participation may start as early as age 10. The age hierarchy looks like this:

1. *Peewees.* The youngest, represent potential full-fledged members. These recruits often live in the gang's neighborhood and are heavily influenced by brothers, sisters, relatives, or friends already involved in the gang subculture.

2. *Junior gang members* are usually 12 to 14 years old and are full-fledged gang members. They write gang graffiti on notebooks, lockers, and clothing and participate in the subculture.

3. The *Homeboys* or *Gang Bangers* are usually between 14 and 20 years old and are the associates and hard-core members. Their activities are geared toward planning and managing the organization.

4. *High Rollers*, 20 years of age and older, and are the veterans who provide drugs to associates and hard-cores to distribute to the streets (Williams, 1992).

Why Youths Join Gangs

Gangs typically are composed of youths who have joined because their basic needs of respect, support, family recognition, protection, identity, belonging, money, and control have not been met through other aspects of their lives (Lacayo, 1994).

Although gangs have been male-dominated for centuries, females become involved for the same reasons as their male counterparts and female involvement in gangs has been on the upswing since the mid-1980s. Females, too, join gangs to fill a void in their lives, often because gang affiliation offers status, guidance, identity, protection, excitement, and attention. Even though their reasons for joining are similar to those of males, female roles within the organization are quite different.

Male and female gang members have similar backgrounds that contribute to the attraction to the gang subculture. Most gang members come from single-parent homes, in which the parents have separated, divorced, or were never married. There is a continuing debate over family structure and its contribution to delinquency.

In an early study, Hirschi (1969) concluded that strong ties to both parents were not necessary to provide an effective buffer against delinquency. Hirschi also argued that broken homes should have no impact on increased delinquency as long as the child is strongly attached to the custodial parent.

Various social-control theories focus on the family as the primary source of attachments, commitments, and disciplinary controls in preventing delinquency. According to these models, the family acts as a buffer against deviant influences by providing a source of basic ties and commitments to the conventional order (Rakin and Kern, 1994). Although Hirschi made some valid points in regard to single-parent families, at-risk youth that are prime targets for gang recruitment primarily feel alienated or neglected by their guardian or custodian. When these youths feel a need to communicate, they often turn to people in the streets of their neighborhood because their family is not meeting their needs.

Another commonality among gang members is that they most often come from violent backgrounds. Most members have had poor role models who have responded to conflicts with violence, and the youths learn that this is the way to handle conflicts in their own lives. Another common characteristic of gang members is that, prior to recruitment, they have had few social outlets at their disposal. Gangs offer members many social opportunities, including parties to entice prospective members. These parties, used heavily as a recruitment tool, generally have readily available drugs and sex. Finally, members of gangs traditionally have lacked interest in education. They do not recognize the value of education and often lack the support and encouragement necessary to continue in an academic environment.

According to Lingren (1995), peer relations expand to occupy a central role in young people's lives, and new types and levels of peer relationships emerge in adolescence. During this time, peers typically replace the family as the center of a young person's socializing and leisure activities. Youths progressing through adolescence tend to have multiple peer relationships and confront different peer cultures with different norms and value systems. Adult's tendency to view their children's peers as having a negative influence is usually unfounded. More often than not, peers actually reinforce family values. Still, one has to consider families that do not socialize their children properly and fail to instill socially acceptable values and norms.

Lingren (1995) also pointed out that the peer group is a source of affection, sympathy, and understanding; a place for experimentation; and a supportive setting for achieving the two primary developmental tasks of adolescence:

1. *Identity*—finding the answer to the question, "Who am I?"
2. *Autonomy*—discovering self as separate and independent from parents (p. 1).

These natural developmental milestones may well be healthy and natural for most adolescent youths, but under unstable, unsupportive family conditions, these normal milestones may open the door for youths to become involved in delinquent groups. According to Lingren, gangs typically are associated with inner-city neighborhoods in the recent past, though gangs have been moving to smaller cities, suburbs, and even rural areas, arising not only from poverty but also from parents who are in constant conflict with their child, distant, and unavailable.

YOUTHS AND GUNS

The use of guns and the proliferation of gun sales in the United States continue to rise. Between 1988 and 1992, firearm fatalities had increased 127% among males 15 to 19 years of age, and the National Death Registry data showed that Black teenage males in this age group comprised 60% of the deaths related to firearms. By comparison, 23% of the deaths from firearms consisted of White males 15 to 19 years of age, 22% were Black females, and 10% were White female fatalities (Albanese, 1996).

These statistics offer a grim picture. The demand for guns among youths has been fueled by an "ecology of danger," consisting of street gangs, an expanding drug market, and different lifestyles and perceptions about gun possession and carrying guns. Often, guns have become symbols of respect, power, identity and manhood. In crime-ridden communities many youths carry guns not so much for respect, power, or identity as for survivability. Studies of adolescent violence show that teenage males, whether in schools, gangs, or correctional institutions, report "self-defense" as the most important reason for carrying a gun (L.H. Research, 1993; Sheley, McGee, and Wright, 1995).

Just as adolescent playgroups evolved into gangs, production of hand-held guns also evolved. When smaller and more portable guns were developed, they became an important part of the gangs' means of operation.

As the homicide rates of adolescent youths continue to climb, so does the fear of victimization within the teenage population. The infusion of guns into the teenage population may have motivated gun acquisition as a form of self-defense (Kennedy, Piehl, and Braga, 1996).

Although guns are used mainly as a means of protection, they also are used to settle conflicts, to show dominance in matters of honor, and to protect territory. As a society, the United States has raised its young people to accept violence as normal, and toughness as part of the adolescent masculine identity. This mindset has been passed from generation to generation in families from various socioeconomic conditions, from upper-class White families to poor, underprivileged Black families. The propensity to resort to violence to resolve interpersonal conflict, some argue, has been the foundation of male adolescent upbringing for hundreds of years and will continue into the future.

An example of violence that has been perpetuated for decades can be seen in the warrior culture that began in prehistoric times. During this era, humans resort to violence to satisfy many of their basic needs, which included some of the same needs that promote violence today. Prehistoric humans had to fight for food, land, and possessions. This culture and its use of violence to obtain material goods have continued throughout history and can be connected with modern violence.

This history of violence raises the question that many criminologists and sociologists have contemplated for centuries: Is violence an innate characteristic in humankind? Do humans have a predisposition to violence? As American society has evolved into a more civilized people, the violence that was commonplace in precivilized cultures has been prohibited by law in modern communities. Still, violence exists, and delinquent playgroups and gangs are beginning to proliferate in many communities.

YOUTH GANGS AND THE DRUG MARKET

The drug market in the United States has grown by leaps and bounds over the past 40 years, mainly as a result of which was the crack epidemic, introduced on the streets of major cities in the 1980s. With crack becoming drug users' and addicts' answer to a quick fix, the popular drug heroin was pushed to the side in favor of the cheapest and most intense high that money could buy. Crack, a solid, smokable form of cocaine, has wreaked havoc on American streets, moving from the major cities where it was introduced to suburban and rural neighborhoods and communities. Over time, the connection between drugs and violent street gangs has reflected changing economic, cultural, racial/ethnic and community factors. According to Fagan (1990), the involvement of youth gangs in volatile drug markets (such as crack) has signaled a transformation of youth gangs from transitory adolescent social networks to nascent criminal organizations.

Over time, gangs that were involved in the drug market have come to utilize juveniles as dealers, manipulating them by flashing money and material goods as a means of gaining their help on the street. Juveniles have been used as look-outs, drug runners, and handlers in drug sales, because the juvenile justice system tends not to incarcerate juveniles for long periods. Although the juvenile justice system has become stricter on criminal youths, juveniles are aware that if they are charged as a juvenile, their criminal record will be sealed at age 18. For these reasons, juveniles have continued as key players in the sale of street-level drugs.

Many scholars believe that the structure of the economy has been largely responsible for the entry of gang members, as individuals and cliques, into drug trafficking (Spergel, 1995). One example is the single mother whi is aware that her son is selling drugs but this activity helps to pay the bills and put food on the table. Therefore, it becomes an issue of survivability. Another example is the scarcity of other means of making money. In economically deprived areas where adults lack work, this in turn results in a lack of work for youths who wish to make money. This makes drug sales an appealing alternative. The quick sale, the abundance of money, and material goods that can be gained from working less while making more makes the drug racket an appealing option.

HOW GANGS MOVE INTO A NEIGHBORHOOD

Broken-Windows Theory

"A man's home is his castle," has become a common cliché that expresses individuals' protective natures over their dwellings. As neighborhoods age, structures (social and physical) sometimes begin to dwindle. Buildings begin to show signs of age, homes are not cared for as they once were, and the overall appearance of the area declines. With aging communities and an aging population that is unable to care for the neighborhood, the probability of crime slowly moving in increases along with aging of the community. These communities are the breeding grounds for criminally minded youths and youth gangs that wish to gain a foothold and take advantage of these deteriorating conditions.

When looking for a possible explanation for why crime and juvenile gangs emerge in such neighborhoods, James Q. Wilson and George Kelling's (1989) classic *Broken Windows* theory may shed some light on the problem. They postulated that, as communities age and buildings and homes are left vacant, they become targets for petty vandalism (i.e., a broken window). As a result of the decline of the area, the vandalized buildings and vacant homes are not repaired. This creates a snowball effect, encompassing more vandalism and crime-related problems for the area.

A common theme for neighborhoods in this situation is that the inhabitants lack the commitment to their community to ward off potential vandalism and other crimes. As the area declines, businesses and organizations that have provided economic stability in an area seek more profitable environments and leave. Along with these businesses and organizations, families move and teachers relocate, leaving the older population to maintain the community. This older population is unable to maintain control of the neighborhoods, and community organizations fall by the wayside. As a result, these communities become targets for unsupervised adolescents and delinquent youths. Unable to take the reins and fearful of retaliation from the intruders, elderly people become prisoners in their homes and at the mercy of those who wish to wreak havoc on their streets. Another possible reason for the downward spiral of impoverished communities is that those living in poverty cannot keep pace with technology and an advancing society and thus lack the resources and opportunity to advance as the more affluent communities do.

Differential Association

Coupled with the *broken windows theory*, Edwin Sutherland's classic differential association theory (Siegel, 1998) becomes important when analyzing delinquency and youth gangs. The theory of differential association suggests that negative and positive behaviors are learned by persistent and consistent reinforcement by significant others. Coupling this theory with the broken windows theory, negative behaviors such as drug dealing, prostitution, vandalism, and gang activity are reinforced. As the result of gang membership, youths receive negative reinforcement to carry out delinquent acts.

The youths involved in delinquent acts are engaging in activities that the community at large prohibits and thus considers negative, but receive positive reinforcement or praise for their acts by the peer group, which at this stage is a dominant influence in the child's life. As the cycle continues, a circular pattern begins to emerge between the broken windows theory and the differential association process that drags the community farther and farther into poverty and victimization.

Labeling Theory

Another possible answer to delinquent acts or gang involvement is proposed by the labeling theory. According to this theory, the youths' continuing delinquency stems in part from the reaction of others to the act committed (primary deviance). If those reactions are negative, the youths may come to view themselves as "bad" and continue to engage in behavior that is consistent (secondary deviance) with that self-image or emerging stereotype.

The labeling could cause the youths to act upon the newly acquired tag, resulting in their downward spiral into more delinquent acts. Many youths who do this are primary targets for recruitment by local gangs. Gangs also may recruit or attract individuals who are predisposed to aggressive and acting-out behavior and, in turn, delinquency and violence. Existing evidence suggests that gang membership does indeed intensify delinquent behavior. And having delinquent friends clearly contributes to one's own delinquency (Batton, Hill, Abbott, Catalano, and Hawkins, 1998). Thornberry, Lizotte, and Wierschem (1993) examined the delinquent acts of gang members before and after membership and compared them to individuals who were not gang members. They found that the gang members did not have higher rates of delinquency before entering the gang but, upon joining a gang, their delinquency rates increased significantly. This suggests that participation in gangs is an important factor in increasing delinquency.

Over the years, many youths have been labeled as "bad" by adults in positions of authority, including parents and teachers. This can have a profound impact on the child so labeled. In most cases, the relationship between teacher and student is a helping one that focuses on the child's development and future. Some teachers, however, label children who do not meet the instructor's expectations. If a child is viewed as uncontrollable, impulsive, disrespectful, or ill-mannered and is described in these terms, a child who seeks attention may begin to take on that role. In some cases, the child receiving the negative attention views it as better than no attention at all.

Parents have a primary influence on their child's life. Parents who verbally compare their child's behavior with that of others may serve as a catalyst for the child to act out. One example is illustrated in the book *All God's Children*, by Fox Butterfield (1995). The main character is a boy named Willie Bosket. He lives with his grandmother and is constantly compared to his father, who has an extensive criminal past and is serving a life sentence for murder. As a result of this continuous comparison, Willie comes to idolize his father's "badness" and assumes many of his father's behaviors. This example offers food for thought about the impressionable nature of children.

Under the labeling theory, persistent negative stimuli from authority figures seems to be at the root of the child's fulfilling of the label. Not only is this potentially harmful, but the child's self-esteem also may fall. Loss of self-esteem can lead to other problems, such as depression, worthlessness, delinquency, and even suicidal tendencies.

Children are impressionable and look to the adults in their lives for love, guidance, support, and the necessary nurturing to develop into healthy and productive adults. At face value, voicing one's opinion about a child's behavior may seem trivial, but the long-term effects of how the child views himself or herself can have a huge impact on the child's life.

A NEW ERA: WWW.GANGS.COM

Gangs, like American society, are dynamic in nature and, as such, are constantly changing, driven by technology, material goods, and money. With the evolution of the computer industry and implementation of the Internet, gangs across the nation are now more accessible. At the push of a button, computer users can access the homepage of some of the more high-profile organizations such as the Bloods and Crips. Upon visiting a gang's web site, users have an abundance of information at their fingertips, including recruitment information, gang signs, members' street names, graffiti, and more.

The information highway has opened many doors in terms of accessing information. Some sites on the Internet are attractive and appealing to youths at risk for gang recruitment. Recently, gang-related web sites have come under fire by law enforcement officials. One such group with a web site that recently received national attention in connection with the massacre at Columbine High School in Littleton, Colorado, is the "Trench Coat Mafia."

Most people have an image of youth gangs as being composed of minority males from underprivileged homes in the inner city. In the late 1990s, this stereotype was shown to be far from the truth. Gangs stretch across all racial, cultural and socioeconomic lines. Gangs can be found in affluent communities, crime-ridden neighborhoods, and small farming towns. This expansion across classes of people makes society more vulnerable than ever. Turning a blind eye to the possibilities of youth gangs moving into middle- or upper-class neighborhoods only invites victimization. The mainstream mindset that youth gangs are a big-city problem makes middle- and upper-class communities more vulnerable to gang infiltration. Educating communities about their vulnerability is a key to preventing youth gangs from infiltrating areas that now are free of gang activity. A continuing roadblock to prevention has been the lack of community interest and support of gang-reduction initiatives (Albanese, 1996). Denying the problem could prove to be most costly roadblock of all.

TELEVISION, THE MEDIA, MUSIC AND VIDEO GAMES

Over the years, television, movies, music, and, more recently video games, have come under fire by officials claiming that viewing violent acts through these means has an extremely negative effect on youths. These modes of entertainment are easily discernable to an adult as real or fictional, but impressionable children may have problems discerning fact from fiction, and the violence portrayed in many movies, video games, and music similarly confuses right from wrong. This is especially true if parents do not take an active role in helping the child differentiate the two.

In regard to gang activity, movies such as *New Jack City*, *Colors*, and the popular 1980s movie *Warrior*, glamorized the life of gangsters. These movies portrayed a life of money, fine cars, nice homes, power, women, and invincibility. Although they provide pure entertainment for most people, children at risk may see these movies as a carrot within their reach. The reckless use of weapons and disregard for authority also are heard in the music recorded by rap artists. In the mid-1990s, music artist Ice T released a compact disc, "Cop Killer," that was later removed from store shelves because of its negative message against law enforcement.

Television in many homes has taken the place of involved parents; the parenting has been left to producers of the popular shows. The nightly news draws in viewers with the glamour and limelight that criminals elicit. On April 20, 1999, a worldwide spotlight focused on Columbine High School in Littleton, Colorado, where a school shooting claimed the lives of a teacher and 14 students, including the two gunmen. Images of the Littleton massacre, as it soon was labeled, appeared on TV, and in newspapers and magazines throughout the country, giving details of the horrifying event. Although the goal of the media is to keep people informed of current events as they unfold, one side effect emerged: During the days following the Columbine incident, other reports of bomb threats, violence, and Trench Coat Mafias "wannabees" began to appear around the country.

As one spin-off from the Littleton incident, another school shooting in an Atlanta, Georgia, high school left six students injured and hundreds horrified and asking questions. If the Columbine incident had this effect, why wouldn't a graphic shoot 'em up gang movie boost local gang recruitment? If the news can give rise to copycat incidents, why wouldn't the release of a glamorized gang movie lead to an increase in gang membership? Video games also have been blamed for violent incidents involving youths. Some claim that the violent nature of modern video games represents negative stimuli that may train children how to act out violently. Children who cannot separate fiction from reality may actually see these games as reality and use them as training for their own future Littleton Massacre.

As the latest news stories come and go the graphic details are imprinted in the youths of America. Therefore, parents need to be cognizant of what their children are watching on television playing on their Nintendo or Play Station, and what Web sites they have access to. Even though monitoring these favorite pastimes may impede social ills from infecting youths, *nothing* can take the place of parents spending quality time and talking with their child.

FEMALES AND GANG MEMBERSHIP

Historically, females have been seen as auxiliary appendages to male gangs, and ignored in systematic analyses in the field of juvenile research. Most of the attention has been given to male adolescents, for males comprise the majority of delinquent offenders, although more and more attention is being paid to female delinquency. The extent of female involvement in gangs, especially those that are independent entities is still much debated. In one national survey conducted by Irving Spergel, females committed only 5% or less of all reported gang crimes (Siegel and Senna, 1990).

Even though females are taking a more active role in gang activities, their primary role in male-dominated gangs historically has been that of gun handlers, drug runners and dealers, and sexual partners for gang members. Females are generally seen as property and are accorded much less status than male members. In a few cities, female gangs are found to be as violent, aggressive, and threatening as their male counterparts.

Although many believe that females are becoming more active in gang activities, perceptions of the level of female participation in more serious aspects of the gang organizational structure vary. In her study of female gangs, Anne Campbell (Crews and Counts, 1997) found that, of the 8,000 to 40,000 gang members in New York City, approximately 10% were females, ranging from 14 to 30 years of age.

The pattern of female initiation into male-dominated gangs differs somewhat from that of males. A feemale is less likely to be pressured or coerced into joining. Unlike the male, she is simply "likely to hang out and attach herself to a group which participates in gang behavior" (Harris 1988, p. 112). Unlike male members of gangs, females have the luxury of coming and going from the gang, and female involvement in the organization can change rapidly because of this. Although some gangs allow females to attach themselves to the organization by mere affiliation with the gang, many gangs require females, as the males do, to show their loyalty to the group. In some cases, females are "beat in"—defined as an arranged fight between gang members and the individual who wishes to become part of the organization. In other cases, females are required to take part in a shooting or other criminal activity as a show of loyalty and commitment to the group. Most females seeking membership are searching for companionship, a sense of love, belonging, support, respect, and a sense of control in her life.

Beginning in the 1980s, a growing body of research emerged as researchers focused more and more on possible unique causes of female criminality. Much of this research had taken traditional male-based theories and applied them to female criminality. One theory with a possible link to female criminality is the Strain theory. According to this theory, juveniles are "pushed" into delinquency as a result of lack of access to legitimate avenues or paths to the attainment of one's goals. Some say racism or sexism are barriers. Those whose access is blocked in some way may seek other avenues to goal attain their goals—which can be criminal behavior and gang involvement.

Historically, this theory was not applied to women because females were not seen as having goals in life. Males traditionally were the leaders, husbands, and fathers, and therefore the ones with power to make family decisions and set goals for the future. In the 1990s, researchers contend the Strain theory impacts females more than males because females are more likely to be victims of blocked access simply because of their sex (Crews and Counts, 1997).

Another possible cause of female criminality can be attributed to what has been called the economic marginalization of women. According to this theory, the absence of employment opportunities for women is what seems to lead to increases in female crime. This theory suggests that poverty is the most predominant force in female criminality. Men still tend to be paid more than women in the workforce. Coupled with the increasing number of female-headed households with dependent children, female criminality has emerged at times out of mere survival (Landis and Simon, 1991).

There is an explanation for why female criminality has not received much attention: Over the years, most deviant acts have been committed by men. As society has evolved, women started to take on jobs and responsibilities that for decades have been the province of men. With the women's liberation movement, women's fight for equal rights and the less passive role of women are beginning to be seen differently in the eyes of the criminal justice system. As women have struggled for equal treatment, the criminality of women also has come to the fore. As women continue to assume roles of single parent, head of household, employee, and mother, crimes committed by females will continue to gain ground and more closely resemble male criminal statistics.

GANG SUPPRESSION AND COMMUNITY INTERVENTION

As discussed, youths seek gang membership for a variety of reasons, from a lack of respect to a lack of love from a parent or guardian. Much research from sociologists and criminologists points to the family as the primary influence on youth affiliation with gangs. Many experts on gangs, however, suggest that gangs and the problems they present are best viewed within their entire social, economic, and cultural context rather than an "us-versus-them" approach. It is evident that many youths continue to seek opportunity in environments where opportunity is lacking and many times this leads them down the path to gang membership. Unemployment, poverty, and the flight from cities by Whites and upwardly mobile Blacks alike have left the underclass behind in the inner city (Regoli and Hewitt, 1997). As these people leave the community, gangs emerge as a dominant power and draw on youths who have dropped out of school, the underemployed and the unemployed.

Five basic strategies have evolved in dealing with youth gangs: (1) neighborhood mobilization; (2) social intervention, especially youth outreach and work with street gangs; (3) provision of social and economic opportunities, such as special school and job programs; (4) gang suppression and incarceration; and (5) a law-enforcement strategy, such as police gang and specialized probation units (Crews and Counts, 1997).

The *neighborhood mobilization approach* to the delinquent group or gang, which evolved in the 1920s and 1930s, was an early attempt to bind together local citizens, social institutions, and the criminal justice system in a variety of informal and, later, formal ways. Neighborhood adults and youth agencies often worked to socialize youths in general and did not specifically target delinquent or gang youths.

These efforts led to the *social intervention approach*—a more sophisticated outreach to street gangs in the 1940s and 1950s. In the 1960s, large-scale resource infusions led to *special school and job programs* designed to change institutional structures and reduce poverty. Although programs such as Head Start and the Job Corps seemed to have had a positive effect on reducing delinquency, it is not clear to what extent these programs addressed the youth gang problem (Office of Juvenile Justice and Delinquency Prevention, 1994).

In the 1970s and 1980s, a new strategy, *gang suppression*, emerged and remains prevalent. This strategy can be related to several factors: the decline of local community and youth outreach efforts, at least with respect to the youth gang problem; the insufficiency of opportunity-provision approaches to target or modify gang structures; the changing structure of a labor market that no longer can adequately absorb unskilled and poorly educated older youth gang members; and the consequent increased criminalization and sophistication of youth gangs (Office of Juvenile Justice and Delinquency Prevention, 1994).

These factors have resulted in more reliance on a *law enforcement* approach including specialized police units. Youth gangs are increasingly viewed as dangerous and evil, a receptacle for sociopaths that social institutions could not rehabilitate. Community protection has become a goal in most gang-suppression projects. Gang members, especially leaders and serious offenders, increasingly have been arrested, prosecuted, and removed from the community to serve long prison sentences (Office of Juvenile Justice and Delinquency Prevention, 1994).

Many programs target at-risk youths who have not yet joined gangs. These programs seek to help youth develop positive social relationships, build self-esteem, and handle conflict in a socially acceptable manner. The programs combine community, school, and family-based strategies, including (Regoli and Hewitt, 1997):

- Youth outreach programs
- Community centers
- Employment and training assistance
- School dropout services
- Multicultural training for teachers
- Family intervention and training
- Substance abuse counseling
- Conflict mediation programs
- Recreational activities.

An Overview of Youth Programs

Several programs target at-risk youths. Some are general approaches to combating delinquency, and others, such as gang suppression, are more specific. Past research has shown that the most effective programs dealing with juveniles are proactive in nature. This type of program intervenes early and seeks youths that are at risk before they become involved with delinquent peer groups or the criminal justice system.

In reviewing many programs, evidence points to early intervention in the lives of at-risk youth as the best approach. Gangs start to recruit members who are as young as 8 or 9 years of age, and many programs do not include this age group. Another common deficiency in delinquency programs is that those implementing the program pick those they want in the program, thereby setting themselves up for success (i.e., statistics that reveal a low recidivism rate). As a result of stringent selection, many programs eliminate youths who are truly in need of some form of intervention.

Current Gang-Suppression Programs

Gang Resistance Education and Training (G.R.E.A.T.)

The G.R.E.A.T. program was designed to reduce youth violence and gang membership using a curriculum taught by law enforcement officers to elementary and middle-school students. G.R.E.A.T. students are given the opportunity to discover for themselves the ramifications of gang violence through structured exercises and interactive approaches to learning. Included in the curriculum are many optional and extended activities that reinforce classroom instruction. Law-enforcement representatives and teachers work together to teach students to become responsible members of their communities, set goals for themselves, resist peer pressure, and resolve conflicts and problems. By 1995, G.R.E.A.T. had trained more than 2,700 police officers in a 1- to 2-week training session, and as a result, more than 1,300 communities had been exposed to the G.R.E.A.T. program.

In 1995, the University of Nebraska completed a cross-sectional survey of 53,935 eighth graders, 45% of whom had participated in the G.R.E.A.T. program; the rest were used as a comparison group. Preliminary results suggested that G.R.E.A.T. had a significant impact on changing the behavior of students to include more prosocial behaviors and attitudes, less involvement in delinquent activities and fighting, and less likelihood of engaging in risk-taking behavior after participating in the program. The most significant results of this program were that after participating in the G.R.E.A.T. project, participants were less likely to perceive blocks to their academic success and expressed stronger antigang attitudes. Although these results were obtained after only 1 year of implementation, further analysis was scheduled for concurrent years 1996–1999 (Office of Juvenile Justice and Delinquency Prevention, 1998)

Gang Prevention Through Targeted Outreach

In 1991, the Boys and Girls Clubs of America (B&GCA) connected local clubs with courts, police departments, schools, social service agencies, and other organizations in the community. Local Boys and Girls Clubs involved in this targeted outreach program identified and recruited at-risk youths 6 to 18 years of age into clubs. The clubs used direct outreach methods to approach youths in the community. This program focuses on enhancing youths' communication, problem-solving, and decision-making skills. Noting monthly progress, the club professional staff helps youths focus on specific developmental goals such as staying in school and out of the court system, improving scholastically, bonding with positive adults, and participating more frequently in club events and activities.

In 1997, B&GCA provided training and technical assistance to 30 existing gang-prevention and 3 intervention sites and expanded the gang prevention and intervention program to 23 additional clubs. In 1998, B&GCA projected that it would provide training and technical assistance to 22 new gang prevention sites and 3 new intervention sites. An evaluation of the program found that, once enrolled, 90% of the youths came to the club once a week or more and 26% began to come in daily. As a result of participation in the program, 48% of the youths involved improved their academic performance (Office of Juvenile Justice and Delinquency Prevention, 1998).

Adolescent Social Action Program (ASAP)

The ASAP program, based at the University of New Mexico (UNM), uses peer resistance and decision-making training to increase self-efficacy, social responsibility, and life skills. Youth participants engage in social-action activities to address conditions that lead to high-risk behaviors, such as substance use and abuse, gang involvement, and violence. Preliminary research findings indicate a significant impact on the development of positive coping skills, the ability to influence others, and reduced rates of teen drinking behaviors.

For more than 14 years, ASAP has operated in more than 30 communities in New Mexico, including American Indian reservations and small, rural Hispanic communities. This program takes small groups of students on three supervised visits to a local or regional hospital, one visit to a detention center, and one visit to the Metro court. The students interview hospital patients and inmates and listen to their stories. Then, using critical-thinking strategies, they examine the consequences of patients' and inmates' actions through dialogues led by trained graduate and undergraduate university facilitators and reflected upon their own lives.

ASAP staff also conducts and develops local and national training for teachers, community groups, and health professionals. Topics include empowerment-based education, peer education, and working with youth (Office of Juvenile Justice and Delinquency Prevention, 1998).

Gang Resistance Is Paramount (G.R.I.P.)

G.R.I.P. was established by the City of Paramount, California, in an attempt to curb gang membership and discourage future gang involvement. Formerly known as Alternatives to Gang Membership, it combines the resources of families, schools, and local government. The program attempts to discourage gang membership by teaching children the harmful consequences of this lifestyle and persuading them to choose positive alternatives. Initiated in 1982, G.R.I.P. has three major components:

1. Neighborhood meetings that provide parents with support, assistance, and resources as they try to prevent their children from joining gangs. These meetings, conducted in both English and Spanish, focus on educating parents about gang activity, increasing family involvement, supporting sports and recreation programs, and increasing neighborhood unity to combat gang proliferation.

2. A 15-week course for fifth-grade students and a 10-week course for second-grade students. The lessons deal with graffiti, peer pressure, tattoos, the impact of gang activity on family members, drug abuse, and alternative activities and opportunities.

3. A school-based follow-up program implemented at the ninth-grade level to reinforce what children learned in the elementary grades. The program builds self-esteem and also focuses on the consequences of a criminal lifestyle, the benefits of higher education, and future career opportunities.

This program has undergone several studies to measure its effectiveness. The most significant finding was that 50% of youths prior to participation were undecided about gang involvement. Once involved with the program, 90% of the youths studied responded negatively toward gangs. The final study conducted on this program cross-checked the names of 3,612 former program participants with local police records and found that 96 percent were not identified as gang members (Office of Juvenile Justice and Delinquency Prevention, 1998).

Youth Gangs and Juvenile Corrections

It has long been established that conditions within the prison system mirror free society. Juvenile correctional facilities across the United States, like their adult counterparts, house gang members. Many youths who are members of gangs and are incarcerated in youth facilities continue to correspond with other gang members within the communities in which they left. Many times, gang members use their time of incarceration to promote their organization and seek out other youths to join their gang. This time of idleness gives the youths time to teach potential gang members about the organization, duties, responsibilities, and history of the organization. In some cases, youths who are inducted into the gang while still incarcerated are branded or tattooed upon release from the institution.

Juvenile correctional officers play a key role in gang suppression in juvenile correctional facilities, for they are the ones who spend the most time with this youthful population. In doing so, the officers become aware of common behaviors among those tho whom he or she is assigned. This takes time, so reassignment of officers to other housing units inhibits the gang suppression effort. The supervisory staff should strive to maintain continuity with the officers who work in the various housing units. And officers should be aware of the backgrounds of the juveniles they are assigned to supervise, including any past gang involvement. One common practice in the Department of Corrections that some juvenile correctional facilities utilize is to photograph tattoos. This gives the staff and administration a record of gang markings and helps to track members within the system.

Juvenile correctional officers can implement several actions in their daily routine to help in the fight against juvenile prison gangs. They may wish to

- Talk with known gang members, to learn as much as possible about the organization.
- Talk with other juvenile correctional officers and exchange information concerning gangs and their experiences.
- Keep all confiscated gang paraphernalia and make duplicates to share with other officers.
- Call local law enforcement personnel to gain information or background on specific youth gangs.
- Don't discard or overlook drawings as "just art," but also do not look at all art as gang symbols.

- Separate gang members and members of the same gang.
- Conduct thorough contraband searches of each room or cell, including the offender, to identify gang markings, drawings, or recruitment materials.
- Educate yourself about gang hand signals and street language so you can intervene properly if you see gang hand signals or hear street language associated with gangs.

In the struggle to maintain control in juvenile correctional centers, the education of juvenile correctional officers and the consistent assignment of officers to housing units is paramount. Training beyond the initial basic instruction should be made available to correctional employees who have direct contact with the juvenile population to ensure that correctional officials continue to have the upper hand in their respective facilities. Also paramount in the effort to suppress gang involvement and recruitment is to inform known gang members about facility rules that directly address gang recruitment and written material related to gang involvement.

Suppressing youth gangs in juvenile correctional facilities is a constant struggle, and its success depends on all employees who work with the youthful population. As juveniles are released, new youths are admitted, and the process continues. This cyclical chain of information and education is the only defense against the proliferation of correctional gangs within the juvenile correctional facilities. Firm, fair, and consistent treatment of all offenders, regardless of gang affiliation, continues to provide the best possible treatment results and gang suppression in American youth facilities.

Crisis in American Juvenile Correctional Facilities

In 1995, 69 million persons in the United States were below age 18—the group commonly referred to as *juveniles*. Earlier, during the late 1970s and early 1980s, the juvenile population declined. Since 1984, however, it has been increasing and is projected to reach 74 million by the year 2010. This population growth will produce more juvenile victims of abuse and neglect, more juvenile offenders, and more cases entering the juvenile justice system. According to the Office of Juvenile Justice and Delinquency Prevention, the juvenile population in the United States will be more diverse than it was 10 years ago. Table 2.1 describes the projected juvenile population in the United States.

As a result of this projected increase in juvenile population, further strains on juvenile correctional facilities also should be projected. As American juvenile facilities continue to be overcrowded, conditions within these facilities have begun to deteriorate. In the recent past, conditions in the Virginia Department of Juvenile Justice, for example, have bordered on Constitutional violations. The Beaumont Juvenile Correctional facility in Powhatan, Virginia, lost its accreditation for facility conditions that included understaffing, overcrowding, and potentially abusive conditions for the juveniles and the staff members alike (Problems at Juvenile Centers said to Persist, 1999). David Ress, a staff writer for the *Richmond*

TABLE 2.1   Projected Juvenile Population Increase by the Year 2010

	Population		Increase	
	1990	2010	Number	Percent
All juvenile	64,185,000	73,617,000	9,432,000	15
Ages 0–4	18,874,000	20,017,000	1,143,000	6
Ages 5–9	18,064,000	19,722,000	1,658,000	9
Ages 10–14	17,191,000	20,724,000	3,533,000	21
Ages 15–17	10,056,000	13,154,000	3,098,000	31

Source: Office of Juvenile Justice and Delinquency Prevention, June 1996.

Times Dispatch, reported the overcrowding at the Beaumont Juvenile Correctional Center to be 25% above operational capacity, and Bon Air Juvenile Correctional in Chesterfield County to be 28% to 35% over capacity.

Along with the increasing juvenile populations in U.S. juvenile correctional facilities, problems have begun to fester that may have stemmed from overcrowded conditions. The South Carolina Department of Juvenile Justice has been accused of serious injuries to juvenile detainees inflicted by other juveniles incarcerated at three facilities. According to *The State*, South Carolina's newspaper, in a 6-month period, 10 boys were sexually assaulted by other boys in prison dormitories (Advocate Seeks to End Violence, 2000). Records indicated that from January through November 1999 approximately 1,200 youth had to be taken to prison infirmaries for treatment after other juveniles had attacked them. These problems are only examples of the violence, substandard conditions, and overcrowding in juvenile prisons. Further examples demonstrating the breadth of this problem are

- The *High Plans Youth Center* in Colorado shuts down after being plagued by violence among inmates and between inmates and staff. High staff turnover and poor employee training were to blame. (Colorado Closes Down Juvenile Facility, 1998)

- At the *Robert Rivarde Juvenile Detention Center*, Baton Rouge, Louisiana, six inmates riot when a search for a cigarette lighter prompts an inmate to throw a chair, striking a counselor in the head. (Six Juveniles Placed in State's Custody, 1998)

- At a *maximum-security juvenile detention center* in Portland, Oregon, four teenage inmates attacked guards. A 7-1/2-hour standoff ensued after the inmates barricaded themselves in an office. (Teen Inmates in Custody, 1998)

- Drugs smuggled into the *Catalina Mountain School* in Arizona helped ignite a gang fight among 17 youths. Some of the youths appeared to have taken drugs, according to correctional officials. (Officials Glossed Over Brawl, 1999)

The incidents in these facilities provide a glimpse into the larger problem. Many states and counties have similar, and sometimes more severe, problems than the ones outlined. There has been a trend in the United States to treat sentenced juveniles more severely, with longer periods of incarceration and with less focus on rehabilitative treatment and more focus on incapacitation. The deteriorating conditions of facilities throughout the country, coupled with inadequate staffing and lack of staff training, have challenged the philosophy behind the juvenile justice system, which for decades has been rehabilitation. Longer sentences in counterproductive conditions actually may lead to higher incarceration rates.

Studies conducted by the California Youth Authority demonstrate that over a 10-year period, as the length of incarceration increased, the recidivism rate increased proportionately (Shepherd, 1998). This points to a possible saturation point or point of optimal incarceration beyond which incarceration becomes counterproductive. Longer sentences in a system that is not treating the juvenile offender population are surely setting ip the youths for failure.

CONCLUSION

Although no one is sure why or when youth gangs started, one thing is evident; juvenile involvement in gangs has been renewed in recent years with much enthusiasm. By the late 1990s, youth gangs had spread from poor, inner-city environments to small towns and middle- and upper-class communities. The migration of these groups into uncharted territory may have been fueled by the growing complexity of childhood and adolescence and the upward mobility of society made possible by technological advances. The computer industry and the evolution of the Internet have made gangs more accessible to the at-risk population in terms of gang recruitment.

Although the nation's technological advancements may provide part of the answer to the proliferation of membership in youth gangs, the family structure and its functioning remain paramount when searching for an origin to the gang problem. Gangs offer an alternative to fill needs for belonging and sense of acceptance of some youths.

The gang subculture continues to be of much interest to scholars, law enforcement officials, and politicians. In addition, the people whom gangs affect the most—those who inhabit communities where gangs thrive—should take note and be aware of what is happening in their neighborhoods. Gangs, once occupying inner cities, are moving next door. Communities in denial about the presence of gangs are in their neighborhood are prime targets for gang infiltration and victimization.

chapter 3

FROM GUM CHEWING TO GUN TOTING

School Violence

I hate Mondays.

> Brenda Spencer, 16, January 29, 1979,
> in response to a question of why she opened fire at
> Cleveland Elementary School with a .22-caliber rifle,
> killing two and wounding nine

I just said, "Mom, I'm okay. I love you." I had to be sure I told my mom I loved her in case I died.

> Zak Cartaya, 17, a senior at Littleton, Colorado,
> Columbine High School, April 20, 1999

No one, especially children, just becomes a murderer. Something had to happen to push them to that point.

> Luke Woodham, 16, Pearl Mississippi High School
> shooter, during an interview on why the shooting had occurred

INTRODUCTION

Although very often perceived to be a new phenomenon in the United States, it is not. School disturbance and violence have existed since the first schools opened their doors. There has, however, been a major change in how this type of violence has evolved over many decades. In the seventeenth and eighteen centuries, school violence appeared as teacher-on-student violence exhibited through extremely harsh and brutal disciplinary practices. This evolved into student-on-student violence in the early twentieth century, as students began victimizing each other. In the late twentieth century, this violence evolved into student-on-teacher violence, coming full circle in the ways it manifests itself (Crews and Counts, 1997).

From an examination of school violence in the United States, a myriad of disturbing trends has become apparent in society. The possibility that a disagreement between students will be settled with some type of weapon rather than the traditional fist-fight has increased significantly. Students seem to be much more inclined to use a weapon to settle a score than ever before in the history of American education. Further, many of these scores that are being settled are for something that happened days, months, or even years before. A quiet school day can suddenly erupt as a result of an argument between two students a month ago off school grounds, catching educators off guard.

Also, many have believed until recently that school violence was just an urban inner-city problem. Now it has become clear that public, private, upper-class, and nonsectarian schools all have seen an increase in school violence. Not only is violence prevalent in all types of schools, but it also is increasing in every geographic region of the United States. Communities large and small across the country are struggling with the problem of school violence (Violence in Schools, 1993). If for no other reason, the rash of school shootings in the late twentieth century taught this to the American public.

The public's concerns about discipline and violence, both inside and outside of the school building, reached a record high in the late 1990s. Crews and Counts (1997) described three types of students in American schools in the late twentieth century:

1. The vast majority who rarely broke the rules or committed any acts of violence.

2. Those who broke the rules somewhat regularly by refusing to accept classroom rules and restrictions, thereby disrupting the learning process for the other children in a classroom.

3. The small percentage who were chronic rule-breakers, out of control most of the time and committing violent and criminal acts in school and in the local community.

Offenders represent all racial, ethnic, and economic groups. Therefore, violence can be found in all schools across the country. Although males are still more likely to be involved in acts of violence, females are engaging more frequently in violent acts.

The motivation for school violence has changed, too. It has become painfully apparent that a logical reason for a violent incident is no longer necessary. More and more often, perpetrators do not have a serious or possibly justifiable reason for striking out against a teacher or a fellow student. Something as simple as a glance, a stare, or an accidental bump in the lunch line can trigger a violent reaction. Teachers are reporting an increasing number of incidents arising from idle gossip, dating problems, feelings of rejection, or the desire to impress others. A student's dislike of the appearance or actions of another student may be all that is required for an assault. Many students in modern American schools are quick-tempered, and the results are often disastrous.

HISTORICAL ASPECTS OF SCHOOL VIOLENCE IN THE UNITED STATES

Much insight can be derived through historical examination of an issue. This is no less truer when discussing school violence.

School Violence in the Seventeenth and Eighteenth Centuries

The first school disturbances occurred as soon as the first schoolhouses opened their doors and began accepting students. The first juvenile offenses included rebelliousness and disobedience. The rules were extremely strict, and even sledding on the Sabbath or playing ball on public streets was forbidden. In some colonies, the penalty for rebellion against parents was *death*. In actual practice, however, the courts and juries often were lenient toward the young. Even if found guilty, children often were acquitted after a nominal trial, or pardoned. In rare cases, children were severely punished or put to death (Rothman, 1971).

In early eighteenth-century America, discipline problems were a daily occurrence in schools. Teachers often controlled students through threats, intimidation, and beatings. A sign of those times can be found in lists of punishments the first schoolmasters administered. Reported punishments included blows with a cane, blows with a rod, blows with a ruler, blows with the hand, blows on the mouth, boxed ears, raps on the head with school books or the Bible, kneeling on peas, and kneeling on a triangular block of wood (Regoli and Hewitt, 1994, p. 252).

The belief grew that deviancy could be traced back to early childhood and a breakdown in family discipline. Also, people of the time believed that orphaned children and the children of drunk or licentious parents were those most likely to fall prey to temptation and vice. The typical philosophy of the time was that the road to crime was paved first by a lack of discipline, then by drinking, and finally by lawbreaking itself (Rothman, 1971).

School Violence in the Nineteenth Century

Behavioral expectations (Hyman and Lally, 1980) continued to be extensive in schools during this period. Male students were required to brush their feet on a "scraper," be punctual, and bow when leaving or entering a room. Female students received similar treatment for their perceived misbehavior. For example, girls caught "dropping their heads" in class were forced to wear a necklace of sharp weed burrs for the rest of the school term.

Punishments often were extremely punitive. Some teachers would lock their students in windowless closets for even a whisper in class; other students were tied to a chair for hours. Twisting of ears, snapping on the heads and slaps on hands reminded students that the most important requirement of school was to sit quietly in their seats. Some teachers did not favor the extreme punishment of flogging children but still defended punishments such as boxing or striking the ears or head. Other teachers believed the rod or whip was better because of less chance of "injury" to the student than using one's hands (Kaestle, 1983).

Educational books written in the middle 1800s (e.g., Kellogg, 1893) included definitions of what constituted the typical "unruly pupil." The problem student was described as almost always large males with an aura of lawlessness who had "shut their eyes" to teacher authority. They were described as "brazenfaced, full of despise for rules, and banded with others for mischief."

School Violence in the Twentieth Century

1900–1920s

Society was changing rapidly in the first decades of the twentieth century. The 1920s have been said to be marked by the "first youth rebellion." This rebellion initially was not viewed with alarm because the country was basking in prosperity and growth. This generation, especially its youth, began to question adult authority through increased independence and behavior different from practices of the past (This Fabulous Century, 1920–1930, 1988). These changes carried over to the classroom.

Out of this time came a breed of youngsters who were said to be hard-boiled, heavy drinking, and daring. The most drastic changes seem to have been in females. Skirts were shorter than ever before. Cloche hats, silk stockings, fake jewelry, and bobbed hair replaced the osprey plumes, hobble skirts, and flowing tresses of the previous decades. The advent of Prohibition made clandestine drinking appealing. Females also took up smoking, which resulted in the doubling of cigarette sales in the 1920s (This Fabulous Century, 1920–1930, 1988).

A classic study conducted in 1927 examined children's behavior and teachers' attitudes. The teachers surveyed regarded the following as the most serious behaviors in their students: transgressions against authority, dishonesty, immorality, violation of rules, lack of orderliness, and lack of application to schoolwork (Regoli and Hewitt, 1994).

1930s

In the 1930s, vagrancy became the number-one crime committed by children, as a result of the harsh economic conditions created by the Great Depression. Many young people left their homes and lived on the streets. More than 250,000 juveniles—nearly all boys—walked through U.S. cities in search of shelter and food. This crime of vagrancy strained the resources of the new juvenile system that had been developed in Cook County, Illinois, at the turn of the century (Drowns and Hess, 1990).

The only type of school disturbance documented in the late 1930s and early 1940s was truancy. As early as 1939, the relationship between truancy and juvenile delinquency was being investigated. A study conducted by the New Jersey Delinquency Commission (1972) found that of 2,021 inmates in prisons and correctional institutions in that state, two in five had first been committed for truancy.

When teachers were asked in the 1930s to describe the "problem child," they reported things such as one who was antagonistic to authority, not applying self to schoolwork, and dishonest. Boys were considered to have more behavior problems than girls did. When asked to report student misbehavior that disrupted schools, the teachers stated immorality, dishonesty, disobedience, disorderliness, and failure to learn (Douglass, 1940).

In the 1930s, an estimated 200,000 children appeared in juvenile court each year. Boys were guilty of offenses such as stealing, running away, truancy, and excessive lying. For girls, the leading offense was immorality (Douglass, 1940).

1940s

A study conducted in the mid-1990s examined the leading school discipline problems in the 1940s. The following were the most reported types of school disturbance: talking, chewing gum, making noise, running in the hallways, getting out of place in line, wearing improper clothing, and not putting paper in wastebaskets (Goldstein, Apter, and Harootunian, 1984). Although many of these behaviors were not considered necessarily intellectual in nature, it was thought that by teaching students simple virtues such as industry, truthfulness, and honesty, these problem behaviors could be overcome (Stendler, 1949).

1950s

During the early 1950s, the list made up of problem behaviors had changed. The 10 most reported school disturbances were: stealing, temper outbursts, masturbation, nervousness, lack of respect for authority, cruelty, lying, fear, obscenity, and lack of responsibility (Stouffer, 1952, p. 271).

The National Education Association conducted a Teacher Opinion Poll from 1955 to 1956, asking teachers if they had been "attacked" by a pupil that academic year (Rubel, 1977). In this poll, 1,141 (1.6%) of U.S. teachers reported that a student had attacked them. This was an important study in that few researchers during this period sought to estimate the amount of teacher victimization or school crime nationwide. Between 1950 and the late 1960s, no nationally comparable records were kept on the amount of student crime.

The first glimmerings of school violence, which ultimately resulted in formation of internal security forces in the public schools, began to come to public attention in the late 1950s (Burgan and Rubel, 1980). In ghettos of major urban centers, unruly student misbehavior became sufficiently noticeable by the mid-1950s to warrant hearings by the U.S. Senate in cities throughout the nation to determine the scope of the disruptive behavior. Books written in this era tended to lump mis-behavior into the general category of "discipline violations." Not until 10 years later did educators begin to separate infractions of school rules from crimes. The popularized public view of urban school violence during this period was exemplified in a major motion picture, "The Blackboard Jungle."

During this decade, buildings were, with alarming frequency, defaced, vandalized, and even burned beyond repair. Equipment and supplies were destroyed and stolen at an immense cost to taxpayers. And, as inflation spiraled ever upwards, taxpaying citizens' concern evolved into alarm over this senseless and nonproductive loss of property (Burgan and Rubel, 1980).

1960s

Table 3.1 depics the increase in some categories of crime between 1964 and 1968 in elementary and secondary schools across the United States. These results were developed by a U.S. Senate Subcommittee to Investigate Juvenile Delinquency, from November 1970 to 1975. Many believed that the data that school districts supplied to the subcommittee were incomplete, and little reliance has been placed on these findings, except by the media. Nevertheless, the results made headlines in many newspapers and news shows across the country. Although these percentages have been placed in the literature as hard facts, they may represent grave exaggerations of what actually was occurring in the 1960s (Rubel, 1977).

Both houses of Congress conducted extensive hearings on school violence and vandalism in the late 1960s. Their reports on violence in schools shocked the nation's conscience. There were 70,000 assaults on teachers annually, some ending in death. Among 757 major school districts, more than 199 school-related student

TABLE 3.1   Increase in Crimes

Category	1964	1968	Increase (%)
Homicides	15	26	73
Forcible rapes	51	81	61
Robberies	396	1508	306
Aggravated assaults	475	680	43
Burglaries, larcenies	7604	14,102	86
Weapons offenses	419	1089	136
Narcotics	73	854	1069
Drunkenness	370	1035	179
Crimes by nonstudents	142	3894	2600
Vandalism incidents	186,184	250,549	35
Assaults on teachers	25	1801	7100
Assaults on students	1601	4267	167
Other	4796	8824	84

Source: The Unruly School, by R.J. Rubel (Lexington, MA: D.C. Heath, 1977).

deaths occurred in one year. According to figures presented at the House hearings by the National Association of School Security Directors, there were 12,000-armed robberies, 270,000 burglaries, 204,000 assaults, and 9,000 rapes in U.S. schools in 1974 (National Center for Education Statistics, 1974).

A conservative estimate of the annual cost of vandalism to public schools was $600 million. According to testimony before the House Subcommittee on Education in 1974, this included $243 million for burglary, $109 million for fire, and $204 million for other destructive acts. In 1973, the average cost per school district nationwide was estimated at $63,000 annually (National Center for Education Statistics, 1974).

1970s

In 1975, a Safe School Report was released by the Bayh Senatorial Subcommittee (Goldstein, Apter, and Harootunian, 1984). This survey of 750 school districts across the United States found the following increases between 1970 and 1973 (p. 2):

- 19.5% increase in homicides on school grounds
- 40.1% increase in rapes and attempted rapes
- 36.7% increase in robberies
- 85.3% increase in student-to-student assaults
- 77.4% increase in student-to-teacher assaults
- 37.5% increase in alcohol and drug offenses
- 54.4% increase in number of weapons confiscated on school grounds

The national scope and seriousness of youth gangs increased sharply during the late 1970s and early 1980s. Gang violence rose drastically in a number of large cities during this time. Gangs emerged in many mid-sized and smaller cities and suburban communities across the country during this same period. Youth gangs continued to become more violent, and increasingly a way for members to engage in illegal moneymaking activity, including street-level drug trafficking (Moles, 1987).

In the mid-1970s, Miller (1975) conducted the first nationwide study of youth gangs. The study found youth gang problems in 50% of the nation's large metropolitan areas. The 10 largest gang-problem cities contained about half the gangs. Miller estimated that 300 U.S. cities and towns contained about 2,300 youth gangs comprising nearly 100,000 members. About 3,400 youth gang-related killings were reported for some 60 cities during a 13-year period ending in 1980.

The movement of gangs from urban to suburban areas has continued since that time. Gangs move to suburban and rural areas to escape police pressure and enforcement or to find more lucrative areas for their moneymaking activities. Also, in mid-size and small towns where factories close or businesses fail, unemployment, poverty, and unrest create conditions conducive to gangs (Tursman, 1989).

1980s

Some have labeled the 1980s as a period when the United States condoned "violence and punitiveness toward children" (Hyman and Lally, 1980). The 1980s saw severe cuts in educational programs combined with reports of increased juvenile delinquency and child abuse. At the same time, there was a growing of resentment and anger against the youth of America. Older adults especially began to push for more severe and harsh treatment of youths.

A study conducted in 1988 found that the number of schools with serious drug problems had declined considerably from 1980 to 1985 (Moskowitz and Jones, 1988). The results still showed that students' drug use was more problematic than alcohol use before and during school, whereas both alcohol and drug use were problematic after school. The proportion of students attending schools that had serious drug problems declined from about one in four students in 1980–81 to about one in seven students in 1984–85. The most common explanation given for the decreases in student alcohol or drug use was a change in the school's discipline policy or increased enforcement of existing policy.

Between 1985 and 1988, adolescents aged 12 to 15 were about twice as likely as older teens to be involved in crimes in a school building or on school property. About 37% of violent crimes and 81% of crimes of theft against younger teenagers occurred at school, compared with 17% of the violent crimes and 39% of the crimes of theft against older teens. Although younger teens were more likely than older ones to be robbed or assaulted at school, the two age groups had a similar proportion of robberies and assaults on the streets. Violent crimes against teenagers that took place in school or on school property were much less likely than street crimes to have been committed by an armed offender. Violent street crimes against teens were three times as likely as crimes in school buildings to have been committed by an offender with a weapon (37% versus 12%) (National Crime Victimization Survey, 1991).

In 1988, some experts estimated the yearly cost of school vandalism at $5 million. Targets of vandalism included buildings, equipment, and furnishings. Other types of vandalism reported included painting on walls and property, theft, lavatory damage, driving cars across lawns, and defacing school furniture. The schools' students committed most of the acts of vandalism, and they were as prevalent in affluent suburban schools as they were in inner-city schools. The typical vandal was a White male, about 15 years of age (Sadler, 1988).

1990s

An estimated 21.6 million students aged 12 to 19 lived in the United States in the early 1990s (National Crime Victimization Survey, 1993). An estimated 9% of students were victims of crimes in or around their schools. Overall victimization rates were similar for males and females. Of the survey respondents, 2% reported being victimized by one or more violent crimes, and 7% reported at least one property crime. Violent crimes consisted largely of simple assaults. Nine percent of public school students and 36% of private-school students reported that they could not obtain drugs at school (Bastian and Taylor, 1991).

Further, 15% of the students said their school had gangs, and 16% claimed that a student had attacked or threatened a teacher at their school. Of 700 cities responding to the survey in 1993, 38 % said school violence had increased noticeably over the preceding 5 years. The largest cities were the most likely to report increasing violence during the past 5 years (National Crime Victim Survey, 1993).

A University of Michigan study (Violence in Schools, 1993) reported that 9% of eighth graders carried a gun, knife, or club to school at least once a month. In all, an estimated 270,000 guns were brought to school every day. Inner-city schools had started adding drive-by-shooting drills to traditional fire drills. Schools had fenced in their campuses, installed metal detectors, and started locker searches and student shakedowns. In October 1993, the Los Angeles School Board decided to put its armed, plainclothes security officers in uniforms, and to add nightsticks to their weaponry.

The actual number of teachers who were victims of violence nationwide during this time is not known but probably was underreported. Many teachers were injured attempting either to break up student fights or halt robberies. The "psychic violence" against teachers—intimidation and verbal abuse—is unmeasured but nevertheless present in the classroom. This caused many teachers who were new to the system and did not have much invested to give up and quit (Foley, 1990).

Nearly 20% of the student respondents to a survey in 1991 reported that they had carried a weapon during the previous school year. Boys were more likely than girls to have carried weapons, and Hispanic and Black males more likely than white males. An estimated 71 weapon-carrying incidents per 100 students occurred per month. Students carried knives and razors more often than clubs or firearms (Weapon-Carrying Among High School Students, 1991).

In 1993, Hill and Hill (1994) reported that 135,000 students on average brought a gun to school each day. During this same year, 20% of students in a national survey expressed fear and concern about the number of guns in their schools, and 31% of their parents feared that their children would be victims of a handgun assault on their way to school.

A CNN Gallup Poll of 400 parents across the country in 1994 reported the number-one concern (78% of respondents) as drugs in schools. Violence in general was the second concern (68% of respondents). The quality of teachers (59% of respondents) and poor curriculum (50% of respondents) were of lesser concern.

In the late 1990s the suburbs were providing fertile ground for juvenile gang movement from inner cities (Hill and Hill, 1994). Schools in nonurban areas could see gangs forming after only one student had transferred from an urban school that had a gang problem. Schools also were observing that younger and younger students were involved in gangs.

Also, schools were being randomly targeted for pulbic aggression (Hill and Hill, 1994). Thirty cases in which a person entered a school building and began shooting were documented between 1984 and 1994. Most often, the offender was an estranged spouse of an employee, an angry parent, or a disgruntled former employee, but the number of random shootings by people who have no connection to the school is increasing.

EXTENT OF SCHOOL VIOLENCE IN THE UNITED STATES

Even as government officials, political candidates, and law-enforcement officials across the country press for stronger anticrime measures, national statistical reports continue to show a decrease in almost all types of reported crime. Although the extent of crime might be stabilizing, crime still remains at a staggering level. The same reports show an increase in random violence and a decline in the age of the perpetrators. This may explain why public fears have continued to increase.

School-Associated Violent Deaths

The National School Safety Center (1992) conducted a study between July of 1992 and May of 1998 to determine the number of school-associated deaths, to include students, teachers, school administrators and staff members, parents, and other citizens whose deaths met four criteria. The death had to occur:

1. on the property of a public or private school (K–12).
2. on the way to or from a regular school session.
3. on the way to or from an official school-sponsored event.
4. as the obvious direct result of a school incident, function, or activity.

The study found the following (p. 1):

Years	Deaths
1992–1993	55
1993–1994	51
1994–1995	20
1995–1996	35
1996–1997	25
1997–1998	32

During this period, 218 total deaths occurred in 38 states. Males accounted for 168 of the victims, and 50 were females. Most of the victims died as a result of shootings (169), and 32 deaths resulted from stabbing. Of the 218 total deaths, 28 were the result of suicides.

In relation to multiple killings, the study found the following (p. 2):

Multiple Killings

Years	Location	Deaths
1992–1993	Langham Creek High School, Houston, Texas	2
1993–1994	East Carter High School, Grayson, Kentucky	2
	Weatherless Elementary School, Washington, DC	2
1994–1995	None reported	
1995–1996	Olathe North High School, Olathe, Kansas	2
	Blackville-Hilda High School (Blackville, South Carolina)	2
	Richland High School, Lynnville, Tennessee	3
	Frontier Junior High School, Moses Lake, Washington	3
1996–1997	Smedley Elementary School, Philadelphia, Pennsylvania	2
	Bethel Regional High School, Bethel, Alaska	2
1997–1998	Pearl High School, Pearl, Mississippi	2
	John Glenn High School, Norwalk, California	2
	Heath High School, West Paducah, Kentucky	3
	Hoboken High School, Hoboken, New Jersey	2
	Westside Middle School, Jonesboro, Arkansas	5
	Philadelphia Elementary School, Pomona, California	2

These figures are startling. Still, though school shootings have a high profile, they occur infrequently. According to U.S. Department of Education statistics released in the late 1990s, only 10% of public schools reported one or more serious violent crimes during the 1996–97 school year (Ballard, 1999). The figure for rural schools was 8%. Although this is an unacceptable amount of school violence, it keeps the problem in the proper perspective.

The statistics (Ballard, 1999) also reported that weapons accounted for almost 11,000 incidents in public schools during the 1996–97 school year; 47% of the schools reported crimes that were less serious, such as vandalism and fights; and 43% reported no incidents of crime at all. Not surprisingly, public middle schools reported fewer incidents of crime than high schools but more incidents than elementary schools. School principals rated absenteeism, tardiness, and fights as the three most common discipline problems among students.

Victimization and Fear of Victimization

In any given year across the United States, approximately 100,000 children take a gun to their school each day and 160,000 students miss school because of fear of injury. On average, in each hour of the school day, 2,000 young people are attacked by other students, 900 teachers are threatened, and another 40 are attacked.

In 1991, the students in K–12 education most often threatened with a weapon were eighth-grade students (19%). The same group also was most threatened without a weapon (31%). Eighth-grade students were tied with 12th graders in reporting property stolen (44%); eighth graders reported more of their property vandalized (34%) than any other grade group (National Center for Education Statistics, 1993).

Of eighth graders threatened with a weapon in 1991, 27% were Black and 22% were Hispanic. Of those actually injured with a weapon, 15% were Black and 16% were Hispanic. During this same year, the majority of teachers who were threatened with injury (15%) and actually assaulted (8%) taught in urban schools (National Center for Education Statistics, 1993).

A contrasting finding emerged from a survey by Louis Harris and Associates (Harris, 1993), in which most public school teachers (77%) felt safe when they were in or around school. Students felt less safe than teachers; 50% of the students felt "very safe" and 40% felt only "somewhat safe." Only a small number of teachers and students believed that violence had increased in the past year, although a substantial proportion of students reported witnessing violent incidents either in or around school very often (6%) or sometimes (31%).

In this same study, teachers, students, and law-enforcement officials agreed that most violent incidents occurred outside the school building. Most teachers and police officials proposed that the major factors contributing to violence in public schools are lack of supervision at home, lack of family involvement in the schools, and exposure to violence in the mass media. Students cited a wider variety of factors contributing to violence, most relating to peer relations. Of the student respondents, 22% reported that their parents devoted any or no time at all to a discussion of school life and homework (Harris, 1993).

Schools are a microcosm reflecting the larger society. Drugs, crime, and violence in local communities infiltrate the schools. Children who live in dysfunctional families and become filled with anger or alienation from their parents are likely to act out in the classroom. Problems of the outside world are leading to disorders in the traditionally protected environment of schools (Shepherd and Ragan, 1993).

The school-related misbehaviors studied most heavily in the mid-1990s were violence, vandalism, and theft. Violence against teachers and other pupils, and the fear it produced, had increased at an alarming rate. During 1992, approximately 8% of urban junior and senior high school students in the United States missed at least 1 day of school each month because they were afraid to attend. About 282,000 students were physically attacked in secondary schools each month and about 125,000 secondary-school teachers (12%) were threatened with physical harm, approximately 5,200 of whom were physically attacked (Berger, 1994).

The tragedy of assaults on teachers extends beyond the personal suffering of any teacher. Assaults destroy the trust upon which the student-teacher relationship rests, and once this trust is lost, teachers cannot teach effectively (Berger, 1994).

A form of school disturbance that often goes unreported is sexual harassment by peers. In junior high and high schools, girls and boys are sexually grabbed, called sexual names, embarrassed by jokes, and forced to perform sexual acts. Often this happens in the presence of adults who fail to react. Of the incidents in 1993, 94% took place in the classroom and 76% in the hallway; 85% of the girls and 76% of the boys reported that they had experienced unwanted sexual behavior that interfered with their lives. Harassment against girls can result in their doing poorly in schoolwork, having lower self-esteem, being depressed, and leaving class or school. Harassed youths become mistrustful of adults who fail to intervene, provide protection, or otherwise safeguard the educational environment (Safe Schools Coalition, 1994).

Recent School Shootings

Another way to examine the extent of school violence is to look at the school shootings perpetuated by students in recent history. The following is a brief chronological review of the school shootings occurring in the 1990s.

- **May 1, 1992:** Eric Houston, 20, killed four people and wounded 10 in an armed siege at his former high school in Olivehurst, California. Prosecutors stated the attack was in retaliation for a failing grade. Houston was convicted and given a death sentence.

- **January 18, 1993:** Scott Pennington, 17, walked into Deanna McDavid's seventh-period English class at East Carter High School in Grayson, Kentucky, and shot her in the head. He then shot janitor Marvin Hicks in the abdomen. Pennington was sentenced to life without parole for a minimum of 25 years.

- **October 30, 1995:** In Richmond, Virginia, Edward Earl Spellman, 18, shot and wounded four students outside of their high school.

- **February 2, 1996:** Barry Loukaitis, 14, turned an assault rifle on his algebra class, killing two classmates and a teacher and wounding one other student, in the central Washington city of Moses Lake. Loukaitis was sentenced to two mandatory life terms for the attack at Frontier Junior High School.

- **February 29, 1996:** In St. Louis, Missouri, Mark Boyd fired into a school bus after its doors opened, killing a pregnant 15-year-old and wounding the bus driver.

- **July 26, 1996:** Los Angeles, California, high school junior Yahao Albert Rivas, 18, shot and wounded two classmates in a stairwell on campus.

- **February 19, 1997:** Evan Ramsey, 16, opened fire with a shotgun in a common area at Bethel High School, Bethel, Alaska. Killed were school principal Ron Edwards and classmate Josh Palacious. Two other students were wounded. Authorities later accused two other students of knowing the shooting was going to take place. Ramsey was sentenced to two 99-year terms.

- **October 1, 1997:** In Pearl, Mississippi, Luke Woodham, 16, was accused of killing his mother, then going to school and shooting nine students. Two of them died, including the boy's ex-girlfriend. Authorities later accused six friends of conspiracy, stating that the suspects were part of a group that dabbled in Satanism.

- **December 1, 1997:** Michael Carneal, 14, opened fire on a student prayer circle in a hallway at Heath High School in West Paducah, Kentucky. Three students were killed and five others wounded. Carneal was described as emotionally immature. He is currently serving multiple life sentences.

- **December 15, 1997:** Joseph Todd, 14, was arrested for a sniper shooting of two students outside their high school. Both recovered. Todd reported that he was tired of being picked on.

- **March 24, 1998:** Mitchell Johnson, 13, and Andrew Golden, 11, opened fire with rifles on classmates and teachers when they came out during a false fire alarm set off by the shooters at Westside Middle School, Jonesboro, Arkansas. Four girls and a teacher were killed, and 11 people were wounded.

- **April 24, 1998:** In Edinboro, Pennsylvania, Andrew Wurst, 14, nicknamed Satan by his friends, fatally shot teacher John Gillette and wounded two students and another teacher at a dance. The suspect, an eighth-grade student at James W. Parker Middle School, reportedly had told students he planned to make the dance "memorable."

- **May 19, 1998:** A high school senior shot and killed another student in the school parking lot at Lincoln County High School, Fayetteville, Tennessee, three days before they were to graduate. Jacob Davis, 18, confronted Nick Creson, 18, apparently because they had argued about a girl. After the shooting, Davis reportedly put the gun on the ground, sat down next to it and put his head in his hands.

- **May 21, 1998:** Freshman Kip Kinkle, 15, one day after being expelled for bringing a gun to Thurston High School, Springfield, Oregon, opened fire with a semiautomatic rifle in the high school cafeteria. He killed one student and critically wounded seven others. His father and mother later were found dead at his rural home.

- **April 20, 1999:** Eric Harris, 18, and Dylan Klebold, 17, entered Columbine High School in Littleton, Colorado concealing a handgun, a rifle, two shotguns, and various explosives. One teacher and 12 students were killed, and 23 others were wounded. Both students committed suicide after the attack.

- **May 16, 1999:** Four boys were charged with plotting a shooting at their middle school similar to the April rampage at Colorado's Columbine High School. Justin Schnepp and Jedaiah Zinzo, both 14, were charged as adults with conspiracy to commit murder for allegedly planning to kill classmates at their 560-student Holland Woods Middle School, Washington. The two others, ages 12 and 13, were charged as juveniles with the same crime. The teens reportedly planned to "top the death toll" of Columbine. The four were arrested after a 14-year-old-girl overheard them talking about an elaborate killing spree.

- **May 20, 1999:** Thomas Soloman, 15, opened fire with a .22 cal. rifle at Heritage High School in Conyers, Georgia, wounding six students. Reportedly, all shots were fired into the floor and ricochet rounds struck the victims. After the attack, Soloman placed the gun in his mouth but was persuaded by an assistant principal to hand over the weapon.

FACTORS CONTRIBUTING TO SCHOOL VIOLENCE

The possible causes of school violence are numerous, complex, and mostly environmentally related. Many teachers, for example, perceive that the major factors contributing to student violence are lack of parental supervision (71%), lack of family involvement with the school (66%), and exposure to violence in the mass media (55%) (Crews and Counts, 1997).

America's children are exposed to a steady diet of verbal and physical violence in the media that begins early and continues throughout their lives. Myriad reports have cited the statistic that children in the United States spend more time watching television than attending school. Much of what children watch, including cartoons, is unsupervised and much of it depicts unadulterated sex and violence. Often, children who behave violently are themselves victims of an overdose of violence.

In too many communities, children are sending signals that they feel isolated from and maligned by society. These feelings know no geographic, social, or economic boundaries. Increasingly, many youths come from communities where the vast majority of the experiences to which they have been exposed has been hostile. They have had to fight to simply survive. These young people become filled with rage and a sense of rejection and, as a result, do not believe they owe society anything (Crews and Counts, 1997).

More puzzling, a growing number of students who have not grown up in mean, hostile environments are becoming involved in some of the most heinous acts of violence upon school grounds. They often cite boredom or the excitement of control as reasons for their actions. Their rebellion against society is difficult to understand.

Parenting Practices

The major factors that have a role in school violence include parenting, peer influences, bullying, alcohol and drugs, and the larger culture. These are discussed individually.

Children often receive mixed messages from parents and other adults about what is right and what is wrong. For example, bribing children to get them to behave in a certain way or to do chores may set a dangerous precedent, causing children to believe they have no reason to do anything unless there is something "in it for them." This attitude conveys strong meanings of roles, responsibilities, and the rights they must learn to assume productive roles in a democratic society.

Parents, too, often do not get involved in their children's schools. These days, with two parents working as the standard, children are not around their parents as much as formerly. Children learn quickly that school officials sometimes have trouble contacting their parents and their parents have difficulty finding time to respond to problems the child may be having at school.

Too, parents do not know how to respond. They may have had bad experiences with their own schooling and be biased against schools in general. They may lack the skills of proper parenting. A growing number of aggressive parents are telling their children that they do not have to listen to the teacher.

Ineffective parenting is evident across the socioeconomic spectrum. Research continues to support the idea that parenting that indulges, neglects, abuses, or ignores children, and that fails to provide strong guidance, discipline, and nurturance, contributes to the spread of violence in American schools. This type of parenting often is found in families that are plagued by chronic unemployment and poverty. Parents in these families often have to be concerned more with economic survival of the family than an individual child's behavior. Poor parenting also is found in affluent families that indulge their children's every wish and in families that simply do not have enough time to spend with their children because of job demands. A survey of American teachers (Harris, 1995) found that 36% of the students surveyed believed the lack of parental supervision at home was the major factor contributing to violence in schools.

Peer Pressure

The second major factor identified (34%) by these students was the presence of gang or group membership or peer-group pressure. Several studies in the early 1990s concluded that peer pressure was perhaps the fastest growing and most disturbing cause of acts of violence among youth, whether in school or out (Crews and Counts, 1997).

Bullying

Bullying is another major problem facing students in schools. Research indicates that male bullies are three to four times more likely to inflict physical assault than girls are. Girls tend to be subtler and psychologically manipulative. As with alcoholism and other forms of abusive behavior, evidence strongly suggests that bullying tends to be an intergenerational problem. Many childhood bullies are abused at home by a parent or witness parents abuse each other. Parents of bullies tend to ignore their children and do not really know what is happening to them (Crews and Counts, 1997)

Contrary to popular belief, victims of bullying are not always different from other adolescents, although victims are often overprotected by parents who encourage dependent behavior. Bullying can lead to school absenteeism because victims fear school itself and the abuse that awaits them there. Victims also are far more likely than other students to bring a weapon to school to protect themselves (Office of Juvenile Justice and Delinquency Prevention, 1991b).

In 1993, about one of every seven children was either a bully or a victim of a bully and approximately 282,000 students were physically attacked in U.S. secondary schools each month. In an average month, about 125,000 secondary school teachers (12%) were threatened with physical harm and 5,200 are physically attacked (National Association of School Psychologists, 1993).

For as long as there have been schools, there have been bullies. Bullying continues to be cited as a major cause of school violence; however, educators must begin to treat bullies as potentially dangerous, just as drugs and guns are. In the mid-1990s, a major effort was directed at finding ways to decrease bullying in schools. Teachers were trained to increase their effectiveness in dealing with bullies and to be able to identify and intervene with children who are bullied.

Bullied children are typically different in some way, such as their weight, ethnicity or clothing. The victims become convinced that they are to blame for their plight and, therefore, do not tell an adult about their problem. Meanwhile, bullies often brag about the abuse they inflict on other students. Being a bully carries no stigma, but those who are bullied carry a massive stigma.

Alcohol and Drugs

Studies continue to find that involvement with drugs and alcohol contribute greatly to school violence. Drug use in schools does not vary significantly by ethnicity, level of family income, or geographic location. Although reports have indicated that the use of drugs such as heroin, cocaine, marijuana, and crack is declining among students in grades 6–12, the consumption of alcohol has not. Alcohol continues to be the number-one drug used by teenagers.

Culture

With the preponderance of school shootings in the South, the so-called Southern gun culture has come under major research and media scrutiny. The debate includes dissention against stereotyping Southerners, as "gun-toting White-trash." Many people who were born and grew up in the South (and in other regions), firearms are an accepted part of life for adults and children alike. Youngsters often go hunting with their fathers and grandfathers, and children sometimes go to school in camouflage clothing.

Upon a closer look, these stereotypes lose much of their impact. Statistically speaking, students still are relatively safer in rural areas than in more urban areas. This may be a result of the traditional elements of small towns and close-knit families. In areas where "everyone knows everyone," children have a harder time "getting away" with unacceptable behavior.

POSSIBLE SOLUTIONS TO SCHOOL VIOLENCE IN THE UNITED STATES

Numerous suggestions have been offered for solving the present state of violence and disruption in American schools. The following is a discussion of various strategies and issues to be considered.

Role of School

Schools can play a central role in preventing delinquency. Every youngster spends considerable time in school; therefore, many delinquent acts are committed within the school setting. Time and time again, researchers have noted that weak commitment to educational achievement and attachment to the school culture, in combination with association with delinquent peers, are closely related to delinquency. Educators have proposed, therefore, that the most effective school-based prevention efforts would be directed toward increasing students' experiences of academic success, stimulating student-to-student and student-to-teacher relationships, encouraging commitments to school culture, and stimulate attachments between students and nondelinquent peers (Hawkins and Wall, 1980).

Theorists have developed six building blocks for preventing student-to-student violence:

1. A shared system of beliefs and values
2. A vision of respect
3. Explicit policies
4. A holistic plan for staff development
5. District statements of policy
6. The use of learned strategies

Additional means of reducing school violence include formulating policies and legislation to protect school employees, providing teacher training in conflict resolution, fostering creation of a school culture and sense of community, developing an emergency school plan, and establishing reasonable precautions to protect school staff. Finally, when assaulted, educators should pursue every legal means possible against the assailant so the attacker will have to face the consequences of violent behavior and the victim will receive full support (Curcio and First, 1993).

Many educational strategies have been developed to prevent violence. Teachers can lead discussions about the nature and extent of violence in society, including hate crimes. This will help students to develop positive attitudes toward minority groups and to reject stereotypes of them. Schools can teach students about the damaging effects of sexual harassment and sexual assault, with reference to specific laws that affect juveniles and the consequences of breaking those laws. Through videos and news reports, teachers can convey to students the lethal impact of guns and the legal implications of carrying or using a gun. Schools can videotape television news stories that describe actual incidents involving guns and provide discussion groups for students to discuss them (Southeastern Regional Vision in Education, March 1993).

Additional educational strategies include teaching problem-solving skills and how to avoid gangs. Students can be taught that anger is an acceptable feeling but that aggression is not an acceptable action. Schools can offer assistance in finding jobs and teaching social skills (Southeastern Regional Vision in Education, 1993).

Impact of Parents

One of the greatest problems contributing to school violence is the lack of parental involvement. Strategies are prevalent for increasing parental involvement in school efforts to reduce violence. Among them (Greenbaum, Gonzales, and Ackley, 1989):

- Parent representatives can be included on school-safety committees and school-improvement teams.
- Meetings scheduled at breakfast, lunchtime, or during the evening make parents' attendance more feasible.
- A copy of the school's discipline code can be sent home to all parents.
- A communication system could utilize strategies such as a parent telephone network, calling parents at work, or sending a brief note home.
- Administrators might get parents and students to help paint and clean up during summer months
- Parent volunteers could patrol schools during the school year.
- School districts could provide transportation for parents to attend meetings.
- Teachers can develop parent-student homework assignments.
- Law enforcement agencies can invite parents to be part of a School Crime Watch Program for their child's school.

School Safety Plans

A relatively new strategy for fighting school violence is the School Safety Plan. This plan requires its developers to determine (Crews and Counts, 1997):

1. What the problem is (identify the problem)
2. How the school is going to prevent this problem
3. What will happen if a problem does occur
4. How the school is going to handle the media
5. What the school is going to do after the problem ends

Some specific activities are as follows:

- Provide student supervision (all hours).
- Call parents often.
- Develop strong discipline policies.
- Involve police when needed.
- Communicate with everyone.
- Develop emergency response teams.
- Teach law-related education courses to students.
- Develop a program allowing students to catch up.
- Practice emergency skills.
- Make counseling available for all after an incident.
- Use block scheduling.
- Limit the number of students allowed in the hall at any given time.
- Limit changes between rooms.
- Determine problem areas in school.
- Develop student leadership.
- Establish parent-student swap programs.
- Require parents pick up report cards.
- Survey as many people as possible for input into problems.
- Provide a crime line so students can call anonymously to report problems.
- Target troublesome grades, primarily middle school.

A school's control or suppression strategy should have at least three components (Schmitze, 1993):

1. Provision for development of a school gang code, with guidelines specifying an appropriate response by teachers and staff to different kinds of gang behavior, including a mechanism for dealing with serious gang delinquency.
2. Application of these rules and regulations within a context of positive relationships and open communication by school personnel with parents, community agencies, and students.
3. Clear delineation of gang and non-gang-related activity.

Schools must have a plan for student supervision before and after school. Often, school personnel leave the school grounds but the students do not. Communities must fight students' boredom by establishing programs that get students involved. Students who are involved in extracurricular activities (e.g., JROTC, band) are much less likely to become involved in crime, according to B. Nesbit (in a personal communication, March 12, 1994). Efforts such as these must be combined with positive after-school, weekend, and holiday activities, positive adult role models, school-based community services and activities, and police-driven efforts to reach out to children prior to the emergence of problems (Majority Staff of the Senate Judiciary Committee, 1994).

Obstacles to the development of effective school safety plans include denial by school officials that a problem exists and insufficient understanding of the problem. Also, many educational systems are reluctant to view school security as a profession (Trump, 1993).

Whatever is done, all efforts must have community support. Schools must have everyone's support for any effort to have a chance at succeeding, according to a personal communication with S. Splittgerber-Wise, March 12, 1994.

Educational Staff Development

Through staff development, teachers must be taught to understand the "signs of the times." Signs of impending conflict include (Brooks, 1993):

- a sudden shift in the clustering of students
- a sudden clustering of rival groups
- unusual movement of a group from its normal territory
- a group of students appearing at an activity they normally would not attend
- isolated racial or intergroup fights
- an incident or disorder in the community at large
- the sudden appearance of underground publications complaining of inequality in disciplinary treatment
- a disproportionate number of disciplinary actions
- a sudden increase in organized demands from students
- complaints about a lack of grievance procedures
- warnings from nonteaching staff
- increase in graffiti at school
- parents withdrawing their children from school

School administrators can reduce violence and develop a safer school climate by being highly visible, establishing and enforcing written rules, actively involving parents, eliminating graffiti, keeping security personnel moving through the building, fencing the campus, keeping the campus grounds clean, and shortening periods between classes. They should keep staff members informed about potential problems, deal with rumors quickly and responsibly, isolate combatants, and deal with threats as if they were acts of violence (Brooks, 1993).

Violence has become more and more frequent at school athletic events and in school recreation centers. This violence often involves physical fights and brawls between rival fans and teams, and even shooting. The threat of violence has become so prevalent that school officials and coaches have developed contingency plans—for example, bullet drills in which students are told that, in the event of gunfire, they are to lie face down in the center of the field, classroom, or gymnasium until hearing the all-clear signal. Violence near high schools also has prompted tighter security at games and special events. Spectators sometimes are searched, and police presence at games has been increased.

The main components of a strategy to curb violence at recreational activities are faculty preparation, an effective communication network, crisis prevention, adult supervision, school/law enforcement partnerships, and active student participation. Effective athletic event management, however, must go beyond intervention and supervision. Violence-prevention programs must clearly identify behavioral expectations and rules for special events. Discussions must take place about proper and improper roles and behaviors for students, coaches, athletes, and school staff. An antiviolence curriculum must be implemented, utilizing peer mediation and conflict-resolution programs to assist students in defusing incidents before they become a major problem (Brooks, 1993).

Security Programs

Schools across the United States are experimenting with many types of security programs. The National Crisis Prevention Institute of Brookfield, Wisconsin, conducts one such program. This institute has a team of experts that trains teachers and administrators to safely defuse disruptive and assaultive students. The teachers learn the telltale signs of a potentially violent situation and the proper verbal and nonverbal responses to calm the situation before it gets out of hand (Brooks, 1993).

As another example, the United Federation of Teachers in New York has provided personal alarms to teachers in elementary schools in Brooklyn. These devices are accessible to teachers and unnoticed by students. By pulling the pin, the teacher sets off an alarm that alerts security (Brooks, 1993).

Modern school planners and architects have committed themselves to the general objective of personalizing space to give each person the perception of ownership. This principle translates to the identification of territories within the school campus. Responsibility for general supervision and care of these newly assigned territories goes with ownership. This is a fundamental concept of space management for crime prevention.

Significant problem areas that require space-management design consideration are school grounds, parking lots, locker rooms, corridors, restrooms, and classrooms.

Problems on school grounds often stem from poorly defined campus borders, undifferentiated campus areas, isolated areas, and poorly located bus-loading areas. Parking lot problems typically stem from poor planning (e.g., conflict with the neighborhood, poor placement and landscaping). Problems associated with lockers and locker rooms include assignment of more than one student to a locker, locker design and color, and isolation. Corridor problems include blind spots because of poor planning and class scheduling that promote confusion and congestion. Restroom security problems typically relate to location. Other problems are multipurpose classroom use and isolation (Crowe, 1991).

Recent Efforts Toward a Solution

Recent responses to school violence in America (*What Can the Schools Do?* 1999) *include the following:*

- Ohio Representative James Traficant tried without success to revive the idea of prayer in schools.
- New Mexico Senator Jeff Bingaman proposed to spend $10 million turning schools into "little fortresses."
- New York Senator Charles Schumer urged stricter gun-control laws.
- California Governor Gray Davis spoke about the importance of more guidance counselors.
- Virginia Governor Jim Gilmore ordered superintendents to report any potentially dangerous students to police immediately.

Two categories for dealing with school violence seem to have developed: nurture and counsel, and crack down and get tough. Many security experts, law enforcement personnel, and frightened school officials have embraced the latter. A large percentage of these individuals want a strong zero-tolerance philosophy combined with security features such as locker searches and armed police officers in the schools.

Some recent security measures that many schools have instituted are:

- Unmanned metal detectors
- Random checks with hand-held wand detectors
- Adopting school uniforms or at least making students tuck in their shirts (to prevent hiding of weapons)
- Surveillance cameras
- Cash rewards for students who report criminal behavior by fellow students
- High-tech fire alarms that guard against false alarms
- Random drug-testing of students, whether drug use is or is not suspected

Many believe that measures such as these undermine whatever trust exists between students and their schools (Ianni and Ianni, 1999). Some question how far we should go in a direction that increases the similarities between juvenile correctional institutions and local schools. Others believe the problem is lazy citizens who do not want to tackle the underlying causes of violence: boredom, despair, depression, impact of home life, pessimism, and so on.

Those pushing the idea of more nurturing propose solutions such as the following:

- Use of more parents as monitors and teacher's aides
- Counseling programs for students and families
- More conflict-resolution programs
- Crisis centers housed at schools
- More use of teacher crisis meetings with administration and students' family
- More support for teachers
- Extended school hours
- More classes for parents

In 1999, a group named *Fight Crime: Invest in Kids*, consisting of victims of violence, police chiefs, and other experts (Ianni and Ianni 1999), attempted to pull together some basic remedies.

1. Give kids something to do after school.
2. Make sure young children have access to quality child care.
3. Help schools identify troubled kids early, and provide counseling for them.
4. Prevent child abuse.

As with all solution proposals, most are easier said than done.

School safety can be improved in many ways. Metal detectors are an obvious but minimal solution. The first priority is to gain student support of school safety and safety education. Police can assist in this effort by putting substations in schools and by identifying qualified officers to teach classes on various issues such as conflict management, enforcement of truancy rules, and parent involvement. The school can combat violence by having older students serve as school patrols and also as role models in the schools. Schools can work with local law enforcement to develop a school safety plan that is comprehensive and provides an environment where students can learn and teachers can educate (Crews and Counts, 1997).

Many factors will impact on the issue of police in the schools over the next decade—taxpayer support for educational services, qualified public school teachers in the state, the number of minority students, public concern over violent crime in schools, and the prevalence of dysfunctional families. If police are present, probable measures include restricting students convicted of violent crimes from attending public schools, requiring schools to develop comprehensive school safety plans, and conducting mandatory drug-abuse prevention and gang-prevention programs in the school curriculum (Schmitz, 1993).

Although violence in schools is not new, the number of serious offenses is a new phenomenon. As a result, school administrators are taking an inventory of school security measures and attempting to develop violence-prevention programs for their schools and districts. Developing a violence-prevention plan requires careful examination of what is being done already in the areas of substance-abuse prevention, teen pregnancy, and habitual truancy. The causal factors are similar, if not the same, so the solutions are overlapping. Solutions require keeping factual perspectives about families, communities, and the successes and failures of schools (Rosen, 1994).

A final possible solution to school violence is potentially sad, but possibly prophetic of what may lie in the future of many schools. Tutt Middle School, in Augusta, Georgia, decided to build an 8-foot wall around the school to protect its school grounds from stray gunfire from a nearby apartment complex (Spaid, 1996). This wall may well be symbolic. Schools across America are going to have to do whatever it takes to insulate themselves and their students from an increasingly violent society. Although these walls may keep outside societal violence from entering the school building, they cannot stop the violence in the school building from entering the society outside.

CONCLUSION

In any historical examination of school disturbance and juvenile delinquency, two concepts become immediately apparent. *First*, juvenile delinquency has been around as long as there have been juveniles. *Second*, school disturbance and violence have existed as long as there have been schools. Problems with juvenile misbehavior have plagued societies around the world and throughout recorded history. The history of the United States is no different.

National statistical reports and surveys have found that almost all areas of reported crime have stabilized and significantly decreased over the past two decades. These same reports show that during this time, rates of youth and random violence have drastically increased. The second trend in youth violence has not allowed the American public to derive much comfort from the first trend of crime stabilization: People are still afraid in their neighborhoods, cities—and more so in their schools.

Juvenile Justice Department records show that in the last 10 years juvenile involvement in violent crimes has increased by roughly 62% to 85%. National surveys suggest that hundreds of thousands of weapons are brought to schools each day and the same number of students are threatened by those weapons each day. Surveys conducted by private agencies, on the other hand, find that less violence is occurring in schools than what the popular media report. Surveys of teachers and of students find that high percentages feel safe in their schools.

Sexual harassment and bullying are two new areas of research into school disturbance and U.S. Department of Justice reports show that illegal drug use is increasing dramatically in the 1990s, whereas student self-report surveys and surveys of teachers show that the use actually has decreased steadily since approximately 1982, and that parental involvement and other student issues are the actual root of many, if not all, of these problems. The history of the United States and the education of its children demonstrate how all of these influences have shaped American society, American education, and, therefore, American school violence.

In reducing violence, solid research on the effects of various strategies is sparse. Available evidence, however, indicates positive results from coordinated school and community efforts. Within schools, the best way to reduce youth violence is to create an atmosphere that encourages students to focus their energies on learning with firm, fair, and consistently applied student behavior standards.

Even with the pervasive problems faced by education in the 1990s, strong evidence suggests that the game has not been lost yet. The Metropolitan Life Survey of the American Teacher (1994) was conducted by Louis Harris and Associates during April and May 1994. The survey included two nationally representative sample groups: public school students and parents with at least one child in public school.

The findings of this survey and other research related to school violence do not support the widely held belief that schools are on the verge of destruction, that the majority of parents have lost faith in the U.S. educational system, and that most students go to school in constant fear. Most public school students (78%) and parents (76%) are generally satisfied with their public schools. Most believe their school provides a safe and secure environment as well as a quality education. A majority of students have not been victims of violence and have never been physically hurt while in or around school. Most students have not experienced more serious incidents such as threats with a knife (81% have had no experiences) or a gun (82% have had no experiences). Students generally believe that teachers and students get along (78%); few (3%) think they do not get along well at all. In seeming to care for students, most parents and students assess the teachers in their school as excellent or good. A majority of parents (67%) believes relations between teachers and parents are good or excellent (Crews and Counts, 1997).

Most students do not worry about their own safety going to and from school and say the hallways, classrooms, and other public areas in their school are clean and well kept. In general, students say their school has taken a wide variety of measures to stop or reduce violence. Most schools have implemented disciplinary codes to help stop or reduce violence; only 14% of students say their school has not done this (Crews and Counts, 1997).

Many problems that may impact on school disturbance have little to do with the school. Instead, these problems center on communication between parents and their children. Almost half (47%) of students do not talk to their parents about problems or disagreements with other students because they think adults do not understand their problems; one-third (29%) say their parents cannot help; and nearly one in five (17%) say their parents are uninterested or too busy (Crews and Counts, 1997).

Differences in perceptions between parents and students seem to be common. Parents say they are involved in their child's school life to a greater extent than students believe. At least half of all students believe their parents never exchange notes with a teacher or school official (58%) and never attend meetings of parents' groups such as the PTA (51%). In contrast, less than one-third of parents say they never have these kinds of contacts (Crews and Counts, 1997).

Parents and students have considerably different views about how various environmental issues impact their schools. Parents (71%) more often view factors such as overcrowded classrooms and the mass media as factors contributing to school violence. Only half of all students (51%) concur. One in 10 parents of a high school student says he or she is most worried about drive-by shootings; only 1% of high school students mention concern over drive-by shootings (Crews and Counts, 1997).

Even before problems of drugs and violence disrupted schools, educators desired a disciplined environment. Maintaining a disciplined environment conducive to learning does not necessarily mean adopting tough policies to keep students silent in their seats. Rather, it means principals and teachers working together to develop appropriate curricular and instructional techniques in support of one main goal: to improve students' academic performance in the contexts of appropriate personal and social development. Schools need to create an atmosphere in which students and teachers are engaged in learning and where misbehavior is dealt with quickly, firmly, fairly, and consistently. Most important, a learning environment requires a caring attitude that shapes staff-student relationships. Changes in classroom organization and management may be necessary to maintain such an atmosphere, which in some cases, might involve alternative settings offering disruptive students special attention, counseling, and remediation.

chapter 4

FROM TRICK OR TREAT TO SACRIFICE OR SUICIDE

Occult and Satanic Practices

Satan has been the best friend the church has ever had, as he has kept it in business all these years!

Dr. Anton Szandor LaVey, *The Satanic Bible*, 1969

Cursed be those who practice their wicked designs and establish in their heart your (Satan) evil devices, plotting against the Covenant of God.

Dead Sea Scrolls

The driving force behind black magic is hunger for power. Its ultimate aim was stated, appropriately enough, by the serpent in the Garden of Eden.

Richard Cavendish, *The Black Arts*, 1969

The Gothic community in no way condones the use of violence. We are appalled by the killings and by the inference that the murderers belonged to our culture.

A disclaimer on the door of Inkubus Haberdashery, a Gothic fashion store in Miami's Coconut Grove District, 1999

INTRODUCTION

In the wake of the school shootings that have shocked America, interest has been renewed in alternative belief systems and their impact upon juvenile behavior. Many will remember the hysteria that developed in the late 1970s and early 1980s regarding the impact of satanic music and backward masking of hidden messages in popular songs. The renewed Goth movement of the 1990s rekindled the fires of hysteria in the general public and once again became the catalyst for renewed attention to the occult.

In many ways Goth and its belief systems, practices, and fashion styles actually may frighten the general public more than did Satanism. Satanic movement of the past generally manifested itself in clearly identifiable ways. Goth and the Gothic movement are not as clearly identifiable, and most people cannot readily get a grip on what it entails. What we cannot understand, we may fear.

This chapter explores possible impacts that alternative belief systems *may*—and *may* is emphasized—negatively impact a juvenile's behavior. We hope an understanding of this topic will foster an understanding that is sorely needed.

A BRIEF HISTORY OF OCCULT BELIEFS

McTeer (1976) offered a history of occult beliefs. The human species, he said, evolved as frail creatures, not well equipped for survival on Earth. They were thin-skinned, practically hairless, with no claws, no fangs, and without strong night vision. Because of their physical state, early humans feared the dark and often envisioned "creatures of the night" as evil beings, just waiting to fall upon unsuspecting prey.

Using their higher intellect, humans learned how to defend themselves from animal attacks, to gather food, and to seek shelter from inclement or dangerous weather. As their intellect and experience grew, humans began to question other phenomena in their world—the sun rising and setting, the moon changing shape, the changing tides, earthquakes, floods, and hurricanes.

They concluded that "great powers or gods" controlled all natural occurrences in the world. When the gods were happy, good things happened, and when they were angry, bad things happened. Evidence for these beliefs is found in the myriad of peoples throughout history identifying their "special god." People attempted to appease the gods' anger by building temples and offering sacrifices. Examples are Easter Island, Stonehenge, the Mayan and Aztec altars, and various cave paintings throughout the world.

Some men appeared, claiming they could control the astral forces of nature and influence the actions of the gods. Many of these men were the first philosophers, alchemists, seers, astrologists, and witch doctors. In opposition to Christianity, witch doctors, magicians and seers turned to Satan for their power. Superstition and fear fueled the beliefs that these men had supernatural powers and could bring plagues, droughts, and famine upon a people. As might be expected, churches, kings, and other rulers quickly discovered that a practitioner of these beliefs could easily erode their power. By the seventeenth and eighteenth centuries, these practitioners held much power over kings and rulers of towns, villages, and countries.

During this time, the suppression of alternative belief systems began. Thousands of people were put to death as rulers tried to eradicate people they believed practiced the Black Arts. People who caused any problems for the jurisdiction were often labeled "witches," and witch hunting began to undermine their credibility. Witches were imprisoned or their land and wealth were taken away. This persecution drove practitioners underground into cults or covens that operated outside of the church, government, and society in general. This set the stage for a subculture that continues to be the subject of great mystery and misunderstanding.

OVERVIEW OF OCCULT-RELATED DELINQUENCY AND VIOLENCE

Goths

The enormous tragedy of Columbine High School in Littleton, Colorado (see Chapter 3) brought about renewed interest in the alternative belief systems of some juveniles. One movement that has received massive media coverage in the late 1990s is the Goth or Gothic movement.

By 1999 (Mall Gothics, 1999), "Goths, freaks, and vampires" had caused quite a stir in many areas of the country. Cities such as Phoenix, Dallas, and Nashua (New Hampshire) have reported extensive problems with large groups of Gothic juveniles hanging out in malls and shopping-center parking lots. Storeowners claimed that these juveniles were responsible for panhandling, vandalism, assaults, thefts, and scaring away customers. When interviewed, the juveniles reported that they were simply talking, shopping, and eating.

In Burlington, Wisconsin, in 1998 (Clique of Gothics; Conflict Fueled Talk of Killings, 1999), five Goth juveniles (15 and 16 years of age) were reported to have been planning to kill 15 to 20 people at their high school. Those to be killed included disliked teachers and classmates, the principal, and the "Cowboys," a group of students who wore cowboy hats and cowboy boots and reportedly picked on the Goth juveniles relentlessly. The five juveniles were caught planning to steal guns, attack the school, and developing the list of those to kill. All of these juveniles were described as "outcasts."

In 1998, in Fort Worth, Texas (Two Teens Stab Dad, Cops Report Satanic Ties Seen in Lakewood Attack, 1998), Jay F. Howell, 17, stabbed his 14-year-old girlfriend in the neck at a Satanic altar that he had built in his backyard. Howell reportedly had been watching a Marilyn Manson music video immediately preceding the attack. This act brought about "Marilyn Manson Awareness Training" across the state of Texas. This training was offered by a private company, which reportedly was instructing schools and local law enforcement personnel to consider and deal with Manson fans and other Goths in the same fashion they do gang members.

In Denver, Colorado, in 1998 (Two Teens Stab Dad, 1998), two Goth juveniles (a boy, 14, and his girlfriend, 15) stabbed the boy's father in an attempt to kill him. They were trying to steal his money and car to run away to California. Police reportedly found "hate graffiti," Satanic symbols, and "Marilyn Manson," carved into tables in the boy's room.

Vampires

The most notorious case involving juvenile vampires occurred in Tavares, Florida, in 1996 (Vampire Exchange Network, 1999). Rod Ferrell, then 17, was the leader of a vampire coven from Murray, Kentucky. This group reportedly drank blood, held sex rites, and conducted animal-mutilation ceremonies. All of the members were described as outcasts. In November of 1996, the group took a trip to Florida.

While there, the group inducted Heather Wendorf, then 15, into its coven. The group talked Wendorf into helping to kill her parents. Ferrell eventually was sentenced to die for the beating deaths of the Florida couple.

Satanists

In 1997, in Pearl, Mississippi (Woodham Testifies He Was Involved in Satanism, 1998), Luke Woodham walked into his high school and killed two students and wounded seven others. He reportedly was a member of a Satanic group called The Kroth. Fellow classmates described this group of students as outcasts.

William Sarmento (Man Held in Satanic Deaths, 1987), then 21, killed two of his neighbors in Providence, Rhode Island, because of his beliefs in Satanism. The victims were a 6- and 9-year-old who lived just doors down the street from his home. Prior to his arrest, Sarmento sent a note to both families telling them that Satan had ordered the killings.

Occultists

One of the first occult-related violent acts committed by a juvenile occurred in Newark, New Jersey, in 1987 (Crews, Montgomery, and Garris, 1996). Thomas Sullivan, Jr., then in his early teens, started studying occult books after researching religion for a high-school paper. During his research, he reportedly had a vision telling him to kill his family. The next day, Sullivan stabbed his mother 12 times and set the house on fire in an attempt to kill his father and brother who were still inside. After this failed arson attempt, he ran out into the snow and slashed his own throat and wrists with the knife, committing suicide.

BELIEF SYSTEMS AND PRACTICES

The following is an examination of the most prominent alternative belief systems exemplified in some juvenile behavior. The discussion, we hope, will clear up some terms and concepts that are often misrepresented and misunderstood.

Satanism

Probably the best known of the alternative belief systems in which some juveniles become involved is Satanism. Many definitions have been proposed. The most basic definition of Satanism (LaVey, 1969) recognizes the Christian Devil, Satan, or Set either as a deity or a principal philosophy. The basic premise of the belief system is that people should live out their lusts and desires and explore as many of the seven Deadly Sins (pride, envy, gluttony, lust, anger, coventousness, and sloth) as possible. The main symbol of the religion is a Baphomet, which is a goat's head drawn in an inverted pentagram.

Whether the religion urges the use of violence to do one's will is the subject of much controversy. Traditionally speaking (LaVey, 1972), the religion teaches that victims or enemies should be killed *symbolically* through the use of Magick, not actually taking one's physical life. Contrary to common perceptions, true Satanists hold life sacred. As an example, the highest of all Satanic holidays is one's own birthday. Many of those involved practice Magick, which involves ceremonies and rituals for the purposes of sex, healing, wealth, or destruction.

Probably the best way to obtain a clear view of the teachings of the Satanic Religion is to look at the nine Satanic Statements (LaVey, 1969), which basically revolve around the ideas that practitioners should indulge in their desires and not practice abstinence; that they should concentrate on their own vital existence and not believe in spiritual "pipe dreams"; that they should honor undefiled wisdom and not accept hypocritical self-deceit; and that they should practice kindness and assistance only to those who are deserving. The statements also point out that humans, being "just animals" should accept their own responsibility in the world and expect others to do the same. If what they expect is not experienced in dealing with others, they are to practice vengeance, not "turning the other cheek."

In a Letter to Satanic Youth in 1998, the Church of Satan posted an open letter from its homepage on the Internet to the youth of the world, reportedly in response to mail from many juveniles to the Church of Satan. The letter opened with a suggestion that youths should not use drugs or intoxicants of any kind. This is in contrast to the common perception that Satanists urge members to abuse drugs and alcohol. It also suggested that youths read as much Satanic literature as possible, much of which can be found in local bookstores. Youths were encouraged to be independent and think for themselves but at the same time to listen to their parents.

The letter instructed the youths to hide their beliefs and practices from everyone. It suggested that rituals and ceremonies be conducted alone, in private, and outside in local woods or deserted areas. Youths are reminded that they can make whatever tools they need in their rituals (such as knifes, chalices, altars). The letter closed with the statement that youth should continue their interest and remember that the Church of Satan will be there when they are ready.

Paganism

Some view paganism as a separate religion and spell it with a capital "P." Others view it as an all-encompassing system of beliefs and spell it with a small "p." Basically (Paganism Guide Page, www.uoguelph.ca/~bmyers/pagan/), those who practice this belief system hold a reverence for the Earth and all of its creatures. They see all life as interconnected and attempt to align the self with the cycles of nature. Paganism covers a wide spectrum of belief systems and is rapidly growing in numbers of adherents. Juveniles are reported to be the fastest growing number of those becoming involved.

Druidism

Druidism can be seen as a form of Paganism. The Celtic people (Druidism Guide Page, www.uoguelph.ca/~bmyers/druid/) called their professional class Druids.

These individuals filled the roles of judge, doctor, sorcerer, mystic, and scholar. Most Druidic wisdom and belief systems were lost as a result of destruction and censorship by the Romans, Saxons, and early Christians. In modern times, some use Druidism to connect with early history or become attuned to the natural world. Juveniles often use the term to cover any number of Pagan practices or belief systems.

Witchcraft and Wicca

Much discussion and debate swirls around the true definitions of Witchcraft and Wicca. In essence, Witchcraft, or the Craft as many juveniles call it, can mean anything to anyone. The practice (Morrison, 1989) combines the use of Magick and spells in an attempt to control the environment or the actions of others. Wicca (Buckland, 1990), by comparison, is more of a Pagan folk belief system. It often honors the spirits and gods of nature in animals. Juveniles also use the terms Witch and Warlock to describe a person "who can bend nature to serve his or her purpose."

Magicians and Magick

In addition to Witch and Warlock, many contemporary juveniles refer to Magicians and Magick. Magick (Morrison, 1989) is spelled in this fashion to differentiate it from sleight-of-hand or rabbit-out-of-the-hand entertainment. The term Magician describes one who believes he or she can control the environment and others to his or her will through the use of spells or rituals.

Goths

The Goth or Gothic lifestyle is a modern movement that many parents, educators, law-enforcement officials, and juvenile service providers are trying to understand. Juveniles involved in this belief system define it as embracing the dark, the weird, the bloody, and the morbid in modern life (Rankin, 1997).

Generally they classify themselves into four types (*A Goth primer*, lexicon.psy.tufts.edu/gothic/primer.html):

1. Those just into the "look," being different, or into the music associated with the practice.
2. Those who are into Witchcraft, Satanism, or Paganism, or are fascinated with death.
3. Those who pretend to be or role-play as real vampires.
4. Those who believe they are really vampires.

Many Goths divide themselves into additional groups (*A Goth primer*, lexicon.psy.tufts.edu/gothic/primer.html):

- *Mod Goths:* those who are also into modern fashion and music
- *Fetish Goths:* those who combine Goth with any number of sexual fetishes
- *Geek Goths:* those who are the traditional "nerds" or overachievers
- *Perky Goths:* those who are "cheerleader types" or hyper
- *Vampire Goths:* those who role-play as or consider themselves to be vampires
- *Pagan Goths:* those who also practice Paganism
- *Mil Goths:* those who combine Goth beliefs with guns, bombs, and war

Most of these youths are intelligent and well read (Scolaro, 1998). Many are independent, creative, and like history. The vast majority are articulate but often underachievers. Their appearance often includes white make-up or pale skin. They frequently dye their hair black, dark purple, or red. The clothes are black combined with black lipstick and fingernail polish. Jewelry is most often silver, and accessories are anything "Gothic."

Vampires

A relatively recent addition to the alternative lifestyles of some juveniles is the vampire movement. Most juveniles who are drawn into the vampire movement become involved through role-playing or playing of fantasy games (Arciaga, 1999). Others like the dress and lifestyle that has been portrayed in books and movies. A number of juveniles actually believe they are vampires and practice the traditional behaviors of drinking blood and attempting to control others.

Generally (Vampire Exchange Network, 1999), vampires seek to draw the life force from others, and drinking blood is one of the ways vampires receive energy or the life force from others. Also, many believe they are psychic-vampires and can draw the energy of others psychically. Some drink blood for pleasure or to create bonds between lovers, friends, or groups. When interviewed, most state that, in their view, vampirism and religion are two different things (Arciaga, 1999). They believe that vampirism is a desire they were born with. They also are quick to point out that they are nothing like the ones in Hollywood; they cannot fly, are not immortal, can walk in the daylight, and do not fear crosses.

Numerous groups on the Internet cater to those involved in vampirism. One of the largest is the Vampire Exchange Network, whose motto is "Keeping the Vampiric Community Connected." It was developed and is maintained by the New Jersey Association of Real Vampires. The stated purpose of this site is to establish and maintain a worldwide communication, information, and support network for all blood-drinkers, psychic-energy vampires, and vampire lifestylers. This group also hopes that, by these efforts, they will be able to correct widely held stereotypes and misconceptions. Through this, they will be able to facilitate acceptance of vampires into mainstream society.

ADVERTISEMENT AND RECRUITMENT ON THE INTERNET

As with many venues, the Internet has become a prime way for occult groups to advertise and recruit members. There are sites dedicated to spreading the teachings of Satanism with links to sites such as the Satanic Army, Satanville, Pack Sarama, Morphine Daffodils, the United Satanists Front, and the Mephisto Grotto. The following is a brief overview of this.

Occult Paraphernalia on the Web

The World Wide Web (WWW), combined with a renewed interest in the occult and Satanism, has spawned a marketing frenzy. Many sites offer related paraphernalia. Some sites cater to those in the Vampire lifestyle, offering full sets of vampire fangs, colored eye contacts, and fingernails. Also, a large number of sites cater to those wishing to purchase Goth clothing and jewelry.

The cost of some of the advertised items is astonishing. These seem to be items of interest to only the most serious of collectors. As with the vast majority of Web sites, purchases are easily made from one's home computer.

Currently Practicing Occult Groups on the Web

The following is a brief description of some of the most prominent occult and Satanic groups advertising on the Internet.

Church of Satan

Probably the best known of all Satanic groups is the Church of Satan. Anton LaVey (April 11, 1930–October 29, 1997) founded this organization in 1966 in opposition to what he viewed as hypocrisy in the Christian religion. The church is based in San Francisco. This church and Dr. LaVey's publication of *The Satanic Bible* in 1969 set the stage for a growing Satanic movement across the world. The philosophy of this church is based on the belief that people should do whatever they desire, so long as no undeserving person is harmed by those actions. It also teaches that people should live according to their natural instincts and pursue rational self-interests (Hatfield, 1997). The Satanic belief system is discussed further later in this chapter.

Temple of Set

In 1975, under the opinion that the Church of Satan had become too "commercial," Dr. Michael Aquino left the organization to begin his own group (www.the600club.com/satanic-search), the Temple of Set. It also is based in San Francisco. Based on the traditional view of Satanism but combined with a more elitist view, the organization is dedicated to the advancement and empowerment of all members. The teachings concentrate on the belief that people should focus on their potential while studying the "left-handed path." In the Christian religion, Jesus Christ is believed to have sat at the right hand of God. Lucifer, or Satan, was believed to have sat at God's left hand prior to being expelled from Heaven.

White Order of Thule

Based in Richmond, Virginia, and Clinton, Washington, is an organization called The White Order of Thule (www.the600club.com/satanic-search). Although information about this group is somewhat limited, it promotes Aryan occultism as the only way to revitalize the European Culture. It states that the only hope for the children of the "Northern peoples" is through Aryan high religion.

Werewolf Order

The Werewolf Order (www.the600club.com/satanic-search) is based in Los Angeles. This organization advertises itself as an elite group of black magicians who are creating a new world order based on Satanic principles. This organization says it seeks to eradicate the "sleepwalking zombie herds of Judeo-Christian corruption." As with all of these Web sites, there is extensive recruitment of new members over the Internet, although it is impossible to determine the true impact of this type of recruitment.

Satanic Underground of Washington, DC

The Satanic Underground of Washington, DC (www.the600club.com/satanic-search) advertises itself as an informal circle of Satanists who follow the teachings of Dr. Anton LaVey. Membership is limited to people living in the District of Columbia, Maryland, or the northern Virginia area. The Web site states that the organization allows Satanists to meet for fun, support, and indulgence.

Order of the Nefarious Mass

Not much information is available about the Order of the Nefarious Mass (www.the600club.com/satanic-search). This group is based in Pittsburgh, Pennsylvania. The advertisement for the group centers on its wish to provide a means for direct dialogue regarding the practice of Satanism. It states that the teachings are developed and offered as a celebration of the Satanic principles, heresy, and blasphemy. With this much advertisement, there is no obvious recruitment of new members.

Order of the Nine Angels

The Order of the Nine Angels (www.the600club.com/satanic-search) is an interesting presence on the Internet. It advertises and offers information extensively but has posted that it has "severed all external contact." The group does offer detailed information on how to conduct "Human Sacrifices, How to Choose a Victim, and How to Conduct Satanic Ceremonies."

Church of the Antichrist

The Church of the Antichrist (www.the600club.com/satanic-search) advertises itself as "a group of Satanic orphans who use their Magick for fun and profit." The membership reportedly consists of those who believe in Satanism but are in it just for personal benefit and wealth. The philosophy centers on the belief that there is no right or wrong, just success or failure.

Thee Temple ov Psychick Youth

Another group that is elitist in nature is Thee Temple ov Psychick Youth (TOPY NA Station, www.eskimo.com/~carcosa/topy.html). This group practices a "functional system of Magick and modern Pagan philosophy developed though the implicit powers of the brain." This system apparently is combined with the practice of "guiltless sexuality." The group teaching encourages individuals to maximize their natural potential.

Additional Items Marketed on Occult WWW Sites

In examining these sites closely one can note the extensive marketing by commercial entities to practitioners of items that can be purchased through these sites. Music and musicians are heavily marketed through links from many of these sites, as are posters, t-shirts, and other items of this nature. Some sites also link to Web sites that market cigarette-rolling papers, specially grown tobacco, water pipes and bongs, and marijuana pipes.

LEVELS OF JUVENILE INVOLVEMENT

The following is a brief discussion of the levels of juvenile involvement in the occult and Satanism.

Youth Subculture

The youth subculture (Crews, Montgomery, and Garris, 1996) represents the vast majority of juvenile involvement in these practices. The juveniles involved simply enjoy wearing the clothes and jewelry most often associated with these practices. Although some juveniles are involved in role-playing games and heavy metal or Gothic music, that is generally about as far as the involvement goes. Any deeper involvement in Satanism or the Occult tends to be in connection with a phase the child is moving through and will result in no long-term harm.

Dabblers

Some experts group the youth subculture and the dabblers together. The only difference between the two groups is that often the dabblers are more involved and explore the subjects more deeply out of curiosity (Larson, 1989; Wedge and Powers, 1988). They still have no actual spiritual motivation; they just play at being involved.

Traditional or Religious Practitioners

Those who represent organizations such as the Church of Satan or the Temple of Set consider themselves "traditional or religious" practitioners. They see this as their way of life and hold their beliefs sacred (Crews, Montgomery, and Garris, 1996). These are the "true believers" of the given religion. They are close-knit and private in nature, wary of outsiders. There is no solid evidence of any connection between these individuals and criminal behavior.

Self-Styled Practitioners

Self-styled practitioners (Crews, Montgomery, and Garris, 1996; Wedge, 1988) are the most dangerous subgroup. These juveniles mix many different belief systems to suit their purposes at any time. Symbols mean anything the practitioners want them to mean and change as the activity changes. These juveniles (as well as adults) often use religion to justify antisocial behavior. Adult criminals sometimes use pseudo-Satanic symbolism to cover their crimes and distract local communities and law enforcement. Examples of this occurrence are presented later in the chapter.

WARNING SIGNS OF POSSIBLE INVOLVEMENT IN THE OCCULT

The following is a compilation of possible warning signs of occult or Satanic involvement by juveniles (Crews, Montgomery, and Garris, 1996; Larson, 1989; Wedge, 1988; Hicks, 1991). When studying any list of this nature, a juvenile who meets one of these signs should not be immediately be suspect. Nor can the impacts of adolescence in general be dismissed, as the behaviors listed below may have numerous other explanations.

- Interest in heavy-metal or Satanic music
- Interest in Satanic paraphernalia and literature
- Obsession with horror movies and magazines
- Writing poetry about suicide, blood, death, or Satan
- Wearing all black or occult clothing and jewelry
- Drawing of occult or Satanic symbols on notebooks

- Uncharacteristic displays of anger or aggression
- Abrupt drop in grades or involvement in extracurricular activities
- Self-mutilation or self-destructive behavior

A youth who is simply curious about these topics is in a delicate position, and parents who attack their children for their interests, music, or reading matter run the risk of driving them deeper into the practices.

OCCULT SYMBOLS AND LITERATURE

As in any area of human behavior, anything can be a symbol, and a symbol can be anything. This is never truer than when juveniles are involved. The following lists some of the most popular symbolism found in juvenile activities:

NATAS	Satan spelled backward
NEMA	Amen spelled backward
666	The number of the beast
FFF	The sixth letter of the alphabet
AC/DC	Antichrist/devil child
⚡	Lightning bolt, symbolic of Satan's fall to earth
☨	Inverted cross, symbolic of "down with Christianity"
⛤	Inverted pentagram, symbolic of Satanism

The most popular occult and Satanic-related literature often used by juveniles includes:

- *Candle Burning Magic: A Spellbook of Rituals for Good and Evil*, by A. Riva (Los Angeles: International Imports, 1989)
- Buckland's Complete Book of Witchcraft, *by R. Buckland (St. Paul, MN: Llewellyn Publications, 1990)*
- Crystal Clear, *by C. Church (New York: Villard Books, 1987)*
- Necronomicon, *by H. Barnes (New York: Avon Books, 1989)*
- Practical Candle Burning: Spells and Rituals for Every Purpose, *by R. Buckland (St. Paul, MN: Llewellyn Publications, 1990)*
- The Black Arts, *by Richard Cavendish (New York: G.P. Putnam's Sons, 1969)*
- The Modern Witch's Spellbook, *BY S.L. Morrison (New York: Carol Publishing Group, 1989)*
- The Satanic Bible, *by Anton LaVey (New York: Avon Books, 1969)*

- The Satanic Rituals, *by Anton LaVey (New York: Avon Books, 1972)*
- *The Satanic Witch*, by Anton LaVey (New York: Los Angeles: Avon Books, 1989)

OCCULT AND SATANIC-RELATED JUVENILE BEHAVIOR

Below is a list of the various ways that juvenile involvement in the occult and Satanism can manifest themselves (Crews, Montgomery, and Garris, 1996):

- Vandalism
- Trespassing
- Desecration of churches and cemeteries
- Thefts from churches and cemeteries
- Teenage gangs
- Animal mutilations

There is valid evidence (Crews, Montgomery, and Garris, 1996) of a connection between these practices and some juvenile involvement with activities in the preceding list. In contrast, there is weak evidence to support a connection with the following list:

- Teen suicide
- Kidnapping
- Murder
- Human sacrifice

These activities will be discussed later in the chapter.

Satanic Tourism

In the concept of Satanic tourism, the vast majority of juveniles are involved in occult and Satanic behavior that is actually "pseudo-Satanic" in nature (Fine and Victor, 1994). This means that juveniles sometimes mask traditional delinquency (vandalism, trespassing, and mischief) with occult or Satanic overtones or symbolism. This type of pseudo-Satanic behavior is "collective entertainment" for juveniles. Although this activity sometimes does involve rituals or ceremonies, it lacks any personal identification by the juvenile. Youths slip in and out of the identities at will. Pseudo-Satanic behavior is used to shock classmates, communities, and parents. This is also a unique way to test the boundaries set by parents and society as a whole.

The view of the adolescents involved tends to be that it is a fun way to spend a weekend (Crews, Montgomery, and Garris, 1996). Many researchers believe this type of behavior is no different from the traditional pranks and petty delinquency that many adolescents engage in. It does have inherent dangers, though. Often, juveniles involved in this behavior drink alcohol, they possibly use drugs, and some have unprotected sex. Adults do not have to be alarmists, but they should be concerned, but about the right things.

Legend Trips

The primary activity of Satanic tourists is the "legend trip" (Fine and Victor, 1994). This means that juveniles are generally attracted to sites tied to a local legend of ghosts or occult activity. Juveniles visit the sites like a tourist would and may take or leave something behind (such as graffiti, campfires, or vandalism). Usually, the youth wants to do nothing more than test a local legend.

Legend trips are no more than a form of recreation to these youth, even if they recite spells or perform rituals. No evidence indicates they have any long-term detrimental effects on the juveniles involved. Even so, certain crimes are associated with this type of behavior. To go to these sites, the youths often have to trespass on others' property. Also, the vandalism, graffiti, and theft angers property owners. As with other types of occult and Satanic behavior, juveniles sometimes become involved in underage drinking, drug use, and unprotected sex.

Legend trip sites can be almost anywhere. They most often are abandoned buildings, houses, or barns. Sometimes they are old bridges, graveyards, or old churches. Other sites include "spooky" woods, abandoned bomb shelters, caves, or dangerous tunnels.

Animal Cruelty

Some juveniles who are involved in occult or Satanic belief systems are cruel to animals. Officially, none of the organizations discussed in this chapter condones or encourages animal cruelty. Most of the juveniles involved in animal cruelty are self-styled practitioners who believe they must offer a sacrifice to their god or demon so they can ask for favors.

Human Sacrifice

Some groups report 50,000 to 60,000 human sacrifices a year. The question becomes one of how that is possible. Individuals and groups supporting this wave of violence offer the following "evidence" (Johnson and Padilla, 1991):

- Runaway statistics of 2.5 million each year
- The use of untraceable people
- The use of transient people
- Disposal of bodies by:

cannibalism and using bones in further ceremonies
feeding victims to animals
mass burials
dumping bodies at sea
burning or cremating of bodies

The reality of what is occurring is the following (Johnson and Padilla, 1991; Bromley, 1991; Hicks, 1989; Richardson, Best, Bromley, 1991):

- Police have investigated every report of Satanic sacrifice and mass murder with no evidence of support for these ideas.
- The probability of this many people getting away with this much crime and killing is slim.
- Most academic research finds the number of occurrences to be blown out of proportion.
- Holding people as "breeders" and disposing of bodies is not that easy.
- The logistics of 400 to 500 groups operating and keeping their existence and activities hidden are prohibitive.

VIEWPOINTS

When examining the possible impacts of occultism and Satanism upon juvenile behavior, we can look at the issue from various viewpoints to gain an appreciation for the complexity of this issue.

Parental Views

The view of the parent (Crews, Montgomery, and Garris, 1996) is probably the most important of all perspectives in that it has the greatest impact upon the juvenile. The parent is most concerned with the child's outward behavior. Strange new clothing or reading material often is the first sign that something has changed. Some of the most upsetting confrontations between parents and children involve the child's dress and appearance.

Law Enforcement Views

The major concern from the perspective of law enforcement is that of the criminal behavior that is sometimes involved in occult and Satanic practices (Hicks, 1991). Some law enforcement personnel see this activity as just another form of juvenile delinquency, and others view it as a more serious problem. The number of police officials who specialize in this form of criminal activity continues to grow. The police officers involved have come to be known as Cult Cops or Ghostbusters.

Occult Practitioners

A perspective that often is not represented in serious work is that of the actual occult practitioners. We contacted various leaders in the Satanic movement to obtain their personal views of the possible connections between occultism and juvenile delinquency. Below are brief excerpts from those conversations:

> The causes of juvenile unruliness are society-wide disintegration of the nuclear family, absentee parents, fear of adults to discipline children, children's disillusionment with and contempt for adults and adult institutions, and a cynical and pessimistic outlook toward adult life. (Michael A. Aquino, Temple of Set, March 30, 1999)

> These misguided youths find their symbolism in the shallow and puerile imagery of popular musicians who misuse Satanic symbolism in…lyrics, artwork, and stage presentations. (Nikolas Schreck, The Werewolf Order, April 8, 1999).

> We agree that certain disturbed juveniles utilize material from various belief systems as misguided justification for their behavior, which can often be of a sort we would consider unhealthy, nonproductive, and nonconducive for maintaining the social contract. (Magister Peter H. Gilmore, the Church of Satan, April 30, 1999).

It is interesting to note the basic theme that runs throughout these comments. As many researchers point out, juvenile delinquency is a product of the background, family, and lifestyle of the child more so than any outside influence (such as music, art, or the media).

Practicing Juvenile Occultist View

During Fall of 1999 and Spring of 2000, Gordon Crews of Jacksonville State University began a dialogue over the Internet with 10 individuals reporting to be 18 years of age or younger and practicing occultists. He was interested primarily in why they had chosen this lifestyle. Table 4.1 synopsizes the information provided through this research.

The initial results from this ongoing research appear to support the commonly stated reasons for juvenile involvement in the occult or Satanism. The interviews revealed that the most common reason for involvement of this small sample was, "I finally found a group that understands me!" The second most common reason stated was that the youth had been reared in a strict or fundamentalist home and found the alternative practices to be a good way to rebel against control.

Adolescent View

The vast majority of juveniles involved in this type of activity say they do so as a "lark," for the excitement and entertainment that these activities can provide (Crews, Montgomery, and Garris, 1996). Some disturbed youths are simply drawn to this type of behavior or belief system, not created by it.

TABLE 4.1

Occult Name	Sex	Age	Belief System	Why Chosen?
Lady Malevolence	Female	15	Druidism/Magick	Atheist/enjoys ancient practices
Chris H	Male	17	Druidism/Paganism	Enjoys history and theology
RokyGirlX	Female	18	Goth	Grew into it—it felt natural
Catea Alistair	Female	17	Occultist	Believes in immortality
Jessica C.	Female	15	Vampire	Believes she was born a vampire
Katarina	Female	17	Satanist	Born a Satanist; hates Christianity
Katt Medosphere	Female	16	Goth	Misunderstood life, found group
Sue Shepke	Female	15	Goth	Most friends involved
Damien Demodus	Male	17	Goth	Enjoys lifestyle
Ajah D'Jinn	Male	17	Occultist	Believes in the power of Magick

Data source: Dr. Gordon A. Crews, Jacksonville State University, AL.

In interviews with juveniles involved in these activities, they most often state that their involvement is basically to "spice up a weekend." Others state that they wear the associated clothing and jewelry as a fad or as a fashion statement. In interviews with older individuals who were involved in these activities previously, they report no longlasting effects on themselves or others that they knew.

Satanic Panic View versus Reality

The "Satanic panic" view (Charlier and Downing, 1988; Hicks, 1989; Richardson, Best, and Bromley, 1991) is of a national conspiracy of Satanists trying to take over the world. This view is supported by media hype from talk shows and lecture halls. Adherents believe that any sign of involvement must be attacked immediately.

Rumor panics, especially occult and Satanic-related rumors, are common in the United States. The idea that Satanists may be involved exacerbates the wide-ranging, all-encompassing strength of the rumor. The following is a sampling of Satanic-related rumor panics, each of which was found to have no basis whatsoever (Johnson and Padilla, 1991):

- 1988—Breathitt County, Kentucky: rumors that Satanists were going to kidnap blonde-haired, blue-eyed children.
- 1989—Jamestown, New York: rumor that caused many citizens to arm themselves with clubs and scour local forests looking for bands of Satanists.

- 1990—Los Angeles: Ritualistic Crime Task Force causing a panic by announcing that Satanists were planning to kidnap and sacrifice trick-or-treaters.
- 1990—St. Louis, Missouri: three dead "dogs" found apparently beaten to death and skinned, which panicked a local community into thinking that teenage Satanists were holding rituals; turned out to be three coyotes killed by a local hunter who came forward after seeing numerous television broadcasts about the incident.

These panics are perpetuated largely by those who support these beliefs. Many therapists and counselors specialize in this type of victimization. Cult Cops (Crews, Montgomery, and Garris, 1996) have gained national reputations for their interpretations of the problem. Some Christian fundamentalists say this is a manifestation of the devil at work in the modern world. Some parents and guardians use panics to shift the blame away from themselves. And many stressed-out communities want a simple answer to what is causing problems in the community.

One must be cognizant of those who stand to benefit from this problem. Therapists can get attention, and thus more clients. Others become overnight experts, exploiting those involved. And glorification by the media has allowed many pseudoprofessionals to draw national attention as "experts."

CONCLUSION

Before any solutions to the problem of juveniles involved in occultism and Satanism can be considered, one must understand why youths become involved in the first place. The vast majority of those juveniles involved do so to overcome a sense of alienation. The attendant practices, including certain behaviors and clothing, are one way to rebel against authority and to gain power over others. Many juveniles use it to justify their already antisocial behavior and others use it for sheer shock value. It is an effective means to flaunt the rejections of adult values. As with many types of negative juvenile behavior, extreme involvement is a symptom of a problem, not the cause. With this in mind, to react irrationally may drive the juveniles even deeper into their involvement. The triads to look for in evaluating whether a juvenile is disturbed or not consists of fire-starting, bed-wetting, and cruelty to animals. Violence toward others, rather than mere fads of music or clothing, is a real danger signal. Serious antisocial behavior cannot be ignored.

Focusing on the trappings of pseudo-Satanic behavior is misleading and counterproductive. Instead of allowing the symbols of teenage rebellion to distract, the emphasis should be upon the root causes of any form of teenage delinquency or violence. Those root causes are:

- Depression
- Poor social conditions
- Boredom

- Alienation
- Poverty
- Abuse
- Low self-esteem
- Pessimism
- Hopelessness

Efforts toward solutions should address these issues rather than worrying so much about alternative clothing or music. Each juvenile involved should be approached with confidence, honesty, and concern instead of hysteria, lack of information, and misinformation.

FROM LACK OF DISCIPLINE TO LACK OF CONSCIENCE

Theories of Juvenile Violence

Violence is an admission that one's ideas and goals cannot prevail on their own merit.

U. S. Senator Edward Kennedy

This recent series of killings in our schools has seared the heart of America about as much as anything I can remember in a long, long, time.

President Bill Clinton, July 7, 1998

The Gothic community in no way condones the use of violence; we are appalled by the killings and by the inference that the murderers belonged to our culture.

Sign in window of Inkubus Haberdashery, Miami, Florida
just after the Columbine High School Shooting, April 20, 1999

INTRODUCTION

In this chapter we examine the extremely controversial topic of causes of juvenile delinquency and violence in America. The chapter covers the spectrum of many different perspectives and beliefs, and applies them to juvenile behavior, including the response of the criminal justice system.

TRADITIONAL THEORIES

For centuries, theorists and scholars have attempted to pinpoint the origins of juvenile delinquency. These approaches cover the gamut of biological, psychological, and sociological factors. In modern times, new thought-provoking insights enter into the mix of causes of juvenile delinquency, filling newspapers, academic journals, and agendas of professional conferences all over the world.

Traditional theories of why youths become delinquent have ranged from the concept of free will—the belief that all humans are rational and make decisions by weighing the pros and cons and by seeking pleasure over pain—to the hard deterministic view—the belief that some individuals should not be held accountable for their actions because of mental deficiencies or biological factors. In between these two schools of thought are soft deterministic views—that society has an impact upon behavior and influences how people view the world and react to it (Drowns and Hess, 1990).

Cesare Beccaria and the Classical School of Thought

The classical (free will) school of thought, promulgated by Cesare Beccaria (1738–1794), describes people as free agents, pursuing hedonistic aims, and able to rationally decide on all or most courses of action. Offenders are viewed as having free will and being no different from nonoffenders except that are "willed" to commit crimes. It follows, naturally, that punishment is expected to be harsh and immediate so offenders will "unwill" to commit future crimes. The offenders' mental make-up, background, and extenuating circumstances are irrelevant (Vold, 1968).

Cesare Lombroso and the Positivist School of Thought

A secondary movement was the positivism school of thought. Founded by Cesare Lombroso (1835–1909), this school emphasizes the criminal offender's personal and background characteristics rather than just the rational thought process and free will. The positive school rejects the classical school's belief that people exercise reason and are capable of choice and free will, and that offenders are not different from non-offenders. Lombroso believed that offenders are "sick" and their behavior reflects the various determinants in their backgrounds. The determinants are the offender's biological, psychological, sociological, cultural, and physical environments. To correct deviant behavior, one has to *treat* these determinants (Matza, 1964).

Charles Goring's Measurements

In 1913, physician Charles Goring took interest in Lombroso's research and published his own measurements of the physical characteristics of criminals in an attempt to reveal the causes of criminality. In his landmark research, Goring took measurements of 3,000 English convicts and also measured comparison groups (which Lombroso did not include in his research). He found no evidence of a distinct physical criminal type (Albanese, 1996).

William Sheldon's Body Types

In 1949, William Sheldon reported on the extensive physical measurements and background information he collected on 200 boys in a Boston reform school. Unlike Lombroso, Sheldon did not see *atavism* as key in distinguishing criminals from law-abiding citizens, although Sheldon believe that one's basic body structure was linked to delinquency. Atavism is the belief that the criminal is a throwback to the neanderthal man. Sheldon identified three basic body types:

1. Mesomorphic—athletic, active, aggressive
2. Endomorphic—heavy, slow moving, lethargic
3. Ectomorphic—tall, thin, intellectual

Sheldon's findings revealed that delinquency was associated with the *mesomorphic* body type and believed this type predisposed an individual toward delinquency. He attributed the cause of delinquency as it related to body type to "germ plasma." His suggested alternative to criminal suppression and prevention of further delinquency was selective breeding to weed out the socially harmful types (Albanese, 1996).

Abraham Maslow's Hierarchy of Needs

Many believe that Abraham Maslow was made famous by popularizing his theory of psychological humanism. One of Maslow's most important contributions to psychology was his hierarchy of human needs, which he developed in the late 1960s. Maslow believed that people are not merely controlled by mechanical forces—the stimuli and reinforcement forces of behaviorism—or the unconscious instinctual impulses of psychoanalysis but rather, should be understood in terms of human potential. He believed that humans strive to reach the highest levels of their capabilities. At each of the five levels of the hierarchy, the individual has different needs, dependent on fulfilling the needs at the previous level. These seven levels, starting with the most basic needs, are:

1. *Physiological needs.* Basic needs such as oxygen, food, water, protection, and the like.
2. *Safety needs.* The need to feel secure; shown by children who display signs of insecurity.
3. *Love, affection, and belongingness needs.* The need to escape loneliness and alienation and receive love, affection, and a sense of belonging.
4. *Esteem needs.* The need for a stable, firmly based, high level of self-respect and respect from others in order to feel satisfied, self-confident and valuable. If these needs are not met, the person feels inferior, weak, helpless, and worthless.
5. *Self-actualization needs.* The need to feel fulfilled by becoming the best one can be.

Maslow's hierarchy of needs is intriguing to criminologists and criminal-justice professionals. Maslow's perpective challenged many other theories that attempted to pinpoint the root of criminal behavior. Are juvenile delinquents criminal because one or several of their basic needs have not been met? If so, other issues such as societal values and morals and social justice come into play. For example, is it wrong for a child to break into a vacant home or building to seek shelter from the cold? Is it wrong for children to steal food when they are hungry? The law emphasizes that stealing and breaking and entering are unlawful, but what about survival?

Maslow's hierarchy points out that a person cannot progress effectively to the point of self-actualization without successfully moving through or obtaining success in a previous stage. If this is so, one can easily justify one's criminality. In keeping with Maslow's theory, society must consider all social ills, such as poverty, as possibly creating pervasive stress that can encompass all aspects of one's life (Crossen-Tower, 1999). The development of Maslow's theory offers more insight and possibly another step toward understanding the possible reasons for juvenile criminality.

Environmental Impact Theories

The concept of environmental impact upon behavior is not new. Research on the impact of the surrounding environment dates back to a study conducted by Clifford R. Shaw (Regoli and Hewitt, 1994) and his ecological theory of crime. Shaw studied crime and delinquency statistics recorded in Chicago between 1900 and 1927. More than 55,000 juvenile delinquents and criminals were found to live in certain areas of the city. Shaw concluded that many of the law violations recorded were acceptable behaviors within the specific setting in which the offender lived. He concluded that most other theories of crime causation must be viewed in the context of the individual's environment.

Environmental impact theories can be classified into at least two groupings. The first is sociological theories, which suggest that society conditions people to act in certain ways and that a person's socialization can precipitate criminal behavior. The second consists of the behavioral theories.

Sociological Theories

One such theory is the social structure and anomie theory by Robert Merton. He built on the work of Emile Durkheim, which focused on the idea of anomie—a state wherein individuals feel disconnected from any group and isolated from the mainstream of interaction and positive peer support. Merton (1938) proposed three conditions that determine whether someone will become a criminal:

1. The cultural goals or aspirations that people learn from their culture
2. The norms that people employ when attempting to achieve the goals
3. The institutionalized means that are available for goal achievement

A second social theory is Frederick Thrasher's gang theory, which suggests that gangs often evolve naturally from spontaneous playgroups. The major factor that transforms a playgroup into a gang is conflict with other groups. As a result of that conflict, it becomes mutually beneficial for individuals to band together to protect themselves and to satisfy needs that the social environment and family do not. By middle adolescence, the gang has distinctive characteristics—a name, a specific mode of operation, and usually an ethnic or racial emphasis (Thrasher, 1936).

Behavioral Theories

Behavioral theorists believe that people act in certain ways because their lifestyle and behavior is taught and not fixed. One well-known behavioral theory is Edwin Sutherland's differential association theory, which states that criminal behavior is learned in interaction with other persons. The principal learning of criminal behavior occurrs within intimate personal groups. This learning includes not only techniques for committing the crime but also a specific direction for motives, drives, rationalizations, and attitudes (Cohen, Lindesmith, and Schuessler, 1956).

Biological and Genetic Theories

Biological theories center on the belief that criminal behavior is inherited, not learned. Biochemical research has demonstrated how dietary intake, allergies, and body chemistry can impact behavior. A case in point is the 1979 "Twinkie Defense" used to justify Dan White's killing of San Francisco Mayor George Moscone and City Councilman Harvey Milk. Mr. White claimed his behavior was precipitated by an addiction to sugar-laden junk foods. This defense prompted the jury to find him guilty of the lesser offense of diminished capacity manslaughter rather than first-degree murder (Siegel, 1998).

In addition, neurological dysfunction may cause learning disabilities. The presence of learning disabilities is linked to a higher rate of criminal behavior (Drowns and Hess, 1990).

According to Siegel (1998), criminal or deviant behavior is not learned but is an innate characteristic present at birth. His "evolution theory" explains that as the human race has evolved, traits and characteristics have become ingrained. Some of these traits make people aggressive and predisposed to commit crime. With a more sophisticated and technologically advanced world, in modern times, the scientific research involving genetics has produced some specific findings.

Early biological theorists believed that criminality runs in families and that children of criminals are destined to breed criminals and continue the cycle of criminality, thereby perpetuating criminal behavior. Although the early theory of the contribution of genetics to criminality has been dismissed for the most part, the notion of a positive correlation between crime and genes has concentrated of late on the fragile X chromosome. On June 9, 1996, the *London Sunday Times* reported that England's Department of Health had undertaken a study targeting individuals who carry what has been identified as the Fragile X chromosome. Passed from unaffected mothers to their sons, and occasionally to their daughters, the defect stems from a lack of a brain protein, which can produce mental defects and aggressive or antisocial behavior. One in every 259 women is thought to carry this gene.

The rationale behind the testing, according to the London researchers, was that mass testing would allow authorities to determine who had the genetic defect embedded in their DNA. A second rationale was that the test would enable female carriers of the condition to abort affected babies. Dr. David Thornton, head of program development at the prison service in England, argued that this would purify the human race—a rationale used by Adolf Hitler's Nazi organization. In addition to killing millions of Jews, Blacks, homosexuals, and drug users, the Third Reich planned to purify the German race by eliminating the handicapped, the elderly, the diseased, and the insane (Neill, 1996).

In the 1970s, (Neil, 1996) a mind-control researcher from the Central Intelligence Agency by the name Dr. Louis Jolyon "Jolly" West worked to develop plans for a Center for the Study and Reduction of Violence, originally proposed by *then* Governor and past president Ronald Reagan. According to West, the program was an attempt to predict the probability of occurrences of violent behavior among certain population groups. He defined the group with the characteristics of male, youthful, black, and urban.

Upon identifying individuals with the predisposition to violent behavior, West prescribed the treatment for the behavior or probability to become violent as consisting of (1) chemical castration, (2) psychosurgery, and (3) the use of experimental drugs that would be used only on involuntarily incarcerated individuals. Thereafter, the Center's findings would be coordinated with a California police computer database, which would maintain files on "predelinquent" children so they could be treated before they developed full-blown delinquency. This program was scuttled by the California legislature because of its moral ramifications.

THEORY APPLIED TO ADOLESCENTS

From the foregoing discussion, it is clear to see that many different beliefs have been proposed as to why youths become deviant. Many of the research-based findings point to issues of boredom and alienation. Some delinquent youths may actually be hyperactive and need extra stimulation to satisfy their need for risk and excitement. Some youths see themselves as being forced into becoming good citizens by society and their parents. Freedom, for them, means testing the limits to see what they can get away with. Some get trapped in delinquent behavior because they are unhappy with themselves or with the outside world and crime may be one way to find something at which one is competent. Some delinquent behavior stems from parental abuse, indifference, and neglect (Wooden, 1995).

An attendant problem is the lack of communication. For example, few students talk with teachers about their personal problems or problems at home (22%) or about where they can get help with personal or family problems (13%). Most students do not talk with teachers about problems they are having with peers.

Students do not discuss their personal problems with teachers for a wide variety of reasons: because they believe there is no privacy or confidentiality in school (26%), because they feel that adults do not understand them (22%), because they think teachers cannot help (20%), and because teachers do not seem interested in or do not have time for their students (24%) (Crews and Counts, 1997).

Impact of School on Delinquency

The U.S. educational system as a whole could be contributing to school violence. Budget cuts have severely reduced education resources in many communities and curtailed state support for local school systems. Spending on elementary and secondary education trails that of other nations. Sweden spends 7% of its gross national product on education, Austria 6%, and Japan 4.8%, whereas the United States spends 4.1%. As a consequence, the United States does not provide some of the classroom services routinely available to children in other nations (Sivard, 1989).

> The worst thing seems to be for schools to work with methods of fear, force, and artificial authority. Such treatment destroys the healthy feelings, the integrity, and the self-confidence of pupils—Albert Einstein

Many educators believe that allowing corporal punishment of children by school officials results in students directing violent actions toward other students. Each year more than 1 million incidents of corporal punishment occur in U.S. schools, 10,000 of which require medical attention. Educators have postulated that corporal punishment teaches children to use force when trying to control another's behavior. Therefore, schools that use corporal punishment should not be surprised when students act out and become violent; it is what they have been taught (Curcio and First, 1993).

Regoli and Hewitt (1994) have suggested that four factors contribute to students' delinquent behavior at school. The first is loss of teacher authority. Teachers must maintain their authority, and they need a strong principal to maintain this authority. When principals and parents do not support teachers, teachers' authority is lost—and control of students along with it.

The second factor is regimentation and revenge. As students age, they are given much more independence and control, but not in school. School rules often do not "grow" with the students. Faced with strict rules and degrading experiences in class, some students try to save face and regain their self-esteem by lashing out at the perceived cause of their embarrassment. Teachers then become victims of attack, and school property the objects of vandalism (Regoli and Hewitt, 1994).

Tracking students is the third problem. Tracking students in a college track, a technical track, or a vocational track has inherent inequities. Students often are placed often by appearance and socioeconomic status rather than ability. Low-track students tend to receive lower grades, even for work of equal quality, based on the rationale that students who are not college-bound are obviously less bright and do not need good grades to get into college. Teachers of high-ability students make more of an effort to teach in an interesting and challenging manner than those who instruct lower-level students (Crews and Counts, 1997).

Tracking, too, calls into play the concept of self-fulfilling prophecy. Students from whom little achievement and much misbehavior are expected tend to live up to these often unspoken assumptions about their behavior. Placement into a low track leads to loss of self-esteem and increases the potential for academic failure and disturbances, both in and out of school. Students segregated in lower tracks easily reflect a value system that rewards misbehavior rather than the academic success, which they feel they cannot achieve. Lower-track students are less inclined to conform. Because they see no future rewards from their schooling, they do not realize a record of deviant or low academic achievement can threaten their future.

The fourth aspect cited by Regoli and Hewitt is IQ scores and their connection with delinquency. IQ and delinquency seem to be strongly related (Regoli and Hewitt, 1994).

Early criminologists trained in medicine or psychology that used intelligence tests made some inflated and, in some cases, ridiculous claims about the relationship between intelligence and crime. They suggested that people of low intelligence were easily led into law-breaking by more clever people, and did not realize that committing an offense in a certain way often led to getting caught and being punished (Slawson, 1926).

Research has consistently found a relationship between IQ and delinquency. Hirschi and Hindelang (1977) reported that the average delinquent has an IQ about 8 points lower than that of law-abiding juveniles. They also reported that IQ was associated with the type of crime the juvenile was likely to commit. Bribers, embezzlers, and forgers scored higher than auto thieves, burglars, and substance-abuse offenders, who in turn scored higher than those who committed assault, murder, and rape. These findings continue to emerge in more contemporary research (Crews and Counts, 1997).

Another area of contemporary research that is emerging is the investigation of the possible effects of the inclusion of special education students in the classroom. Mainstreaming is a very popular concept that has had some positive impacts on the special education student and the other students in which the inclusion has occurred. Research in this area is weak, but there is evidence that some of the more advanced students get bored and think low achievers are holding them back. This feeling can possibly increase feelings of boredom and lack of motivation. As discussed throughout this work, this lack of interest and motivation can lead to a myriad of problems—not the least of which is juvenile delinquency.

Theories of delinquency generally ignore these findings, and just how IQ affects delinquency remains a mystery. One possibility is that IQ has no effect. It may be that both IQ and delinquency are caused by some third variable such as social class (Chambliss and Ryther, 1975). Another possibility is that low IQs do not lead to higher rates of delinquency per se, but merely to higher rates of apprehension which contribute to delinquency (Haskell and Yablonsky, 1978).

A third possibility is that IQ has a direct effect on delinquency. Wilson and Herrnstein (1985) believe that adolescents with low intelligence may be more impulsive or lacking in moral reasoning. They argue that people with low intelligence favor impulsive crimes with immediate rewards and those with high intelligence, the inverse.

Hirschi (1969) suggests a fourth possibility—that IQ does affect delinquency but not directly. Instead, the effect of IQ is transmitted through school-experience variables. The original purpose of IQ tests was to predict how well a person would do in school and, though they are not perfect, IQ tests do have a reasonably good prediction record: Students who perform well on IQ tests tend to get good grades.

Psychological Factors

The developmental period of adolescence is probably the most well researched correlate of juvenile delinquency. Adolescence brings biological, psychological, emotional, and social stress. Adolescents pretend to be adults by doing what they think adults do (dress like adults, talk like adults, smoke, have sex, and drink alcohol [Drowns and Hess, 1990]).

Adolescents who become delinquent are more likely to be socially assertive, suspicious, defiant, destructive, ambivalent to authority, impulsive, resentful, lacking in self-control, and hostile (Drowns and Hess, 1990). And they are more likely to act out, defined as the free, deliberate, often malicious indulgence of impulses. It frequently is associated with aggression, as well as other manifestations of delinquency including vandalism, cruelty to animals, and even murder. There is a desire for immediate gratification and an absence of self-control (Drowns and Hess, 1990). Acting out may result from an early history of severe parental reaction or deprivation or from witnessing or experiencing physical abuse and violence. Adolescents may strike out to hurt the world they see as hostile, and to gain a sense of importance by overcoming feelings of inferiority. This can be found in all socioeconomic levels of society (Drowns and Hess, 1990).

Also, vulnerability to peer pressure peaks in early adolescence, usually between sixth and ninth grades. This often leads to conflicts with parents; adolescents report the greatest number of disagreements in the ninth grade. Too, self-esteem declines, particularly in girls. At a time when adolescents are seeking stronger peer associations and a supportive climate for resolving identity issues, they are confronted with an educational environment that is more impersonal (Elkind, 1984). Most of this occurs when adolescents are moving from elementary to middle school to high school, where many students are strangers to each other and new relationships must be formed. In addition, the peer group does not remain constant during the day, which makes establishing relationships even more difficult. The fear of not knowing anyone is anxiety-provoking. Finally, the transition in schools frequently coincides with other life changes such as the onset of puberty, dating, family disruptions (such as divorce), or a move to a new neighborhood (Garrin and Furman, 1989).

Conforming to the norms of peer groups and becoming accepted meets many of the socioemotional needs of young adolescents for affiliation. The parents may inadvertently drive adolescents to their peer group. For example, when parents are restrictive and limit their children's opportunities for decision-making, the children tend to turn to the peer group for advice and support.

Whenever children of any age are confronted with transitions, they adjust best if they have emotional and social supports. Students who have strong relationships with peers and teachers show higher academic performance, less anxiety, and more favorable attitudes toward school. It follows that these students are less likely to commit acts of violence or to drop out of school (Garrin and Furman, 1989).

Although many adolescents have the cognitive competence to think logically, they often do not do so, especially when in regard to themselves when their thoughts tend to be flawed by "adolescent egocentrism" (Garrin and Furman, 1989). Adolescents often create an "imaginary audience" for themselves as they fantasize about others' reaction to their appearance and behavior. They assume that everyone notices and judges their appearance and skills. The imaginary audience tends to be composed of peers rather than adults. When adolescents become more comfortable and secure in their social world, they are more secure, more realistic, and more positive, and they rely on their own opinions and beliefs rather than those of an audience. Girls more than boys, and younger teens more than older teens, tend to be concerned about the imaginary audience. Delinquent boys, however, think more about imagined opinions than do nondelinquents of either sex (Elkind, 1984).

Adolescent thought processes are characterized by the propensity to imagine possibilities and to deny reality when it interferes with adolescent fantasy. This results in the "personal fable" and particularly the aspect of the "invincibility myth," in which adolescents feel they are immune to laws of probability and mortality. Adolescents engage in risk-taking, secure in the belief that they will not get killed, sick, pregnant, hurt, or caught. They imagine their lives as heroic and see themselves as destined for greatness. They may have decided already that school is a waste of their time. This facet of the personal fable is influenced by what they deem is their value in their peer culture (Elkind, 1984).

By late adolescence and early adulthood, young people are better able to reason logically. Consequently, they become more secure and more realistic. As a result, delinquent behavior decreases because of cognitive maturity rather than punitive measures (Elkind, 1984).

Two Types of Delinquency

Theoriests have described two types of delinquency—addictive and chronic.

Addictive Delinquency

If children are born into organized crime and learn delinquency as a way of gaining pleasure, or if they learn to identify with a delinquent father who has been irresponsible to family, friends, or society, children can learn delinquency as a way of life, much as children learn language. This has been called addictive delinquency. According to Weil (1992), this way of life is reinforced when parents fail to offer children consistent, helpful, and empathic controls of delinquent behavior.

According to Weil (1992) addictive delinquency emerges if children are rewarded by parents for delinquent acts and if the children also gain the approval of peers for those acts. He believes that adolescents who have been severely deprived of empathic care during infancy run a statistically greater chance of manifesting addictive delinquency. These children will more likely adopt delinquency as a supply line of *pleasure*.

Another factor associated with addictive delinquency is the presence of physical abuse during infancy and childhood. Presumably, the abuse generates so much hate and antagonism toward the perpetrator that it in turn is discharged upon other human beings, perpetuating the "cycle of abuse." Clinical cases observed by Weil (1992) suggest that the earlier in life a child incurs abuse, the more diffuse, exaggerated, and deeply ingrained the subsequently destructive delinquent behavior.

More widespread early contribution to addictive delinquency derives from chronic deprivation of empathic care during infancy. Among the symptoms are an "emptiness of pleasure"; a compensatory "greed for pleasure"; a need to "manipulate the environment"; "frozen empathy"; and "a readiness to turn away from human care" (Weil, 1992). The children turn to delinquency as a "compensatory supply line" to restore the state of pleasure. The addictive aspect of the delinquency, like the addictive aspects of alcoholism and of compulsive sexuality, for example, can be understood in terms of the driven need to keep pressing "pleasure buttons" to compensate for triggered recordings of chronic deprivation and emptiness. In this sense, the psychology of the addictive juvenile delinquent is comparable to that of individuals who indulge in shopping binges, borrowing binges, and gambling binges in an attempt to compensate for triggered recordings of chronic deprivation and emptiness.

Chronic Delinquency

Although youthful offenders come from various backgrounds and experiences, the typical profile of a chronic delinquent is that of a male who has abused drugs (75%), has committed at least 50 felonies, is impulsive, began crime at an early age

(5 or 6 years), and shuns responsibility. His behavior has caused his family to give up on him. He skips school and is prone to drop out. His friends typically have the same profile (Drowns and Hess, 1990).

Two identifiers of chronic juvenile delinquency are:

1.   Starting criminal activity prior to the age of 12

2.   Coming from poorer, inner city, disorganized neighborhoods.

The Office of Juvenile Justice and Delinquency Prevention (1994) hypothesized three pathways to chronic delinquency:

1.   *Overt*—from aggression, to fighting, to violence

2.   *Covert*—from minor covert behavior, to property damage, to serious delinquency

3.   *Authority conflict*—from stubborn behavior, to defiance, to authority avoidance

It is believed that these chronic offenders commit 75% of the juvenile crime in any given year.

Other characteristics of chronic violent juvenile offenders include less attachment to and less monitoring by their parents. Offenders are more likely to reside in poor, high-crime areas. They have less commitment to school and attachment to teachers, have more delinquent peers, and are more apt to be gang members and to act out in school (Office of Juvenile Justice and Delinquency Prevention, 1994).

Juvenile offenders are sometimes said to demonstrate psychopathic or socio-pathic behavior. These concepts relate to failure to develop a socially appropriate conscience. To differentiate: Psychopaths do not know the difference between right and wrong. Sociopaths know the difference between right and wrong but do not care; they do not have guilt feelings appropriate to society. These adolescents often lack a positive role model, parental control, or parents with social values (Drowns and Hess, 1990).

Antisocial and At-Risk Youth

The turn of the twenty-first century is seeing more antisocial youths. These youths expect school to serve their purpose, choose not to apply themselves, and perceive school as a place to socialize. They use drugs as a shortcut to excitement, or to escape from reality. They seek the easy way to go, digging themselves one hole after another, and not heeding warnings. The only time when they are inclined to seek another lifestyle is after a severe personal tragedy. Although many are thought to have learning disabilities, most of them are illiterate because they will not take the time to learn (Crews and Counts, 1997).

The 1990s saw the emergence of what was termed "at-risk" students. These students displayed clearly identifiable physical, cognitive, or emotional conditions or had background and family circumstances that made their potential to learn bleak. They would require special assistance. Large numbers of students also were classified as being at-risk in certain educational situations, and changing their classroom and school characteristics would improve their chances. This encouraged many educators to move beyond an epidemiological perspective and its attempts to identify personal characteristics and conditions that predicted at-riskness. Instead, educators began to focus on the characteristics of schools and classrooms that encourage success or failure. Educators could more easily control school and classroom variables than they could the personal, socioeconomically based variables traditionally associated with the term at risk (Donmoyer and Kos, 1993).

Group Membership

Many times delinquency originates from the child's group. Sometimes a child's membership in a certain group is not of his or her choosing. Instead, the perceptions of or stereotyping by others label that child as belonging to a particular group. One of the earliest theories of causes of juvenile delinquency causation involved the concept of labeling. Edwin Lemert is believed to be the most important contributor to the delinquency labeling approach. In this view, the deviant label is attached and the juvenile becomes stigmatized. This label becomes a self-fulfilling prophecy. There is primary deviance, which is the original act, and then secondary deviance, which results from the labeling (Drowns and Hess, 1990).

Groups such as punk rockers may feel alienated from what they perceive as the complacency and mindless conformity of peers. Groups such as skinheads often are motivated by the changes in racial composition of their community and disapprove of minorities. Although most of these youths eventually outgrow their defiance, some do not (Wooden, 1995).

The school itself often becomes the setting where this separatist grouping occurs. Exclusionary grouping is known as a clique. The following presents some examples of the cliques found in a typical U.S. high school (Wooden, 1995, p. 51):

1. Jocks—boys who participate in sports
2. Cheerleaders—attractive, school-spirited girls who support the jocks
3. Tweakies—boys who have an extremely laid-back attitude
4. Trendies/socs/preppies—youths who are desperate to fit in and spend much time shopping
5. Drama freaks—students who are engrossed in acting
6. Bandos—students who are engrossed in band
7. Smacks/brains—students who have high grade point averages
8. Dirtbags—middle-class students but considered "low-lifes"

9. Sluts—girls who wear provocative clothing

10. Punks—youths who dress in torn jeans, combat boots, and mohawk haircuts

11. Death rockers/metal heads—youths who live and act like the music suggests

12. Loners—students who have no peer group with whom to socialize, always alone

The attraction to those who are like oneself is natural, but those who are seen as "different" are pushed aside and alienated from the cliquish groups with no thought of the repercussions. An example of the alienation that some students feel is demonstrated in the Littleton, Colorado, massacre on April 20, 1999. Eric Harris and Dylan Klebold, students at Columbine High School, were considered "different." Their not fitting in with the other students, mainly jocks, is considered to be a factor in their shooting rampage. Harris and Klebold declared an all-out war on Columbine High, which claimed the lives of 12 students and 1 teacher, plus their own lives.

THE FAMILY AND DELINQUENCY

The study of parental impact on children's behavior has two traditional approaches:

1. The *genetic heredity approach*, in which a genetic predisposition is passed on to the child. To separate the effects of heredity from environment when families live in similar social situations and often in the same home or community is difficult (Walters and White, 1989).

2. The *social approach theory*, currently more popular, which emphasizes modeling of behavior for the child. In this approach the antisocial trait in parents is related to their disciplinary practices, which in turn result in the child's antisocial behavior. In effect, the parent produces the antisocial norms in the home. A "culture of deviance" is established through antisocial talk and behavior modeling (Drowns and Hess, 1990).

Albert Bandura and Richard Walters (1963) developed the concept of modeling, which holds that children copy the behavior of people whom they hold in high regard and who provide rewards. Primary among models are the children's parents. Models also can be siblings, peers, athletes, and television personalities.

The impact of the family upon children cannot be overstated. The structure and patterns of interaction at home influence prosocial or antisocial behavior. The family can have a positive impact by insulating children from antisocial behavior, using rewards judiciously, and maintaining positive relationships. Delinquency most often occurs when positive family interaction and control are weak and conflict is high. The family can be a primary cause of delinquency. Family influences on the child's sense of security have a bearing on the attractiveness of negative or positive groups (Drowns and Hess, 1990).

The family is considered the first teacher, first role model, first social institution, first classroom, and first educator. If parent and child do not communicate well, the child may not learn appropriate behavior. A family establishes a sense of right and wrong. Within the family, children learn attitudes and values that they keep throughout life (Drowns and Hess, 1990).

Another major area of concern is socialization outside the family. Nondelinquent children learn respect for others and the rights of others, social and moral values, honesty and fair play, and conformity to social norms. The family ideally reinforces these virtues and rushes to correct violations (Drowns and Hess, 1990).

Shaw and McKay (1969) theorized that disorganization in society and disorganization within the home can have the greatest impact upon delinquent behavior. They believed that economic status has a great deal to do with delinquent behavior. The more economic deprivation, the more delinquency; and the less economic deprivation, the less delinquency. They believed that persons living in disadvantaged environments often have the same material aspirations as those living in advantaged environments, but residents of disadvantaged areas learn that legitimate access to their goals is difficult. The disparity between their goals and the means available for legitimately achieving them creates a situation conducive to deviancy, delinquency, and crime in urban areas.

Homes of delinquent youths typically are disorganized, have no set routines for family activity, and have no protective shield for the child. Their parents ignore them, and family policies are inconsistent. Adolescents in dysfunctional homes sometimes resort to running away when they feel they can cope only by leaving. They may feel the entire world is against them and they have no other choice but to leave. After they run away, they incur more problems: crime, prostitution, and other illegal activities. Adolescents report the reasons for leaving home as conflict with parents, alienation, rejection, hostile control, lack of warmth, lack of affection, and lack of parental support.

These circumstances also can lead to suicide. Suicidal persons feel unable to cope because the environment is against them. They see themselves as alone and at the mercy of a hostile world (Drowns and Hess, 1990).

A relatively new area of research examines the concept of victimization in children. Major variables that predict victimization levels in children are gender, number of siblings, exposure to violence outside school, and personal violence-related attributes. Across the United States, only about 1 in 10 victimizations seems to be random (not predicted by the aforementioned variables). Victimized students have characteristics that put them at higher risk (Sheley, McGee, and Wright, 1992).

Parents often see juvenile behaviors—dress, body piercing, tattoos, and branding—as adolescent fads. Students see these changes as "look at me" symbols, and parents sometimes think they are sending a visual message to peers, teachers, and other adults that they have no respect for anyone or anything. Many psychologists believe that these manifestations are ways for teenagers to express their individuality and to assert their independence. Psychologists also warn that parents must guard against letting these fashion statements provoke major family battles. A more positive approach is to talk to teenagers and help them consider the consequences of their actions before making permanent changes to their body. Most psychologists believe that nonpermanent changes represent adolescent fads that will change with the times and have no lasting effects (Drowns and Hess, 1990).

A root problem of delinquency remains poverty. Poverty has been correlated with malnutrition, lack of growth, and psychopathology (Drowns and Hess, 1990). The infant mortality rate is higher, as are the numbers of children being reared by teen mothers, unmarried mothers, and incidence of drug use, crime, and unemployment. Test results and other evaluative instruments revealed that the United States is producing a poorly educated adult population, saddled with a job structure of low-pay and low-skill jobs (Hodgkinson, 1990).

Children who grow up without adequate supervision at home are at risk for later criminality. Drugs use accelerates a juvenile's crime rate, and negative peer influences can lead to criminality. Children who do poorly in school or drop out are more likely to become criminals (Regoli and Hewitt, 1994).

Many of the theories attempting to pinpoint the causes of juvenile delinquency have been dispelled by research. In many cases a combination of two or more theories is more plausible. Most recently, the family has been the focal point in the struggle to understand, predict, and formulate prevention strategies concerning delinquency. Children who are rejected by their parents, who grow up in homes with considerable conflict, or who are inadequately supervised are at greatest risk of becoming delinquent (Office of Juvenile Justice and Delinquency Prevention, 1996).

Loeber and Dishion (1983) reviewed approximately 70 studies focusing on family characteristics that seem to be associated with subsequent delinquency. They found consistent predictors in relation to the child's age. For example, at age 6, family functioning predicts delinquency. Antisocial behavior and aggressiveness at age 9 indicated delinquent tendencies, and parental criminality when the child was 10 was a valid predictor. Educational factors predicted delinquency at age 15. At age 16, if the child was involved in delinquency, continued delinquency was predictable. Table 5.1 breaks down the predictors in terms of their strength.

Snyder and Patterson (1987) found that discipline and positive parenting were somewhat related to delinquency. Parental monitoring of the child had a stronger association, which Snyder and Patterson labeled as "moderate." In comparison to these family functioning areas, conflict and problem-solving had the weakest relationship with delinquency but still had a modest association. According to Snyder and Patterson, the association of family structural characteristics including socioeconomic status, parental absence, parental criminality, and family size was unclear.

After reviewing the relationship between family transactions and child psychosocial functioning in 65 studies conducted over a 30-year period, Henggeler (1989) found delinquent behavior to stem from three areas:

TABLE 5.1   Predictors of Delinquency

Strong	Moderate	Weak
Parental rejection	Parents' marital relations	Parental discipline
Parent-child involvement	Parental criminality	Parental health
Parental supervision		Parental absence

Source: "Family Factors as Correlates and Predictors of Juvenile Conduct Problems and Delinquency," by R. Loeber and M. Stouthamer-Loeber, in *Crime and Justice: An Annual Review of Research,* Vol. 7, Chicago: University of Chicago Press, 1986.

1. A low level of parental control
2. Parental control strategies are present, but inadequate or ineffective (at-risk factor)
3. Antisocial behavior of parents, including deviant methods of meeting goals

Divorce and Juvenile Violence

Divorce is one of the most powerful emotional events that can impact a family. The absence of one parent, emotional and financial tension, continuing conflicts between parents, and divorce frequently lead to psychological problems for boys and girls alike. The worst period is the first year after divorce, when aggression, distractibility and noncompliance, academic difficulties, poor relationships with peers, and low self-esteem are common in the children of divorce. These negative effects are most apparent in boys, and generally diminish with time (2–3 years). Using a longitudinal design, however, some studies found many boys still exhibiting the above effects six years after divorce.

Adaptation seems to depend on parenting style and conflict following the divorce. Generally, children who are strongly attached to both parents have a lower probability of delinquency than children who are strongly attached to only one parent. Further, children living in single-parent homes who are strongly attached to the custodial parent have a greater probability of committing delinquent acts than children living in intact homes who are strongly attached to both parents (Garris and Furman, 1989).

As the twenty-first century begins, more than half of all marriages end in divorce, with substantial effects on the youth involved. Dr. Nancy Warren, a psychologist and director of the Family Therapy Program at Baylor College of Medicine, believes that divorce, per se, does not cause maladjustment in children, but their exposure to ongoing, unresolved conflict may. Warren's findings singled out family conflict or inability to deal with conflict as the main culprit behind a child's maladjustment. Dr. Warren explains that the child's reaction to family conflict many times is expressed through misbehavior, depression, delinquency, and aggression.

According to Dr. Warren, about two-thirds of children from divorced families do well or at least adequately when compared to a control group. Researchers have projected that 60% of all U.S. children will live in single-parent homes before reaching age 18. Warren suggested four measures to benefit the child whose parents have divorced:

1. **Reduce family conflict.** Work to maintain the parental bond while ending the spousal bond.

2. **Give the child access to both parents in a comfortable, safe, and homelike setting.** Children should have their own space at each household. They need a place in both parents' homes that is totally theirs, even if it's a closet shelf in a small apartment.

3. **Minimize the number of life changes children have to go through in a short period.** Parents who are forced to move should try to maintain the child's environment as much as possible. This includes schools, social networks, and overall surroundings.

4. **Acknowledge the child's feelings. Some research shows that children have different reactions to divorce depending on their age.** Children up to age 3 seem to adjust better than those ages 9–12. Younger children are not yet dealing with the complex emotions of anger, loyalty, and blame.

Child Abuse, Neglect, and Violence

In a National Institute of Justice brief, Kathy Widom (1992) discussed the correlation between childhood abuse and neglect and violent behavior. The cycle of violence suggests that a childhood history of physical abuse predisposes the survivor to violence in later years. This study reveals that victims of neglect also are more likely to develop common conceptions of physical abuse (Natalucci-Persichetti, 1996, p. 55).

Childhood victimization is a widespread social problem that increases the likelihood of juvenile delinquency and adult criminality. Poor educational performance, health problems, and generally low levels of achievement also characterize the victims of early childhood abuse and neglect. Even neglect alone (not necessarily physical abuse) was significantly related to violent criminal behavior (Natalucci-Persichetti, 1996, p. 55).

One facet of physical abuse is sexual abuse. At the Youth Center in Beloit, Kansas, the state's only institutional facility for female juvenile offenders, 55% to 60% of the female offenders said they were sexually abused at some time in their lives (Moore, 1991).

According to Moore (1991) sexual abuse itself does not lead to delinquency but rather, the way the child deals with the victimization. Moore and his colleagues at the Kansas facility identified the factors that seem to play the most significant role in fostering delinquent behavior as anger and aggression toward others, alienation, distrust of authority and adults, self-blame, substance abuse, and running away. Although sexual abuse does not lead all sexually abused children down a road to delinquency, sexually abused juveniles are at much higher risk of becoming offenders than are nonabused youth.

CONCENTRIC RINGS OF JUVENILE DELINQUENCY

It is said that there are really no new ideas any more, just rehashes of past ideas. This is probably no truer than in criminological thought. The following is a brief overview of a conceptual theory in progress by Dr. Gordon A. Crews of Jacksonville State University. It is not expected to bring the reader into an entirely new arena. Instead, it offers a general perspective on a possible framework from which to begin understanding juvenile delinquency. Figure 5.1 graphically depicts this theory.

An explanation of the figure follows.

- **Child.** The child is the centerpiece of the interaction between the forces of the immediate family, extended family, peers, local community, and society at large. Biological, psychological, and sociological aspects must be considered and ascertained prior to any deeper analysis of why the child is exhibiting a certain behavior.

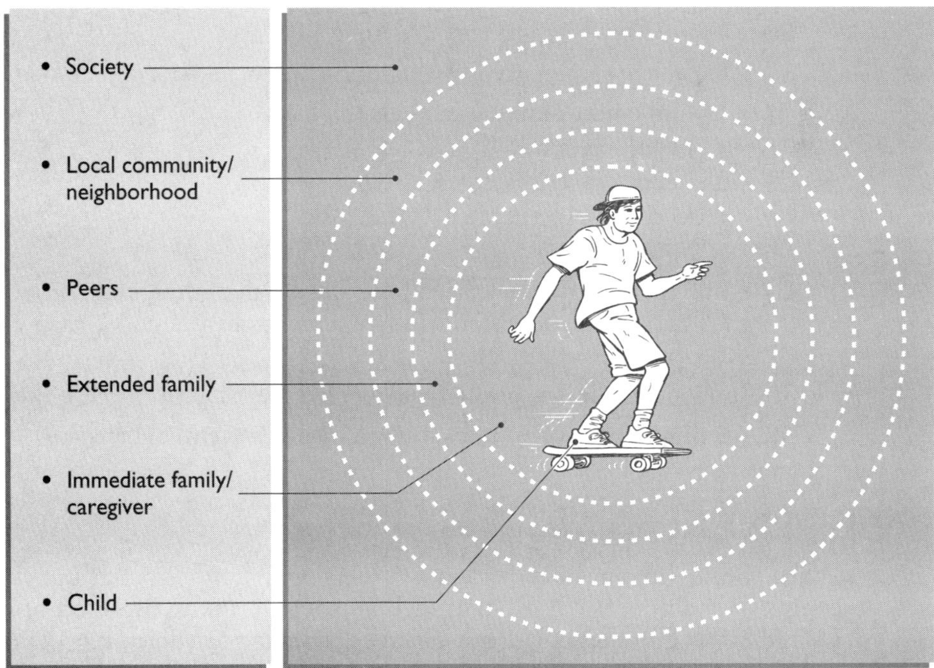

FIGURE 5.1   Crew's Theory of Concentric Rings of Juvenile Delinquency

- **Immediate family/caregiver.** The family structure of the child may be a biological, adoptive, or foster parent, a grandparent, or other primary caregiver. Even though this is the person or persons the child spends the most amount of time with, it is not whole. Every family structure, at one time or another, has "holes or gaps" where children can and/or will look to the next ring for guidance.

- **Extended family.** This family structure consists of grandparents, uncles, aunts, cousins, and other relatives. These people offer opportunities for the child to seek input and support.

- **Peers.** Peers are the friends and associates in a child's life. These relationships are not as strong as those of the immediate family, although important relationships can develop between adolescents.

- **Local community/school/neighborhood.** The local community, school, and neighborhood have an impact of the child but only after all of the other rings have been tapped.

- **Society.** Society as a whole exerts an impact on all the other relationships. It is fluid in that societies and cultures let other cultures in and out. No culture or society is totally self-contained and oblivious to other cultures or societies.

Basic *assumptions* of this theory are the following:

1. Children are influenced by the following societal forces in ranking order:
   a. Immediate family or caregiver
   b. Extended family
   c. Peers
   d. Local community/school/neighborhood
   e. Society
2. Concentric rings can be used to represent all of these relationships in that each totally surrounds and fully encompasses the child, each exerting a different level of influence.
3. Influences whether positive or negative are filtered through these rings.
4. All rings will have an impact upon a child's eventual behavior.

CONCLUSION

When considering juvenile delinquency, no single theory in itself can explain the complex variables related to youth delinquency. In the twenty-first century, the United States is undergoing many changes including rapidly advancing computer technology and the proliferation of street-level drugs, among others.

The *causes* of delinquency continue to challenge scholars, policy-makers, and those charged with the treatment of youthful offenders. As time passes and theories are dispelled, new, thought-provoking ideas are entering the realm of thought on juvenile delinquency. Currently, the dynamics of the family is a focal point of research. Parental supervision, love, affection, and parents' willingness to listen to their children can only help the parent-child relationship and contribute to healthy-functioning children.

chapter 6

FROM FAMILY, CHURCH, AND SCHOOL TO POLICE, COURTS, AND CORRECTIONS

Possible Solutions

Nothing enduring can be built on violence.

Mohandas K. Gandhi

Blessed are the peacemakers for they will be called children of God.

Matthew 5:9

Do not envy the violent, and do not choose any of their ways.

Proverbs 3:31

Never when controversy avoided the subjects which are large and important enough to kindle enthusiasm, was the mind of a people stirred up from its foundations, and the impulse given which raised even persons of the most ordinary intellect to something of the dignity of thinking beings.

John Stuart Mill, *On Liberty*

INTRODUCTION

The problems surrounding violent juveniles are numerous and immense, with no magic pill or simple solution. Hammurabi, King of Babylon, instituted the Code of Hammurabi around 2000 B.C. Section 195 of the 282 clauses of this code presented the following solution for a father faced with a violent son: "If a son strikes his father, they shall cut off his fore-hand" (Miles, 1968, p. 77). This, of course, would not be an acceptable approach for the twenty-first century.

SUGGESTED SOLUTIONS

Suggested solutions are found in programs and initiatives, counseling and treatment strategies, get-tough approaches, and state innovative programs.

Programs and Initiatives

Work is a wise and simple solution that can benefit many youth in the United States. The City of Columbia, South Carolina, for example, established a model work program involving approximately 500 youths each summer in the late 1990s. The official title of the program was the Summer Work Experience Leadership Program (SWELP), and the Columbia Urban League administered the program. Its aims were to build character, a work ethic, and self-esteem. Also, it was hoped that the employer would serve as a role model for the juvenile participant (*Summer Jobs Give Youths More Than Pay*, 1998).

The City of Bridgeport, Connecticut, had a unique way to intervene with juveniles and weapons. If a youth turned in a weapon at one of several church locations, he or she was given a cash-equivalent reward that could be exchanged for gift certificates for food, clothing, or toys. The State's attorney promised not to prosecute for possession or carrying a weapon if people dropped off weapons at one of the churches. John Kardaras, a lawyer involved in this project, pointed out that every gun off the street is a gun that won't kill somebody (*They're Turning in Their Guns*, 1998, p. 10).

In 1997, the U.S. Federal Government established JUMP (Juvenile Mentoring Program), which was administered by the Office of Juvenile Justice and Delinquency Prevention (OJJDP) (Grossman and Gary, 1997). Its purpose was to bring together caring, responsible adults and at-risk young people in need of positive role models. Congress has since placed millions of dollars into JUMP initiatives across the country. The Cincinnati Youth Collaborative in Ohio, for example, matched 136 youth and volunteers. Activities included visits to colleges, job shadowing, school beautification projects, and a trip to New York City. Occupations of the mentors included lawyers, postal clerks, college students, and nurses, just to name a few. A follow-up showed that 99 of the 136 youth demonstrated improvement in their grades and 102 improved socially.

Some juveniles apparently are best served by being placed in a group home setting. These homes may be privately owned or State-owned. The basic objective is to provide a stable home environment for groups of 6 to 15 youths. "The group home is for youngsters who are in unresolvable conflict with their parents but are not seriously disturbed or psychotic" (Abadinsky, 1997, p. 84). Restrictions for juveniles could range from low levels (probation supervision, day treatment, and group home) to high levels of restriction (residential treatment centers to training schools). *Probation supervision* may be the proper disposition for children who are not seriously delinquent. In *day treatment*, troubled youths who cannot function in public schools report to the center 5 days a week. At the day-treatment center, youths receive individualized academic programs designed to improve their self-esteem. When a youth completes the program, he or she is returned to the public school system.

Alternatives to incarceration should be used whenever possible with juveniles who have broken the law. In the state of South Carolina, for example, 213 youths were placed in departmental group homes and 335 youths were placed in contractual group homes in 1994 (South Carolina Department of Juvenile Justice, Office of Research and Statistics, 1996).

Group homes might be used for children deemed to be pre-delinquent. An example is the Fremont County Group Homes, Inc., located in Wyoming, which is a nonprofit, state-licensed group. This organization serves adolescents 10 to 17 years old. These youths are nonviolent, but require a structured environment. Youths that exhibit these characteristics living at the group home usually have displayed behaviors that have interfered with their lives, schools, or family relationships. A girl's home, which has a capacity of 9 youths, is located in Lander, Wyoming. The boy's home, which also has a capacity of 9 youths, is located in Riverton, Wyoming.

All youths attend public schools. The workers in these homes "live" at the home for their shift of 5 to 12 days. This work pattern provides for close supervision and structure for the youths. Program components involve peer groups, individual sessions, errors-in-thinking groups, and independent living program, pregnancy program, recreational programs, drug and alcohol education, and evaluations on each youth.

Residential treatment centers provide residential care for youngsters who need constant supervision. In the late 1990s, the San Francisco Juvenile Court reported on a residential facility named the Log Cabin Ranch, for boys 15 to 18 years of age. The youths have four choices of vocational programs (mechanics, electronics, building maintenance, or culinary arts). After completing their training, they are placed in apprenticeship job programs.

First-time nonviolent offenders are sometimes given a second chance. The State of South Carolina established one of the first Juvenile Pretrial Intervention (PTI) programs in the country. A juvenile who was arrested for the first time on a nonviolent charge could come to PTI from the court on a personal recognizance bond. This system allows the defendant to be diverted from incarceration, enter a program of restitution, receive counseling, and then return to society without a criminal record. The individual must be at least 17 years of age.

This program has been popular because it is self-supporting. The application fee is $100, due at the time of application for the program. If a person is accepted into the program, there is a $250 participation fee. Other requirements for the program include performing a minimum 30 hours of volunteer work, taking part in counseling sessions, paying back the victim for any losses incurred, and not being rearrested while enrolled in the program. Depending on their performance, individuals can be required to enroll in the program anywhere from 90 days to one year. Upon successfully completing the program, no further action is taken on the charges. Those who are rearrested are tried on the charge for which they were accepted into PTI, as well as the new charge. Each year, approximately 8,000 citizens of South Carolina complete this program.

Drug-Related Programs

A major obstacle facing many youths is drug use. The Clinton Administration allocated about two-thirds of anti-drug spending for law enforcement and the remaining one-third for prevention, treatment, and other programs. Vice President Al Gore (*Gore Announces $18 Million*, 1999, A-12) "calls for greater efforts to improve schools and create greater economic opportunity for young people, especially in minority and low-income communities." The centerpiece of this Administration's prevention strategy is a multi-medium advertising campaign designed to alert adolescents to the dangers of illegal drug use.

The National Drug Control Strategy (Office of National Drug Control Policy, 1998) reported that 34.8% of Americans age 12 and older have used an illegal drug in their lifetime (p. 5). Marijuana continued to be the illegal drug of choice. Alcohol was the legal choice of drug for youth. Furthermore, 4.5 million American children under age 18 now smoke cigarettes." (p. 16).

A major goal of the National Drug Control Strategy is to educate parents and other caregivers, teachers, coaches, clergy, health professionals, and business and community leaders to help youths reject illegal drugs and underage alcohol and tobacco use (p. 24). Research had found that when parents and other concerned adults are involved, drug prevention efforts are more successful. An additional component of this national strategy is to provide more drug treatment for the addicted population (Fields, 1999, p.7A).

Winik (2000) points out the importance of having parents involved in the effort to prevent teen drug use:

> Parents should help their children establish realistic personal goals in academics, athletics, and social life. Then they should encourage and help them to achieve their goals....Parents at the same time should be aware of the warning signs of drug abuse, from physical changes to hostility to loss of interest in school or hobbies. (p. 4)

The U.S Department of Justice took the lead in developing juvenile and family drug courts. The Office of Justice Programs Drug Court Clearing House (1998) reported that there were 97 programs at the juvenile drug court level and 20 programs at the family drug court level in the United States as of June 1998. A juvenile drug court was defined as "a drug court that focuses on juvenile delinquency (e.g., criminal) matters and status offenses (e.g., truancy) that involve substance-abusing juveniles" (p. 3). A family drug court was defined as "a drug court that deals with cases involving parental rights, in which an adult is the party litigant, which come before the court through either the criminal or civil process, and which arise out of the substance abuse of a parent (p. 3)."

A basic goal of these programs is to provide immediate intervention into the lives of children and parents using drugs. These programs also provide structure to assist children "to resist further criminal activity, perform well in school, and develop positive relationships" (p. 5).

A 1998 U.S. Government publication entitled *Guideline for Drug Court on Screening and Assessment* points out the need to complete a drug-court screening at the earliest time after a juvenile has been arrested. The information covers criminal justice, substance use, and mental health. Criminal justice information consists of juvenile criminal history. Substance-abuse items include results of drug testing, prior involvement in treatment, motivation for using drugs, and family history of substance abuse. Mental health information includes symptoms (e.g., depression), prior involvement in mental health treatment, and family history of mental illness.

U.S. Surgeon General Dr. David Satcher (2000) is quoted in *Psychology Today* as saying "few Americans are untouched by mental illness, whether it occurs within one's family or among neighbors, co-workers or members of the community. In fact, in any one year, one in five Americans—including children, adolescents, adults and the elderly—experience a mental disorder (p. 32)."

Another example of juvenile drug courts is the Richland County Juvenile Drug Court in Columbia, South Carolina. This program provides an alternative to the traditional court process for nonviolent juvenile offenders. A youth may be in this program from 9 to 12 months. The objectives are to help juveniles stop using alcohol and other drugs, stop their involvement in crime, and improve their school performance. The juvenile must be between the ages of 12 and 16½, a resident of Richland County, have a history of using alcohol or other drugs (besides nicotine), have no history of violent behavior, and have no history of incarceration in a long-term juvenile justice facility. Juveniles admitted to the program must have submitted to random drug tests, attended family counseling sessions weekly, appeared before a judge weekly for a progress report, and attended treatment sessions three times a week. Additional services include primary health care, tutoring, and psychiatric/psychological counseling.

The staff in this program makes in-home as well as in-school visits to see what progress the juvenile is making. Both sanctions and rewards are used to bring about behavior change. Sanctions include curfews, community service, house detention, and facility detention. Rewards include verbal praise, certificates, and advancement in the program. The ultimate responsibility for making program decisions concerning a juvenile resides with the family court judge in charge of the case. The judge also decides if a juvenile is admitted to the program in the first place. If juveniles successfully complete this program, the initial charges are dropped.

The Bridge Program (1999) is another unique program for juveniles in South Carolina. This program is a "bridge" for juveniles from the institutional setting (drug inpatient or correctional facility) to their home. The program is tailored to each participant. It is designed to reduce drug use (alcohol, tobacco, and other drugs), criminal involvement, school dropout, sexual activity associated with teen pregnancies and sexually transmitted diseases, and violent behavior, and to improve life skills. This program also assists parents who might receive training in parenting skills, vocational or employment assistance, and drug treatment, if necessary.

As of 1999, six South Carolina counties had participated in this program. Generally, someone in this program does not stay active longer than one year. Research revealed that 60% of the juveniles needed intervention or treatment services for alcohol or other drug abuse. The data further showed that 90% of the individuals who had successfully completed the program avoided reincarceration. Also, 31% of successful clients earned their GED or completed high school.

The State of South Carolina developed another unique program to assist parents and their high-risk students in grades 7 through 12—the School Intervention Program (SCIP). The annual report of South Carolina Department of Alcohol and Other Drug Abuse Services (1998) for 1996–1997 showed that 5,154 adolescents had received services during the year in this program (p. 18). Students in this program were identified through the school system as having a wide range of personal or behavioral problems.

A national school-based program that has been popular is the Drug Abuse Resistance Education Program, better known as D.A.R.E. These programs use uniformed police officers in the classroom. The National Institute of Justice (1994) reported that the popularity of D.A.R.E. cuts across racial, ethnic, and socioeconomic lines. D.A.R.E. uses a core curriculum consisting of 17-hour-long weekly lessons taught to fifth and sixth graders, with some programs added to reach middle- and high-school students.

Teen Courts

Another unique approach for handling student disputes and arguments is the Teen Court. These courts are not designed to determine guilt or innocence. Instead, they function as a disposition alternative. Teen jurors hear details of the case and recommend a constructive sentence. Typical participants in Teen Court are between the ages of 14 and 17. The only adult is the judge, who is usually a retiree from a district court.

The teen jurors listen to a case, then adjourn to the deliberation room to discuss the case. A foreperson is elected, and the case is discussed until reaching a unanimous decision. Upon returning to court, the bailiff instructs the defendant to face the jury. The foreperson reads the constructive sentence to the defendant, who receives the completed jury form and meets with the teen court coordinator to finalize sentencing arrangements. If the jury sentence is unacceptable to the judge, jury deliberations must begin again.

Teen courts have been used in Arizona, Colorado, Oregon, California, Michigan, New York, Georgia, Indiana, and Florida (Collins, 1992). Teen courts have had encouraging results. In Odessa, Texas, 15% of juvenile traffic offenders and 1% of other offenders recidivated. The failure rate for the Teen Court in Montgomery County, Indiana's Teen Court was between 10% and 15%, and Gila County, Arizona's was less than 12% (Collins, 1992).

Yes Initiative

Kristen Kracke (1996) has studied another government initiative entitled YES—Youth Environmental Service Initiative (1996). This program was created to work with at-risk and delinquent youth, providing environmental work and education opportunities on federal land.

The program has been tried in Florida, Washington DC, and Utah. The Florida model was established at the Banyan Halfway House Work Release Program in West Palm Beach. The selected youths stayed in this program from 4 to 6 months. They worked on the Loxahatchee Environmental Project, of which exotic plant eradication was one of the many skills in landscape that the youth experienced.

Another example of the YES programs is the Genesis Youth Center in Salt Lake City, Utah. The center can house 72, and youths in this program pay restitution to their victims. Males ages 14 to 18 serving 30- to 120-day sentences are eligible to take part in the program. The youths work on projects in the Wild Horse and Burro Center.

In the District of Columbia the YES program is located in the Boys and Girls Clubs of Greater Washington. Ages served range from 8 to 14 years. The participants come from low-income families. The youths have worked, for example, with the National Park Service at Rock Creek Park, attended educational workshops, and assisted with trail clean-up and park maintenance.

After-School Programs

Another approach involves programs for after-school. The Carnegie Council on Adolescent Development (1994) recommended that these programs explore issues "such as health and physical well-being (ex. physical fitness); personal and social competence (ex. preparation for parenthood; cognitive and educational competence (ex. homework clinics); preparation for work (ex. career awareness), and leadership and citizenship (ex. youth advisory boards)" (p. 21). An example is the Brooklyn Children's Museum, which established the Teen Interns Program. This program is for teens ages 14 to 18, who are paid for part-time work after school. The program helps the interns to develop higher-order thinking and problem-solving skills.

Counseling and Treatment Strategies

Among the counseling and treatment approaches are mentoring group counseling, career counseling, art therapy, religious retreats, school counseling, community-based interventions, and youth volunteers.

Mentoring

Hamilton (1990) described mentoring as a one-on-one relationship between a pair of unrelated individuals—one adult and one juvenile—which takes place on a regular basis over an extended time. Mentoring has been shown to be effective with many youths. In the late 1970s, Big Brothers/Big Sisters of America was the largest mentoring organization in the United States (Grossman and Garry, 1977). Mentored youths were found to be less likely to skip school, engage in drug or alcohol use, or resort to violence. Furthermore, their school grades improved, along with their relations with friends and family.

Group Counseling

Kelman (1963) proposed in the early 1960s that group counseling could be of great benefit in helping individuals overcome feelings of isolation, increase self-esteem, and accept more responsibility for solving their own problems. This has been validated over time. A group leader guides the group sessions, which deal with general issues or specific issues such as family concerns, employment, or school issues. Co-leaders, or co-facilitators, have been advantageous to have as advocates (Jones and Pheiffer, 1975). One leader works with a group member experiencing significant emotional problems while the other leader assists the other group members. The theory is that two leaders can better facilitate development of the individual within the group and the group itself.

Career Counseling

One area that is paramount for juveniles is career counseling. Youths might be given the *Kuder General Interest Survey* (KGIS), the *Strong Vocational Interest Blank*, or the *Ohio Vocational Interest Survey* to reveal the youths' vocational interest areas. The *KGIS* has numerous interest scales including: outdoor, mechanical, computational, scientific, persuasive, artistic, literary, musical, social service, and clerical areas (Kuder, 1965). Career counseling could be used with delinquents who desire to make a better life for themselves.

Role-playing is a psychodrama technique that can also be used with youths who want to improve their job opportunities. For example, once a juvenile is placed on probation, the probation officer could role-play as the prospective employer. The unemployed youth then undergoes the "employment" interview. The probation officer could videotape this practice job interview to show the youths later what he or she is doing well or could improve in the job interview process. By practicing the job interview, unemployed juveniles increase their chances of being successful during the actual job interview.

Art Therapy

The popular art therapy technique Before, Now, and After can be used in almost any juvenile-offender setting. For example, delinquent youths in a residential treatment center might be given three pieces of blank poster paper and a drawing marker. The youths are instructed to draw on the first poster paper what their life was like before entering the residential treatment center. On the second piece of poster paper they draw what their life is like now that they are in the center. On the third piece of poster paper, they draw what they see in their future once they leave the center.

Each youth then is given the opportunity to explain the meaning of their drawings. The benefits of using this technique in a group are that the youths learn that others have faced similar problems and have common hopes for the future. Leuner (1969) concluded that art therapy enabled individuals to express their emotions with less fear and anxiety.

Religious Retreats

An approach that works with some juveniles is the weekend religious retreats. These retreats help juveniles under detention overcome their problems. Newspaper reporter Peter Buttress (1999) reported that 25 boys imprisoned at the Broad River Juvenile Justice Facility attended such a weekend in Columbia, South Carolina.

The weekend was called the Epiphany Weekend Retreat. The activities included talks, prayers, songs, and discussion. The juveniles learned about the unconditional love of God and his forgiveness of whatever mistakes they had made in the past. A team of 40 adult volunteers from around the state took leadership roles in the program. A unique feature of this retreat was a "birthday party" for the boys, complete with balloons, paper hats, and birthday cakes with candles—"symbolic of one's physical birth in order to be reborn into Christ's family" (New, 1999). The youths also received letters telling them that people cared about them and were praying for them.

During the retreat, each teen was given an Epiphany T-shirt and hat, a Bible, and a cross. Epiphany weekend retreats are held three times a year at the Columbia, South Carolina, juvenile justice facility, and twice yearly at the Greenwood, South Carolina, facility for girls. This program also includes follow-up contact when volunteers return to meet with the attendees twice a month for prayer, fellowship, and spiritual counseling.

School Counseling

Many experts believe we need more school psychologists and counselors. These therapists help students develop motivation and self-esteem, help them deal with crises such as death, provide hands-on immediate assistance in crisis situations in schools, and assist schools in developing conflict-resolution plans. Some schools are using educational television systems to better inform school officials about school safety. The National Education Association (*The State*, January 21, 2000, p. B-3), for example, has developed such a program in response to growing concerns over school violence. Other topics covered are anger management, discrimination, and peer mediation.

Joey Holleman (1999, p. A7) has written about warning signs of violence. Kids, he reported, get very angry and frustrated over routine situations. Teachers often refer students who exhibit signs of depression or anger. School psychologists and counselors decide what action is needed. It might be necessary to send the student to a treatment center.

Peter W. Greenwood (1999) has found that most physical development in the brain occurs by age 3. His research also reveals that special early intervention education programs could improve educational processes and outcomes for the child.

The Office of Juvenile Justice and Delinquency Prevention (May, 1998) stated in his research on serious and violent juvenile offenders that it is never too late to intervene with known serious and violent juvenile offenders (p. 1). Additional findings show (Office of Juvenile Justice and Delinquency Prevention, 1998):

1. Serious violent juveniles constitute a minority of identified offenders in the juvenile court system.

2. Reoffending can be reduced by the use of appropriate interventions, especially interpersonal skills training and cognitive-behavioral treatment.

3. Interventions should be multi-modal to address multiple problems and integrated across the juvenile justice system, mental health system, schools, and child welfare agencies.

4. Aftercare programs are essential to reduce the likelihood of reoffending. (p. 6).

This 1998 study found that "early intervention in at-risk families will reduce serious and violent offending. Families plagued by violence, abuse, and neglect can be helped by nurse home visitation (before and after childbirth), parent training, and early childhood care and education" (p. 7).

Sheila Hotchkin reports that "one in every three women worldwide has been beaten, raped or somehow mistreated. Abuse also has been linked to problems with pregnancies, substance abuse, gastrointestinal disorders and chronic pain syndrome (2000, p. A-1)."

Community-Based Interventions

There is a trend among state legislatures to provide funds for community-based intervention programs for juveniles. Minnesota, for example, passed legislation in 1997 to require the Commissioner of Corrections to begin operating a juvenile sex offender treatment program at Red Wing Correctional Facility.

Youth Volunteers

Another alternative was described by Jones (1999) as YCWA (Youth Crime Watch of America). The concept is based on the view that youth volunteers know what is going on more than anyone else. YCWA sponsors these types of activities:

1. Providing drug- and crime-prevention education
2. Establishing youth patrols
3. Teaching school bus safety
4. Training youth as leaders

5. Facilitating communication and creating anonymous crime-reporting systems

6. Establishing community networks and partnerships.

YCWA supports activities at the elementary, middle, and high school levels. Youth trained in YCWA methods run the program for their school, neighborhood, public housing site, recreational center, and park.

An example of the YCWA program can be found at Miami's Carol City High School. Figures for 1995 showed a 45% decrease in student crime. Another example is Tampa's Leo High School, where statistics indicate a 72% drop in crime for 1994.

In a 1994 government publication, *Partnerships to Prevent Youth Violence*, the following ideas were at the heart of many police-community partnerships to reduce youth violence:

1. Settle arguments with words, not fists or weapons. Don't stand around and form an audience when others are arguing. A group makes a good target for violence.

2. Learn safe routes for walking in the neighborhood, and know good places to seek help. Trust feelings, and if there's a sense of danger, get away fast.

3. Report any crimes or suspicious activities to the police, school authorities, and parents. Be willing to testify if needed.

4. Don't open the door to anyone you don't know and trust.

5. Never go anywhere with someone you don't know and trust.

6. If someone tries to abuse you, say no, get away, and tell a trusted adult. Remember, it's not the victim's fault.

7. Don't use alcohol or other drugs, and stay away from places and people associated with them.

8. Stick with friends who are also against violence and drugs, and stay away from known trouble spots.

9. Get involved to make school safer and better. Have poster contests against violence, hold anti-drug rallies, counsel peers, and settle disputes peacefully. If there is no program, help to start one!

10. Help younger children learn to avoid being crime victims. Set a good example and volunteer to help community efforts to stop crime (p. 4).

Get-Tough Approaches

The training school is generally a severely restrictive approach. Usually a youth is sent to one of these institutions as a result of a juvenile court order. The Warwick School for Boys, located near New York City, is one example. This facility housed 170 residents, living in dormitories and receiving counseling, academic instruction, and vocational training (Abadinsky, 1997).

A major contributing factor to delinquency is school dropout. Ingersoll and LeBoeuf (1997) found that in 1993 approximately 63% of high school dropouts were unemployed. In addition, high school dropouts, over their lifetime, will earn significantly less than high school graduates and less than half of what college graduates are likely to make in their lifetimes. Furthermore, many truants and dropouts who are not in school are engaging in delinquent behavior.

Moreover, teen drinking is on the rise in this population. "The Centers for Disease Control has found that 32% of high-school age children are binge drinkers (more than five drinks at one time) and teens are getting drunk more often (Ciabattari, 1991, p. 17)." Treatment programs must be provided to assist youths in dealing with drinking problems.

Communities need to develop programs to combat the problem of truancy and school dropouts. Milwaukee, Wisconsin, developed a unique program entitled Truancy Abatement and Burglary Suppression (TABS). This program is a joint effort of the Milwaukee County Sheriff's Office, police department, public schools, and the Boys and Girls Clubs of Greater Milwaukee.

Juveniles who are in the community during school hours without an excused absence are picked up by law enforcement, taken to TABS centers at Boys and Girls Clubs, and the parents of the juveniles contacted. The parents and the student meet with school counselors to set goals for regular school attendance. If needed, Social Services arranges to assist the youths and their parents. Police department records showed that as student attendance improved over a 30-day period daytime juvenile crime rates declined. According to follow-up statistics, violent juvenile crime in Milwaukee was reduced as follows: homicides by 43%; sexual assaults by 24%; robberies by 16%; and aggravated assaults by 24%.

Richard (1999) wrote about a unique alternative school in Detroit, Michigan. The school, named the Frederick Douglass Academy, has 300 boys and no girls. The principal is Thomas Woodhouse. Metal detectors and security officers are used to ensure that no weapons enter the school.

Students have to apply to attend this alternative school. Kids who fight are punished by having to do bare-knuckle pushups on a concrete floor. Education is viewed as a serious undertaking. Nine in ten students who graduated in a recent year went on to college.

Many state legislatures believe the answer to juvenile crime is to pass "get-tough" legislation. Torbet and Szymanski (1998) found that many states are making it easier to prosecute juveniles in criminal court instead of juvenile court. Kentucky, for example, passed legislation in 1996 permitting the juvenile court to transfer a juvenile to criminal court if the individual is 14 years old and charged with the felony of possessing a firearm.

Another trend noted by Torbet and Szymanski (1998) is the increasing disclosure of formerly confidential juvenile court records to a wide array of people (such as schools and victims of crimes). Alaska, for example, passed legislation in 1997 permitting the victim to be present at juvenile hearings. In 1997 North Dakota passed legislation adding a provision that if a child is an adjudicated delinquent for a sexual assault, the court must notify the superintendent of the school district and the principal of the school the child attends of the disposition in the court case.

Under a grant from the Office of Juvenile Justice and Delinquency Prevention, the National Center for Juvenile Justice (State Responses, 1996) researched the trend by many state legislatures to increase the rights of victims of juvenile crime, such as:

1. Including victims of juvenile crime in the victim's bill of rights.
2. Notifying the victim upon release of the offender from custody.
3. Increasing opportunities for victims to be heard in juvenile court hearings.
4. Expanding victim services to victims of juvenile crime.
5. Establishing authority for victims to submit a victim's impact statement.
6. Requiring victims to be notified of significant hearings (e.g., bail and disposition).
7. Providing for release of the name and address of the offender and the offender's parents to the victim upon request.
8. Enhancing sentences if the victim is elderly or handicapped (p. 48).

Another illustration of these trends is that of legislation passed by New Mexico. The law provides that if a youthful offender or serious youthful offender commits a felony against a person age 60 or older, or against a person who is handicapped, the sentence may be increased by 2 years (p. 49).

Some cities use curfews as a way to cut down on juvenile delinquency. "Many states consider evening curfews as a viable means to enhance the safety of the community and its children" (Office of Juvenile Justice and Delinquency Prevention, 1996, p.1). A typical curfew is from 11 P.M. to 6 A.M. on school days and from midnight to 6 a.m. on non-school days. Most curfew ordinances apply to juveniles under 16 years of age, and some 16- and 17-year-olds.

An example of curfews can be found in New Orleans, Louisiana, which established a dusk-to-dawn curfew ordinance in May of 1994. To manage this program, the City opened the Central Curfew Center (CCC). The sheriff's office assigned 30 deputies to patrol the streets. Ministers, officers from the Juvenile Bureau, and staff members from the Louisiana State University Medical Center Department of Psychiatry were stationed at CCC each night. Curfew violators are brought to the CCC center. Their parents are contacted and participate in counseling sessions with trained staff. Parents of repeat offenders risk being taken to court and fined for failure to keep their children from curfew violations.

A big part of the New Orleans project is its summer youth programs. The New Orleans Recreation Department provides evening swimming and volleyball. Approximately 100,000 youth take part in this program. Also, the City created 1,300 new summer jobs for youth.

The reason for the success of this program in 1994 was a combination of the curfew, jobs programs, and the new recreation programs. This project resulted in a 27% reduction in juvenile crime during curfew hours in 1994. Armed robbery dropped 33% and auto theft dropped 42% from the previous year.

Innovative Programs by States

Many states have developed innovative programs to deal with the problems of young people. The following is an examination of some of these programs.

The Boys Ranch of Arizona was mentioned in *Alternatives to Incarceration,* published by the National Juvenile Justice Conference (1999). This program serves at-risk youth. The Boys Ranch provides family-style and paramilitary settings that help youths ages 8–18 to develop positive attitudes toward society, continue their education, and learn job skills to help them be competitive in the job market. The main campus is located near Phoenix.

Another unique program is run by the Saint Francis Academy. This Academy has three centers for the treatment of young people ages 12 through 18 who have conduct disorders. Centers are located in Salinas and Ellsworth, Kansas, and Lake Placid, New York. Length of time in the program varies from 1 to 24 months. The staff utilizes individual, group, and intergenerational counseling with occupational and remedial therapies.

Alternatives to Incarceration mentioned a special program named Brown Schools. These schools are located across the United States and in 22 foreign countries. The Brown Schools aim to resocialize, redirect, and psychologically rehabilitate young people. Techniques include positive peer culture and correctional techniques, in a flexible and therapeutic milieu.

Another publication, *State Innovations in Juvenile Justice,* describes additional special programs. New York, for example, has developed the Adirondack Wilderness Challenge. This program uses physically challenging group experiences to educate and build character for youngsters. Activities include projects such as renovating hiking trails. The program has four phases: a 3-month residential phase, a 3-week wilderness challenge component, a 4-month city challenge component, and finally, a community care program.

Tennessee has developed a unique program named Home Ties (Therapeutic Intervention and Education Services). The purpose of the program is to provide home-based intervention for families with a child at risk of being removed from the home and placed in an institution. These kids have a diagnosis of severe emotional disturbance. A Home Ties specialist is available 24 hours a day, 7 days a week, to assist these families. A short-term (4 weeks) in-home program teaches skills to all family members so the family can function more effectively.

VIEWS OF EXPERTS

We interviewed several experts across the United States to learn of their views on violence and juveniles.

Dr. Donald Thomas, an educator with 50 years of experience, volunteered his views on July 1, 1999, in Fort Lauderdale, Florida.

Dr. Donald Thomas, professor and consultant, was interviewed on June 1, 2000, in Fort Lauderdale, Florida.

Question: What is your name, and what type of work experience have you had?

Answer: My name is Donald Thomas and I have served as Superintendent of Schools in Salt Lake City, Utah, from 1973 to 1984. I also was Deputy State Superintendent for Public Accountability in South Carolina from 1984 to 1987, when Richard Riley was governor. I have also been an education consultant to several other governors. Currently I am a professor for the Nova Southeastern University in Fort Lauderdale, Florida, and consult with school districts in about fifteen states.

Question: Is school violence a big concern of school administrators around the country?

Answer: Yes. School violence has become the number-one concern for many school administrators. While it had been a major concern for urban school personnel, it is now a big concern for most school administrators. The recent rash of shootings in suburban school settings has increased concern. Many believe that the increase in violent behavior is related to the loneliness the young people experience both in the home and the school. This condition is discussed in detail in the May 10, 1999, issue of *Newsweek*.

Question: What are some of the actions that school administrators are taking to prevent school violence?

Answer: Prevention is most effective when programs target children prior to school entrance. Programs such as Parents and Teachers, First Steps to Success, and similar early childhood intervention strategies have reduced antisocial behavior. School administrators have tried to create safe schools with the introduction comprehensive variety of actions.

- Expanded counseling services for at-risk students.
- Identification cards for all school personnel and students.
- Metal detectors at school entrances and surveillance cameras within the school.
- Parent education programs to help parents to establish effective discipline.
- Mediation programs to assist students to resolve conflict in a nonviolent manner.
- Fairness committees to resolve issues between teachers and students.
- Police supervision of schools and school grounds.

- Decentralization of school governance with parent councils at each school.
- Zero-tolerance for the use of drugs, weapons at school, and violent behavior.
- Teacher supervision of halls, playgrounds, and parking lots.
- Structured small units within large schools.
- Expulsion programs for repeat offenders.
- Alternative education programs for at-risk youth.
- Extensive extracurricular clubs and school-related activities.
- Citizenship education programs that establish ethics and moral values.
- Programs that reward good behavior.

A model antiviolence program has been established in the Olentangy Public Schools, Olentangy, Ohio.

Question: Do you see an increase in school violence in the future?

Answer: If schools and the society in general continue to "technolize" human activity, violence will increase. Technology creates animosity and isolation as well as an increase in stress and pressure. In addition, public policy related to the care of children must become a substantially higher motivated priority. We cannot continue to have a large number of children living in poverty without adequate medical care and higher quality day-care services. Finally, without strengthening the family, society will continue to see an escalation of troubled men and women with antisocial behavior. This is probably the most difficult social problem we face: the breakdown of a stable family unit. Remedies include economic public policies, marriage and family life education, and community partnerships with churches, schools, and welfare agencies.

Question: What actions should be taken by school administrators by boards of education?

Answer: School administrators must establish greater contact with parents and community agencies. There is a strong need to coordinate services to children and youth. I suggest that all agencies that provide services to children and youth be governed by *one board* to provide educational, health, and social services. The superintendent of schools would then be the executive officer of this one community board. Boards of Education should present the superintendent of schools stronger security, greater control over personnel matters, and extensive latitude in coordinating all services to children and youth. The current fragmented approach to providing services to our children is obsolete and contributes to both adult and youth antisocial behavior. Time for change has already passed us by.

Dr. Bob Heckel, a retired Psychology Professor at the University of South Carolina at Columbia, also an expert in working with juveniles, was interviewed concerning delinquent youth on June 30, 1999, in Columbia, South Carolina.

Question: What are some of the causes of violence among youth?

Answer: Many people have described a series of contributory factors: abuse, unstable home, violent role models, witnessing violence, low self-esteem, hatred and prejudice, drugs and alcohol, peer pressures (gang), lack of success experiences in school or sports, the lack of appropriate moral values, and a feeling that the person has nothing to lose (or to live for).

Question: What are some signs for parents to look for?

Answer: Signs for parents are kids who show a lack of empathy, show anger, are secretive, withdrawn and perhaps most important a dehumanization of others and cruelty to animals and people.

Question: What is the best treatment for violent youth?

Answer: No one treatment stands out as being the best, but a combination of behavioral and cognitive (problem-solving) has a slight edge. Prevention, though, is the best approach.

Question: Will you describe the book you are writing about teens that murder?

Answer: The book deals with the incidence of preteens who murder, how they are dealt with, suspected causes, assessing them, treating them, and their rehabilitation. We also see moral development and family issues as central.

Question: What can schools do to deal with violent youth?

Answer: Schools have given up their former role (in loco parentis) in which, with family permission, they served as a part of the extended family. It may be impossible to get this back, because teachers are not trained today for being parent surrogates, and even if they were, there is a fear of lawsuits or worse.

Dr. David Kleckley, Department of Special Education at Sequoyah Middle School in Doraville, a suburb of greater Atlanta, Georgia, gave his views in an interview conducted on June 29, 1999, in Atlanta, Georgia.

Question: What do you believe may be some of the causes of school violence?

Answer: In the small community where I grew up, it was not so rare during deer season to see a pickup truck with a shotgun hanging in the back, parked in the student parking lot at the local high school. Today, such an occurrence would be cause for great alarm. There was a time also when it was rather customary for boys to have pocketknives and bring them to school. They used them for such things as sharpening pencils and cleaning fingernails. Nobody thought much about it then, but if a student is caught today carrying a pocketknife in school, he or she will most likely be suspended or perhaps even expelled for carrying a deadly weapon. In many schools, even having book bags is now forbidden, for fear that youngsters might conceal dangerous items. Something has definitely changed.

Children have been fighting for as long as there have been schools in America, and before, but extreme acts of violence like we have witnessed at Columbine High School and other places seem to be more of a recent phenomenon. The tragedy at Littleton, Colorado, on April 20, 1999, was followed by many copycat threats around the nation.

In light of these current events, as highlighted in national news, many commentators have tried to pinpoint an exact cause for increases of violence within schools; and they typically seize the opportunity and use the issue to promote their various agendas. In actuality, however, there are probably many factors which contribute to the prevalence of senseless hostilities in our educational facilities and throughout our society.

There has been a growth in human population here and around the world. Crowded conditions, especially in large cities, could be having some impact. Certainly, our nation's forty-eight million students are being vicariously exposed to scenes filled with violence, which most likely results in subtle but pervasive desensitization. The institution of family has become more fragmented and perhaps less functional; and due to much litigation, there has been gradual erosion of the power of school personnel to effectively discipline a child.

Religious leaders and a few politicians debate the presumption of a moral breakdown in our society, while others point their fingers at the availability of guns. Perhaps as many as one in one thousand students in the United States are routinely armed. Some are not aggressive, but afraid. However erroneous the idea, they carry weapons for self-protection. Obviously, the price we pay for maintaining our Second Amendment right in a free society is the risk of accessibility to guns by those who should not have them. Nevertheless, the presence of firearms cannot be solely to blame.

What we do know is that youths that are abused then do become abusive themselves, and those who grow up in harsh environments, where there is much violence around them, often become violent as well. Culture definitely plays a part. In some neighborhoods young people are compelled to join gangs, often linked with drug activity.

On the other end of the spectrum there is at least a proportion of children and adolescents whose comfort and affluence characterize conditions, but who, for one reason or another, feel profoundly isolated and estranged from their families or peers. A small number of these become real loners or form…associations who share extremist and destructive ideas. They are the ones we need to watch when our concern relates to bizarre possibilities.

Question: What measures seem to work to end incidents of school violence?

Answer: Schools reflect the cultures and conditions around them. A broad spectrum of groups should take an active role in addressing the problem. Among those who need to become more involved in the issue are families, places of worship, community-based organizations, businesses, and government. Without giving up First Amendment privileges per se, greater responsibility could be assumed by the motion picture industry, the creators and manufacturers of some electronic games, and mass media in general.

Statistics can be used to show trends and variances, but we never really know precisely what has been averted, in contrast to simply not happening. All we can really do is make attempts at addressing the problems and hope that our efforts are working. Various organizations around my locale have begun to tackle the issues.

Recently, the Southern Christian Leadership Conference sponsored a gun buyback in Atlanta. Local citizens exchanged guns for vouchers worth fifty dollars. The firearms were ceremoniously deposited in a coffin.

A North DeKalb County, Georgia, cable provider, Comcast Communications, announced plans around the end of May 1999 to start a pilot program to curb school violence. Through the Comcast challenge, "Youth Against Violence," they hoped to inspire competition between two DeKalb County high schools, each working toward the goal of submitting a five-page summary of an action plan to combat school violence. The winning school was to receive a grant for five thousand dollars. Student involvement is believed to be the key to effective strategies. Around the same time, the Chamblee, Georgia, Mayor and City Council issued the proclamation that May 26, 1999, would be designated as "Youth Violence Prevention Day."

A yearlong antiviolence campaign was begun recently from a partnership of the U.S. Department of Justice and Education, and MTV—Music Television. The campaign, "Fight for Your Rights," is intended to elevate awareness and provide answers to youth violence. Special programs, new features, and public service announcements will continue throughout the current year.

Perhaps the most effective means we have found to curb school violence is to elicit the support of the student population. It may sound like an oversimplification of the matter, but teaching students to be good citizens and to share in the responsibility for their own well-being is important. It is impossible for teachers, staff, and school administrators to effectively police schools alone. In my experience, I do not know of a single situation where a student has been caught wearing a weapon that it was not the result of some young person sharing information with authorities. We do not want to encourage our students to be little tattletales, as such, but when circumstances are truly critical, it behooves everyone to take a stand.

The American Psychological Association (APA) produces a guide called "Warning Signs." It is intended to help young people recognize when a friend or classmate might be a potential danger to themselves or others. The guide addresses such topics as reasons for violence, dealing with anger, and controlling your own violent behavior. The guide is not intended as a substitute for qualified mental health care or assistance for a psychologist or another licensed professional.

Question: What treatment programs seem to help juveniles who have problems with violence?

Answer: My school district operates facilities for students who cannot seem to adapt to regular schools, including those who may be harmful to themselves or others. Included are several psychoeducation[al] facilities and an alternative school for adolescents whose behavior does not minimally meet the district's criteria for acceptable conduct. A small percentage of high-school students elect to attend what is called open campus. There, they must adhere to a few strict rules but are afforded much freedom otherwise. Most of them are not troublemakers but rather, individuals who seem to function better in a more open environment.

Closer to the mainstream are in-house special education programs, as they are almost everywhere throughout the country. Among the special education classes taught where I work is decision-making, a class where students are free to discuss personal concerns and ways to appropriately channel their aggressions when dealing with classmates and others. Part of the difficulty is correctly identifying the ones who really need special attention. Often, they are quiet and are not so readily noticed. Counselors and psychologists are also available to assist students who are struggling with personal concerns.

One approach that has proven to be most effective is our mentoring program. Individual students are paired with chosen adults, mostly teachers, but some outsiders as well, to receive friendly support and guidance. Rapport and a bond often develop between the mentor and mentee as they meet informally to talk and share pleasant experiences. Good relations between the faculty and students help to ensure open lines of communication, essential to the maintenance of a secure environment.

On June 28, 1999, Dr. Steve Katsikas of the Carlos Albizu University (Miami, Florida) gave his views on causes of juvenile violence for inclusion in this book. This interview was developed, conducted, and transcribed by Burt Hayner, a doctoral candidate in clinical psychology at the Carlos Albizu University.

Mr. Burt Hayner, M.Ed.

Question: Please, tell us what your name and job titles are.

Answer: My name is Steve Katsikas. I am Assistant Professor of Psychology and also co-director of the Community Partner's Program.

Question: Have you worked with any juveniles in any regard?

Answer: I've worked in inpatient psychiatric settings that often had transfer cases or referrals from juvenile detention or the court system. I currently work primarily with younger children on an outpatient basis.

Question: What in your opinion are some of the causes of violence among juveniles?

Answer: The more I read about it and the latest research, the more I am convinced that it is a multi-determined phenomenon. There are a lot of different ways to become aggressive—many different pathways. There seems to be a genetic component involved. It's related to aggression, and we know that through some of the hereditary studies, the adoptive studies, and twin studies, there does seem to be a genetic component to violence, but that does not explain the variance very much. One of the big factors that predict which children are going to become conduct-disordered is actually the additional presence of attention deficit hyperactivity disorder. That seems to be one of the largest risk factors that predict a child becoming conduct-disordered, so that seems to be significant. Other factors include poor family functioning and variables associated with growing up in poverty.

Question: Along that same line of questioning, what other factors increase the incidence of violence among juveniles?

Answer: It seems that a lot of youthful offenders have a non-optimal family. There are a number of risk factors you can talk about in these families. There are a number of factors that are sociological—for example, poverty, single-parent homes, younger mothers, and neighborhoods where violence is predominant. All those factors seem to highly correlate with the emergence of violence. Other things, in terms of the actual interactions in the families, are also predictive.

For example, there seems to be a high correlation between harsh physical violence and youth aggression. I'm not talking about just corporal punishment but, when it is excessive, corporal punishment seems to be associated with the development of aggression down the road. Part of that seems to be explainable through a social learning model. These parents don't mean to injure their children, but they get out of control and they are overwhelmed by stress, and when the child does something they don't want them to do, they react by lashing out physically while they're angry.

What's being communicated to the child is that when you get angry this is how you can handle your problems. This is what's being modeled. When someone doesn't do what you want him or her to do, this is how you can get him or her to comply. It is a powerful negative message.

One of the interesting things about conduct disorder and about childhood aggression in general is how well we can predict which children are going to become delinquent down the road. One of the impressive predictors seems to be playground bullying. I read a recent study—and I do apologize for not having the reference—but a large proportion of children who are identified as bullies in the third grade will enter the legal system with some sort of changes by adolescence. To me, that's a very powerful predictor.

In terms of what causes the increase, I think that a lot of it has to do with the social deprivation and the cycle of poverty. Even though the economy is doing well, the poor are still very poor and the inner cities are still very unpleasant places to live. There is still a lot of violence in these places; there's still a tremendous amount of illiteracy. However, my understanding of the statistics is that violent crime has actually been decreasing among youth. I think what's happening, though, is that there are more spectacular examples of violent crimes, like what's been happening in some of the school systems. I like to keep in mind that overall violent crime in youth is on the downturn, but whether that's a function of our society improving or that we're just incarcerating a lot more, I'm not exactly sure.

Question: Are there any particular treatment approaches or recommendations that you have found to be successful with violent youth?

Answer: I'm going to start backward and then move my way up to your question. I'm a strong believer in prevention. Prevention is not really a treatment per se, but I think we can identify risk factors very early. We can identify kids who become pathologically aggressive in kindergarten or first grade. What I'd like to see are diversion programs for children who are starting to have these behaviors at an early age. Intervene, go in there and provide some sort of treatment. As they get older and their behaviors become more entrenched, treatment becomes less and less effective and becomes more expensive.

If we're talking about acting-out adolescents, and we're trying to think what's the best treatment for an adolescent who's already engaging in these things, I'm a strong believer that a family system approach, especially one that is multi-systemic—that's intervening at multiple system levels—is really your best choice. I think that the research suggests that it is even superior in terms of outcome to inpatient residential treatment, but it's very difficult to do. It requires a lot of training, and the therapist really takes on the role of the case manager too. They have to intervene with so many different systems, and do interventions at so many levels, that it's difficult to do. But again, I would love to treat the problems before they become that serious. That says to me we should have prevention programs in all the elementary schools.

Question: How about involving the parents in prevention or treatment programs?

Answer: Absolutely essential. I cannot picture individual psychotherapy for an acting-out adolescent being very effective at all without taking a systems approach. I'm really talking about a family therapy model. There are other systems that you intervene with, but you have to work with the family. I understand the aggressive behavior often fulfills a systemic role for the family, or that aggressive behavior within the family may also reflect lack of some parental skills. One of the biggest problems is that the parents don't monitor their children's whereabouts. If you can improve parental monitoring, you are going to make significant impact into these delinquent behaviors.

I believe in teaching parents parenting skills and I see a lot of kids getting onto this pathway because the parents don't have the skills. I see also that a lot of these parents don't know how to discipline correctly, where they end up using ineffective ways of disciplining their children like harsh physical punishment or threats that never get carried through. That can have a negative impact on their children's behavior.

Question: Are you aware of youth being placed in treatment by the courts and what effectiveness this carries with it?

Answer: Not directly. It's not the kind of work I've been doing. I haven't worked with any court-ordered juveniles. But, interestingly, one of the things I think you can read from the literature has to do with the boot camp idea. I really haven't found compelling evidence that the boot camp approach works as long-term treatment. I know that courts are sentencing juveniles to this kind of treatment, but from my reading—and this is not my personal experience—the literature hasn't really found it to be an extremely effective approach.

Question: Do you think that many of the youths have substance-abuse problems?

Answer: The ones who do are becoming even more dangerous than the ones who don't. There is a similar pathway in becoming a youthful offender as becoming a youth with substance-abuse problems. Often you see an underlying psychiatric disorder like depression or anxiety that also accompanies the conduct problems. Substance abuse in a sense becomes an attempt on the part of the adolescent or child to self-medicate, to sort of treat his or her own symptoms. Again, the best treatment for a substance abuser has been an intense multi-systemic approach.

Question: I think we've sort of covered my next question, but I'm going to ask it anyway and see if there's anything you might want to add. Do you see any solution to the problem? I know you have already spoken of some solutions such as early intervention, but are there any other solutions you might want to add to your list?

Answer: I think we can make the living environment better for children, but as a society, we need to prioritize that. I think from a political point of view it is easier for these elected officials to authorize the building of prisons. They can walk out to that prison in the ground-cutting ceremony, cut the ribbon themselves, and everybody says, "Look what so and so is doing about crime." Now, from a politician's point of view, do you want to pour tons of money into prevention when you're not even going to get credit for a reduction of crime that will not be seen for ten years? Do you really want to get involved in that?

What we have to do as a culture and as a society is to start becoming a society of preventionists. I think a dollar spent in prevention is so much more effective than a thousand dollars spend in treatment. Prevention dollars are a lot cheaper. Michenbaum has data that says you can spend a dollar now or thousands of dollars later on the same problem. It's more cost-effective to treat at the earliest stages of the disorder. So what does that mean?

How do we become that culture? I think, as psychologists, we have to be politically active by being members of APA, by being in local government, advisory boards, et cetera. We have to keep pushing that point that we need to do these prevention tactics and we all benefit. Our whole society benefits from this. We just need to educate our communities about the role of mental health services and how early intervention has a tremendous payoff.

Question: Are there any special projects that you're involved in that are in this same area?

Answer: Dr. Rodriguez and I wrote a grant that was funded by Miami-Dade County to do what I've been talking about—an early prevention program. This is the Community Partners Program, and we've just been funded, for another additional year. We'll be starting our third year of this program. It's an out-patient-based program for elementary school kids. It's funded by the County, so the services are free for the families.

The kids are referred by teachers and guidance counselors in nineteen area elementary schools, which are within a five-mile radius of Miami Institute of Psychology. It is a psychoeducational program with eight structured sessions. The children get four sessions of anger-management in group therapy and four sessions of social-skills training and self-esteem building. While the kids are in group therapy with a team of therapists, the parents are at the same time having parenting groups. The parenting groups are a parental support program that also gives these parents specific skills to use with their kids. The skills have to do with helping the parents be more effective. It's not only disciplining more effectively, but also enhancing their children's self-esteem, helping parents help their own children mediate conflict. After eight sessions, the children and parents graduate. We refer any families that need more intensive intervention.

We have data on our program, and we have found out that the parents who have participated have been very satisfied with the services they have received. They seem to consider it to be valuable. That really matches what I see in the sessions. The kids are happy to be there. They come week after week with stories of how things are going better in school, how somebody did something and they were able to ignore that, and the parents come in and report decreases in aggression, plus positive phone calls from teachers, better grades, and so on. That's the program we are involved in. It's a very low-dose kind of intervention. We conceptualize it as a form of prevention for later, more serious problems.

IMPACTS OF THE FAMILY

Children must feel like they are valued and cared for. If they are not valued by family, church, community, and school, they often look to be valued by street gangs or other negative peers (Crews and Counts, 1997).

An issue that should not be underestimated when discussing problems faced by juveniles is that of divorce. The absence of one parent, the emotional and financial tension, and sometimes continuing conflicts between parents that accompany divorce frequently lead to psychological problems for boys and girls alike. The worst period is the first year after divorce. Some resulting effects on a juvenile in that first year might be aggression, distractibility and noncompliance, academic difficulties, poor relationships with peers, and low self-esteem. Generally, children who are strongly attached to both parents have a lower probability of self-reported delinquency than children who are strongly attached to only one parent. Further, children living in single-parent homes who are strongly attached to the custodial parent have a greater probability of committing delinquent acts than children living in intact homes who are strongly attached to both parents (Garrin and Furman, 1989). Thus, some juveniles of divorced parents might need the services of community mental health centers to deal with issues causing them pain, depression, anger, or guilt.

A poor family life might influence a juvenile to emotionally escape by using drugs and alcohol. The Office of Juvenile Justice and Delinquency Prevention (1998), in its fact sheet, reported that approximately 9.5 million drinkers in 1996 were youths ages 12 to 20. Of this number, 4.4 million were binge drinkers, including 1.9 million heavy drinkers. In addition, alcohol was a factor in 50% to 65% of suicides among youth. A major problem is getting juveniles with drug problems to seek treatment. "Getting addicts to see that they have a problem is often half the battle against the problem" (Whitehead and Lab, 1990, p. 434).

In the following interview, David Jameson provided some helpful insights concerning the juvenile drug and alcohol problems he has worked with.

Parents are on the front lines in terms of guiding youths through adolescence into adulthood and serve as role models for their children. Therefore, parents' behaviors, whether socially acceptable or not, will often be copied. For example, if a parent drinks, smokes, or uses drugs, the child is likely to copy that particular behavior. It is also true in regard to parents' attitudes. Attitudes are often passed on to children through example, and parents who have poor or negative attitudes about themselves or the world may pass on that belief or attitude to the child. Attitudes are often seen as the views to be held and practiced, since the parent is the one who serves as the child's role model. In essence, parents serve as the moral compass for the child.

The *Juvenile Justice Bulletin* (Rafael and Pion-Berlin, 1999) dedicated an issue to a unique organization that could benefit many parents, Parents Anonymous. This nationwide organization, founded in 1970, assists

Mr. David Jameson, Executive Director of the Lexington-Richland Alcohol and Drug Abuse Council in Columbia, South Carolina

Question: How do you process a teenager who is a binge drinker?

Answer: We do an assessment with the teenager and his or her parents. He or she could be a school referral or court referral. Some are even self-reported. We do a family history and develop a treatment plan. The individual could be placed in an inpatient program or an outpatient program. He or she might also be referred to a self-help group like AA (Alcoholics Anonymous) or NA (Narcotics Anonymous).

Question: What are the characteristics of patient intake workers?

Answer: Generally, they are social workers or have a similar master's degree. They must be able to gain the trust of parents and teenagers. They also must be certified as an addictions counselor. Fifty individuals are employed as addictions counselors by our agency.

approximately 100,000 parents and their children each year. Weekly meetings led by parents and professionally trained facilitators have been held at no cost to participants. Many of these groups also operate 24-hour telephone help-lines to assist parents in need.

Parents Anonymous programs are based on the following principles:

1. *Parent leadership.* Parents recognize and take responsibility for their problems, develop their own solutions, and serve as role models for their children.

2. *Mutual support.* Help is reciprocal, in that parents give and receive support from each other, creating a strong sense of community.

3. *Shared leadership.* Parents and professionals build successful partnerships to share responsibility, expertise, and leadership roles.

4. *Personal growth.* Parents make significant long-term positive change through identifying their options, exploring their feelings, and acting on their decisions in an atmosphere of belonging, trust, and acceptance in which healthy interactions are modeled.

The facilitators who lead these groups are mostly practicing professionals in social work, counseling, healthcare, mental health, teaching, and related fields. They have expertise in child abuse, juvenile delinquency, group dynamics, family systems, child development, and local community resources. These experts have donated roughly $10 million dollars worth of services.

A major goal of Parents Anonymous is to prevent or end juvenile delinquency and child abuse in families. Experts believe children who are reared in supportive, affectionate, and accepting homes are less likely to become deviant. Also of concern are children who are born to parents who use drugs. As a result these children are at extreme risk of child abuse and neglect. Jane Hanson (2000) wrote in the *Atlanta Journal-Constitution*:

> Of the 513 children in Georgia who died from 1996 to 1998, approximately one in 10 was born with drugs in the bloodstream. Others died from neglect due to the fact that the parents were too busy getting high to tend to the basic needs of their children. Typical among them was the 3-year-old who died when his mother, high on amphetamines and marijuana, put him in a car unrestrained, then wrecked the vehicle (p. A19).

Most experts place immense importance on the role of the family in the child's development. A unique project is the Parents As Teachers program (PAT). One program is located in National City, California. The Office of Juvenile Justice (1995) sees this program as a model. Its purpose is to provide special services for adolescent parents who remain in the program until their child is age 3. Children who participated in this program were found to be significantly advanced over their peers in language, social development, problem-solving, and other intellectual abilities. In addition, parents in this program knew more about child development than nonparticipants.

The four family-related indicators of risk factors for delinquency or violent behavior are (p. 7):

1. Family history of problem behavior.
2. Family management problems.
3. Family conflict.
4. Favorable parental attitudes concerning crime and involvement in crime.

MEDIA AND INTERNET ISSUES

Many believe that children need protection from Internet violence, smut, and hate. Andrew J. Glass (1999) reported that the Internet industry had developed a Parent's Protection Page that allows parents to:

> (1) limit access to violent game sites; (2) monitor which Web sites their children have visited; (3) set time limits on their children's online sessions; (4) get information

on how to report criminal activity; and (5) utilize pointers to kid-friendly sites that offer good educational content (p. A3).

Many experts are blaming media violence as a factor in modern youth violence. In her article in *Education Week*, Bess Keller (1999) states: "Many researchers stress that the crucial element in the climb of the youth murder rate over the past 30 years has been access to guns and the media's tacit encouragement of violence" (p. 20). Mr. Cornell of the University of Virginia was quoted in Keller's article with his view that "in high schools, there have always been in-groups, out-groups, and cliques; what has changed is access to weapons, and information on the Internet, and the encouragement children receive from music videos, computer games, TV, and movies to engage in violent behavior" (p. 20).

Keller reported that Eric Harris, one of the attackers at Columbine High School, was a master of the shoot-'em-up computer game called Doom. He was so skilled on the computer that he devised variations on his Web site.

An article entitled "Violence Is Preventable" (Elias, Lantreri, and Patti, 1999) reported that "by the age of 18, the typical child will have seen 16,000 simulated murders and 200,000 acts of violence" (p. 45). The same article stated that:

> The causes of violence extend beyond virtual violence and include poverty, institutionalized and individual racism, intolerance of differences, abuse, lack of parental supervision and guidance, and the breakdown of family structures. Many young people today who experience or who are exposed to violence do not think they will live past the age of 20. Their violence is fueled by a lack of hope, a dearth of positive connections to the American dream, and a sense that they have nothing to risk (p. 45).

In the fall of 1993, a citizens' panel in Washington, DC (a coalition of groups including the American Medical Association and the National Parent–Teacher Association) presented U.S. Attorney General Janet Reno with a series of recommendations aimed at curbing violence on television between the hours of 6 A.M. and 10 P.M. These citizens suggested that a major cause of school violence and juvenile delinquency is exposure to television violence. Attorney General Reno informed a Senate panel that government action was needed if the entertainment industry did not take it upon itself to reduce television violence. This represented an effort to get the entertainment industry to limit the violence voluntarily. If the entertainment industry failed to examine the violence problem and propose plans to reduce violent programs, government regulation was suggested (Brooks, 1993).

A study conducted in the early 1990s examined the effect of violence on violent behavior (Agnew, 1994). Data indicated that only a small percentage of adolescents generally approve of violence or express indifference to violence. A large percentage of adolescents, however, accept neutralization (not realizing the full impact of one's violent actions), which calls for justifying the use of violence in specific situations. Both cross-sectional and longitudinal data suggested that acceptance of these neutralizations contributes to violent behavior. Further, the effect of neutralizations on violence is conditioned by certain variables; neutralization is most likely to lead to violent behavior by those who disapprove of violence and associate with delinquent peers. Most of this neutralization comes from watching television.

NATIONAL RESPONSE TO COLUMBINE HIGH SCHOOL TRAGEDY

On Tuesday, April 20, 1999, 12 students and a teacher were killed at Columbine High School in Littleton, Colorado. The suspects were two fellow students described as outcasts. America was in shock and searched for answers.

A reported problem bothering the suspects was the teasing and bullying they received from student athletes; 8.2% of students in 1993 grades 6 through 12 reported having problems with bullying (Sefton, 1999). Therefore, parents should be vigilant in pursuing any persistent taunting of children. Parents also could role-play with their children appropriate responses to bullying. For example, the student could try kindness toward the teaser, which might catch them off guard.

A national poll of 659 adults (Browning and Huizinga, 1999) solicited ideas on effective tactics to stop school violence. More than 50% of the adults recommended stricter gun control for teens, more counseling for teens, metal detectors in schools, and restrictions on TV/movie violence. Other suggestions included Internet restrictions, penalties against parents of children who use parents' guns to commit crimes, school dress codes, body searches of students, and stiffer penalties for parents whose children commit crimes.

The American Civil Liberties Union received hundreds of complaints of school administrators' overreacting to students in the wake of the Littleton school massacre (Jones, 1999). Administrators responded that the ensuing suspensions, expulsions, and arrests were necessary to protect the safety of students.

The Columbine High School shootings have increased the call for greater use of security devices at schools. Take the example of Garrett Metal Detectors in Farland, Texas. The company used to sell its products to airports, courthouses, and prisons. In 1999, approximately 25% of its business was the schools. Random body-checks with hand-held wands were placed in all 170 junior and senior high schools in the Los Angeles Unified School District. Basic metal detectors sell for about $2,500 each, and a hand-held wand goes for $100. After introducing metal detectors and hand-held metal detector wands in many New York City schools, the number of in-school incidents fell 11% city-wide (Parker and Kasindorf, 1999).

Other security strategies include the use of police officers on campus, installing night vision cameras in student parking lots, and bomb-sniffing dogs. Despite the extensive media coverage of the Columbine incident, school shootings are rare. The overall school crime rate for students ages 12 to 18 has continued to decline since 1993 (Parker and Kasindorf, 1999).

JUVENILES AND MENTAL ILLNESS

Depression affected one in every 33 children and one in eight adolescents in the United States in the late 1990s (Roy, 1999). Signs of childhood depression include (p. D2):

1. Persistent sadness and hopelessness
2. Withdrawal from friends and activities once enjoyed
3. Increased irritability or agitation
4. Missed school or poor school performance
5. Changes in eating and sleeping habits
6. Indecision, lack of concentration and forgetfulness
7. Poor self-esteem or guilt
8. Frequent physical complaints, such as headaches or stomachaches
9. Lack of enthusiasm, low energy or motivation
10. Drug or alcohol abuse
11. Recurring thoughts of death or suicide

> Depression can be triggered by a specific event or trauma, or it may be a chemical imbalance in the brain that happens for no apparent reason. It is closely linked to suicide, the third leading cause of death in the United States for 15- to 24-year-olds (p. D2).

It is important to provide information and support to families that have a child who is mentally ill. Furthermore, "disturbed juvenile offenders can cause untold harm to themselves, their peers, their families, and their crime victims" (Glick and Goldstein, 1995, p.185).

A *Time Magazine* article reported on the mental health of many of the shooters/suspects in American school shootings (Cloud, 1999). For example, Barry Loukaitis of Moses Lake, Washington, who killed one teacher and two students, was thought to be suffering from severe depression as well as an inferiority complex. He was 14 years old at the time of the shooting.

Another example is Luke Woodham, who killed two students and stabbed his mother to death in Pearl, Mississippi. He was 16 years old at the time of the murders. His mental health was reported as "erratic coping skills; lack of empathy; and sensitive to insults" (p. 36).

Of Eric Harris (18) and Dylan Klebold (17), who killed a teacher, 12 students, and themselves at Columbine High in Littleton, Colorado, Cloud reported that "Harris took the antidepressant Luvox and Klebold was shy and sad" (p. 37). Thomas Solomon, age 15, wounded six students in Conyers, Georgia. He was "depressed and had been taking Ritalin" (p. 37).

A popular approach to dealing with depression in juveniles seems to be the use of antidepressants. According to Chua-Eoan (1999) "500,000 to 1 million prescriptions for antidepressants are written for children and teens each year" (p. 44). The best known of the antidepressants are Prozac, Zoloft, Paxil, Luvox, and Celexa.

The big question that parents must decide is whether to medicate or not. In any case, many parents "consistently miss the signs of depression" (Chua-Eoan, 1999, p. 46). The problem becomes even more complex if the teens are also using pot or alcohol.

CONCLUSION

Many views are forthcoming as to the best solution to the problem of youth violence. "There is little agreement on the causes of delinquency other than that there is no single cause" (Fagan and Forst, 1996, p. 23). If America is to have schools that are free of drugs and violence, however, strategies must be drawn and actions taken at local, state, and federal levels.

The Denver Youth Study was a longitudinal study conducted in 1999 of urban youths from high-risk neighborhoods. The study found that the best predictors of success were having conventional friends, having a stable family and good parental monitoring, having positive expectations for the future, and not having delinquent peers.

A school climate must be developed to alleviate the problems of school violence. The school must provide a physically safe and emotionally secure environment with curriculum programs that are academically effective and developmentally appropriate. Students need emotional and psychological growth through diversity, self-exploration, meaningful participation in school and community, positive social interaction, physical activity, and other competency development (Allen, Splittgerber, and Manning, 1993). Counselors who work with youths in the schools need to be aware of the concerns of teens. The two major worries of high school students, according to an *USA Today* (Leavitt, 1999) poll are crime and violence.

In dealing with criminal-justice issues, police officers should be part of a community-based team that includes the social, educational, and judicial resources of a locality. The public education system is an ideal base of operation for the community-based team because it provides a logical setting for police officers to deliver education, prevention, intervention, and enforcement services to students, parents, and community. Educational law enforcement—a relatively new idea—builds on the value of community-based policing. This concept asserts that an emphasis on early intervention and the encouragement of citizenship values in youths provides the greatest long-term investment in funding community police services.

Police officers serving as mentors work one on one with students to gain the trust of the youth community. Educational law officers also seek to help students develop higher self-esteem by achieving goals and projects. In addition, young people receive formal instruction designed to improve their decision-making skills. Educational law enforcement relies on restrictive enforcement activities as a last resort (Johnsen, 1992).

Community, home, and school must have a strong presence in a child's life. If any of these key components is weak, the remaining components have to "pick up the slack." Approaches such as school safety plans, conflict-resolution instruction, peer counseling, and peer mediation can help strengthen each of these components (Crews and Counts, 1997).

DUSK BEFORE THE DAWN OR THUNDER BEFORE THE STORM?

A Look at the Future

Peace cannot be kept by force. It can only be achieved by understanding.

Albert Einstein

537 hate groups were identified in the United States in 1998.

CNN Live, August 13, 1999

INTRODUCTION

Throughout history, juvenile violence has mirrored the problems of the greater society. Historically, the three major social institutions—family, community, and school—have evidenced shortcomings in the care of children at one time or another. As one area becomes weak, the other two have had to compensate for the weak component. In the 1990s, the schools were expected to assume even more responsibility as families and society tended not to satisfy the needs of the young people. There is no evidence that this will change as the country enters the twenty-first century. Schools maintain that they are doing the best they can with what they have. Schools are (and have always been) expected to solve problems they did not create and cannot control.

The extent of juvenile violence—and violence in general—in the future is uncertain, of course, but one characteristic of U.S. society *is* evident: History has a tendency to repeat itself. The pendulum of justice has constantly swung between two extremes and has yet to find a middle ground between the "lock'em up" approach and the "pure treatment" philosophy.

At the turn of the twenty-first century, American society is once again following the classical school of criminological thought, in which the majority believe that the root cause of negative behavior is simple—the result of free will—and the only answer is swift, certain, and severe punishment following any criminal act. If it is true that history always repeats itself, where should the United States be on this continuum? Are we headed backward, making no real progress in understanding and learning from past mistakes?

149

BACK TO THE BASICS

Many scholars, scientists, and politicians are continually looking for complex answers to complex social problems. Perhaps this approach may not actually be so complex. As with a complicated home project that is not working out, the basics of what *does* work should be revisited to allow regrouping, rethinking, and then moving forward. Sometimes the answer to complex problems is simple. Still, society *is* a dynamic entity requiring a variety of intervention strategies. But do these interventions have to be as complex as the problem itself?

Many programs addressing juvenile delinquency are elaborate and cost taxpayers millions of dollars. Some successful programs have been brought to the attention of the criminal justice community, only to be replaced by what is new and trendy. The harsh reality behind juvenile delinquency might be the basic notion that the earlier at-risk children are attended to, the less likely they will be to progress into a pattern of antisocial behavior.

Some programs have creative and noteworthy ideas and goals but the target population is not the population that needs the services. On the other hand, some programs are targeting the correct population and intervening at the appropriate time but are "feel good" programs that offer no real assistance.

Elementary and middle-school children who live in decaying neighborhoods that are targets for crime should be the focal point of juvenile delinquency programs. The sooner contact is made with this population, the more likely the program is to be successful (Crews and Counts, 1997).

COMMUNITY INSTITUTIONS

For years the cornerstone of American civilization has been self-discipline. Churches, families, and schools have been interconnected and dependent upon each other. This support seemed to almost guarantee a town or community's survival. The values and morals that once were taught by these institutions instilled discipline not only in the current population, but also the generation that would become the next generation of leaders. These children grew up in environments that taught by example, and criminality was minimal. What criminality there was met with public shaming in forms ranging from the offender being placed in the stockades in front of the courthouse to children standing in the corner at school for misbehavior.

"Can we stop the violence?" is the headline of a newspaper article by Diane Lore (1999). This is the question that will challenge researchers into the twenty-first century. The challenge must be met if the trend of children killing children is to be reversed. Homicides in the past 20 years have become the second leading cause of death for young people between the ages of 15 and 24. Homicide is the third leading cause of death for children ages 10 to 14, according to Lore. The best violence-prevention programs have these characteristics:

1. The program is theoretically sound.
2. The program keeps kids out of trouble.
3. The program is able to sustain a positive effect for at least a year.
4. The program must have worked some place other than where it was created (p. A8).

A primary example of this program in action is Second Step in Seattle, Washington, which has been duplicated in 10,000 schools. The program "teaches younger children not only how to avoid conflict, but to feel empathy for others and control impulses. Additionally, Second Step successfully reduced aggressive behavior and increased prosocial behavior in second and third graders who had gone through the program" (p. A8).

Further, youth-corps–type programs often hope for the future. The U.S. Corporation for National Service coordinated 120 youth corps programs in 37 states in the late 1990s. These programs, according to Stephens (1977), involved 22,000 young people. He wrote, "The programs try to instill a work ethic in participants and help them understand the meaning of working with others toward a common goal" (p. 7).

Children want attention. Attention is a reinforcer of behavior. A national report, "Combating Violence and Delinquency" (1996), encouraged local media to "showcase youth successes in local communities (p. 104)." Positive reinforcement is an effective tool for parents, teachers, and others in the community.

EVOLUTION OF THE SCHOOL ENVIRONMENT

Recently, school violence has taken the lead as a primary societal concern in the United States. This shift in attention has been mainly a reaction to the several school shootings by teens in the 1990s. This reaction has led administrators to take extreme measures to protect students, but at what price?

Safety in American schools may cost millions of dollars in the future, and what continued impact will this have on the student? Many schools have installed metal detectors, initiated book bag checks, and placed restrictions on types of book bags that can be brought into school. Other schools have considered doing away with lockers to prevent students from hiding weapons and bombs there. Already in some schools, students eat in shifts and change classes on staggered time schedules. If these activities do not sound familiar to the reader, they should.

Some of the practices that many schools are following are similar to institutional procedures used in the American prison system. Some of the parallels between these two American institutions are:

School	Prison
Controlled movement	Controlled movement
Metal detectors	Metal detectors
Searches of personal effects	Searches of personal effects (staff and inmate)
Perimeter doors locked	Perimeter doors and internal doors locked
Uniforms (for students)	Uniforms (for correctional staff and inmates)
School resource officers	Correctional officers and counselors
Cameras to observe students	Cameras to observe inmate movements
Overcrowding	Overcrowding

HOMEROOM TEACHER OR SCHOOL RESOURCE OFFICER?

In the near future, high schools across the nation may see a shift in some teaching practices. If school violence continues, the traditional high school teacher might become almost "extinct," replaced by school resource officers with college degrees and teaching credentials in dual roles. These officers will come to work in uniforms and teach in their respective areas of expertise while simultaneously providing security for the school.

Is America trying to protect children more than educating them? With more emphasis on safety and security and less and less emphasis on academics, the future could be bleak. It became apparent in the 1990s, that the wave of violence in public schools had distorted the mission of the educational system and academics have taken a back seat to safety—albeit necessary.

Security in the public schools will continue to be of concern to parents, students, teachers, and school administrators in the years ahead. A high school in South Carolina was to begin requiring students to carry their books and school supplies in transparent backpacks. School officials adopted the requirement to reduce the chance of student-initiated violence (Flash and Robinson, 1999, p. A–1). This school also was to lock more doors and move the attendance office to the front of the school to prevent strangers from moving around the school.

The federal publication *Early Warning Timely Response: A Guide to Safe Schools* (U.S. Department of Education, 1998) suggests these practices to increase physical safety:

1. Supervising access to the building and grounds.
2. Reducing class size and school size.
3. Adjusting scheduling to minimize time in the hallways and in potentially dangerous locations. Traffic-flow patterns can be modified to limit potential for conflicts or altercations.
4. Conducting a building safety audit in consultation with school security personnel and/or law enforcement experts.
5. Closing school campuses during lunch periods.

6. Adopting a school policy on uniforms.

7. Arranging supervision at critical times (for example, in hallways between classes) and having a plan to deploy supervisory staff to areas where incidents are likely to occur.

8. Prohibiting students from congregating in areas where they are likely to engage in rule breaking or intimidating and aggressive behaviors.

9. Having adults visibly present throughout the school building. This includes encouraging parents to visit the school.

10. Staggering dismissal times and lunch periods.

11. Monitoring the surrounding school grounds including landscaping, parking lots, and bus stops.

12. Coordinating with local police to ensure that there are safe routes to and from school (p. 20).

The National School Safety Center (1999) advocates the increased use of peer counseling programs to change the attitudes of youths about violence. Peer helpers would receive training in conflict-resolution skills and empathic listening. Troubled students, therefore, could approach a peer helper to talk about their problems.

This concept has been applied at the Granada Hills High School in California. This school has a Peer Assistance Center where students can talk with peers or trained counselors. The Center is

> a place where a student can get information, counseling or referral regarding alcohol and drug use, child abuse, coping with adult authority, death and dying, divorce and separation within the family, dropping out, improving family communication, family concerns, financial problems, gang violence, handling an emotional crisis, health issues, legal problems, loneliness and friendship, peer pressure, prejudice and discrimination, relationship difficulties and dating, and running away (p. 17).

In an interview, Dr. Sidney Hopkins, Ph.D., Director of Middle/Secondary Education for the Kershaw County School District in Camden, South Carolina, was asked his opinion concerning at-risk youth in the school environment (see p. 154). He points out that the characteristics of a teacher working with at-risk students include sensitivity, honesty, interest and concern, treatment as an individual, and fairness.

In the publication *Preventing Chaos in Times of Crisis* (Association of California School Administrators, 1995), school administrators were advised to develop a crisis management plan for crisis situations that might arise. Experts warned that "an unprepared school is asking for chaos" (p. 4).

This publication points out important items that must be included in a crisis-management plan. For instance, who is to be in charge during a crisis? In a school, the principal or vice principal generally takes this role. The school leader must decide who will be part of the crisis-response team. This team

Dr. Sidney Hopkins, Director of Middle and Secondary Education for Kershaw County, was interviewed on May 5, 2000 in Camden, South Carolina.

Question: What characteristics do you look for in selecting persons to work with at-risk youth?

Answer: O. H. Mower at the University of Illinois conducted research on the characteristics of teachers to motivate students. He concluded that the ability of the teacher to motivate students was related to the degree to which the student felt the teacher had affection for the student. This characteristic was labeled the hope effect. To answer the question, teachers who have this trait will display the following:

1. Treat the student with respect and commit valuing behaviors:
   - Calling him by name
   - Attributing positive verbal statements to the student
   - Assisting the student when asked
   - Reinforcing appropriate behavior positively

2. The teacher will take interest in the student's total life, not just his academic work. This should be manifested by:
   - Showing concern for the student's feelings
   - Knowing something about his or her family
   - Discussing the student's hobbies, recreational activities, and interests
   - Providing curricular materials that might support these interests

3. The teacher will relate to the student as an individual, and not as a member of a group. This characteristic will be manifested by:
   - Knowing the student's birthday
   - Having knowledge of the student's career interests
   - Discussing the student's aspirations for higher education
   - Assisting the student with his/her needs
   - Showing interest in his/her relationship with others

> 4. The teacher is completely honest in assessing the student's progress by:
>   - Providing instructional feedback on individual student work, as opposed to judgmental feedback
>   - Avoiding the use of positive assessment to encourage the student when actual performance may not be quality work
>   - Providing an explanation of how to improve instructional performance and give concrete examples
>   - Continuing always to exhibit confidence in the student's ability

might consist of an administrator, a nurse, a psychologist or social worker, teachers, a counselor, and support staff. The police liaison must be a member, too. The team must be trained and aware of policies and procedures. It should establish a code (phrase or word) to be used over the public address system to alert the staff of a crisis in the school.

Experts advise crisis response teams to hold practice sessions. These role-plays help everyone "to become aware of potential problems and discuss how to respond to them" (1995, p. 6).

WHAT MIGHT SCHOOLS LOOK LIKE IN THE FUTURE?

The highly controlled environment of many public schools lately might only be the beginning of what may be seen in the future. Schools might become more militaristic, or at least continue to evolve in the direction of the penal system with the goal of student compliance and discipline. For parents who fear the victimization of their children, the future may hold more students being taught at home—once again repeating history with many home-schooled children.

In addition to these possible changes, that more military schools might be built, and enrollment may increase significantly in existing military-type academic institutions. This type of institution ensures compliance and self-discipline, which parents want to have instilled in their child. But is this the right direction for the future of education and schools? Some say that it is not.

In an article entitled "Saving the Nation's Most Precious Resources: Our Children" Dr. Gene Stephens (1997) points out the need to expand effective programs in the future. An example is the Community Schools Programs in which the objective is to effectively break the cycle of violence and frustration that many youths experience. This federal initiative has helped keep 675 schools open for extra hours in Missouri, assisted the Boys and Girls Clubs in New Jersey to offer

Dr. Gene Stephens

mentoring programs in public schools, and provided Safe Haven programs in New York City for after-school tutoring and enrichment.

Dr. Stephens also believes character education in schools can help youths learn values such as fairness, tolerance, responsibility, and love. He reports that "schools with large numbers of at-risk youth have reported pregnancy and dropout rates cut in half, along with reduced fights and suspensions, after character education took hold" (p. 56).

If polls are valid, character education is needed. Will Lester (1999) reported, "the Littleton shootings increased the numbers that thought life was worse for teens, from 52 percent before the violence to 61 percent just after" (p. A3).

Howell (1999) stated:

> If students cannot read well by the end of the third grade, their chances for later scholastic success are greatly diminished—including a greater likelihood of delinquent behavior and dropping out of school. Dropping out of high school manifests serious, negative, long-term consequences for youths (p. 26).

Deputy Commissioner Joyce Burrell of the Division of Juvenile Justice Services in Philadelphia developed an Adopt-a-School partnership program between her staff and an elementary school in West Philadelphia. The partnership seeks to help children in the West Philadelphia community read well and independently by the end of third grade. To accomplish this, the staff provides one-on-one reading support to third-graders weekly. More programs like this one are needed to increase the chances for success among youth and divert children from the criminal justice system.

Dwyer (1999) addressed the need to have more school psychologists to deal with the emotional problems of troubled youth, reporting that

> national statistics point out that any school of 1,500 can expect to have 195 students who have serious emotional and/or drug problems, which block success and increase feelings of hopelessness. Without help, as many as 56 percent drop out and become adult problems—some underemployed or on welfare (p. 15A).

Schools need the necessary staff to assist students who have emotional problems. The ratio of one school psychologist per 3,000 students must be improved if schools are to have a chance to help troubled youth.

It goes without saying that any adult who is to be hired to run a program involving youth must be well qualified. The agency hiring this person assumes a great deal of responsibility. A careful background check is necessary to assure that applicants have the proper academic background, have no criminal history, have no drug problems, and are highly recommended by previous employers.

Kratcoski (2000) points out the many skills a person who assists individuals in their efforts to solve their problems must possess. Two of the important skills are listening and feedback. Listening is defined as

> receiving messages from a client by focusing attention on what the client is expressing, both verbally and nonverbally. Feedback is the verbal or nonverbal response that the counselor makes as a result of processing the information received from listening to a client (2000, p. 559).

If those administering a program do not have the ability to listen to troubled youth and provide feedback, they will not be successful.

Another major skill in working with youth is trust. Trojanowicz and Morash (1992) state that "it is essential to develop a basis of trust between the therapist and the youngster" (p. 286). Goleman (1997) describes the effective therapist as someone with interpersonal intelligence and defines interpersonal intelligence as "the ability to understand other people: what motivates them, how they work, and how to work cooperatively with them" (p. 39).

Legislatures of the future are admonished to increase funding for school districts to reduce class size. Viadero (1999) reported on the benefits of students' experience in smaller classrooms, writing:

> The data show that even by the end of 12th grade, years after returning to larger classes, students who were in small classes early in their school careers tended to drop out less frequently, to take more challenging courses, and to be more inclined toward college than were their counterparts from larger classes (p. 5).

She also found in her research that Blacks from smaller classes opted to take college-entrance exams at a higher rate than their counterparts from larger classes.

GANG INFLUENCES IN THE FUTURE

Although large cities and lower-class neighborhoods have long been concerned with gang activity, all areas are becoming increasingly concerned with these gangs. The 1990s saw a transition stage of gang activity, gang sophistication, and gang recruitment. Unlike previous generations of gangsters, new "gangsters" stretched across all economic and class lines. Much of this change can be attributed to the advances in technology and the lower-class people's struggle to keep pace with the evolving technological world.

Computers have made access to potential gang members lucrative and will continue to be a tool utilized in this millennium. With the traditional family fading and the number of single-parent families rising, unsupervised children are at the mercy of gang recruiters. Looking for a sense of belonging, purpose, identity, and their place in the world, these unsupervised children become easy prey. As America continues into an uncertain time, emphasis on traditional gangs is steadily giving way to other groups that threaten communities as much, if not more so, than the traditional gangs such as the Bloods and Crips. In the future, communities will be exposed to groups that are much more violent than the traditional gang.

HATE GROUPS AND CULT ACTIVITY

Violent subcultures have been around for quite some time, masked by the attention to traditional gangs. The "backdoor" approach that some groups take is of most concern as they prey on children's' weaknesses and belief system. Children who are struggling with their religious beliefs are easy prey for Satanic groups, and those that oppose the general idea of governmental authority, may be targets of hate or militant groups. Although these groups are small, they have a tendency to be highly organized and in the future will play a role in societal problems.

According to Floyd Cochran (1999), a former Aryan Nation member, the real threat of hate groups is that they most often emphasize a leaderless group. The hate group simply directs the interested individual to information that supports the group's beliefs. Once this has been achieved, individuals can take the information and principles and apply them to their own way of thinking and lifestyle. Cochran predicted that the future will see fewer hate crimes committed by groups and more by individuals who follow a set of beliefs and act alone. One example of this is the shooting at a Jewish Community Center in Los Angeles in August of 1999. The man apprehended was an unofficial member of the Aryan Nations, a White Supremacy group. The group denied any connection to him.

EXTINCTION OF THE "JUVENILE"

U.S. society has witnessed several negative transitions in its juvenile population. From children who played in the neighborhood and participated in youth groups or Scouts, to the kids who looked forward to watching cartoons every Saturday morning, many youths have degenerated to the point that they are doing time in the adult penal system. More and more youths are being held fully accountable for their actions and adult-type crimes. Penitentiaries across the country are seeing more "throw-away kids" incarcerated for extended periods.

The future probably will see an increase in get-tough laws to deal with troubled youths. Haven (1999) wrote,

Teens caught smoking in South Dakota can be fined once for every cigarette they light up, as can the merchant who sold them the pack. Louisiana passed a law that makes students in kindergarten through fifth grade address teachers with a courtesy title such as "sir" or "ma'am." Also, students in Maryland who plant bombs or make bomb threats can lose their drivers' licenses (p. 11A).

Society is increasingly becoming less tolerant of juvenile crime, but is society's intolerance and meting out of harsh punishments really the answer? Many believe that the brutal environment of the penal system can only produce a resentful, more violent, and ruthless youthful population upon their release. Although the justice system sends a clear message to the rest of society that violent crime by any segment of its population will not be tolerated, the future may be more volatile if the masses allow this merger of juvenile with adult accountability. In the past, juveniles were to be rehabilitated within the justice system with the hope that they would some day contribute to society and become productive taxpayers as adults. Has society lost sight of this once dominant philosophy? Many practitioners argue "no," but the number of juvenile waivers to the adult court continues to increase despite the decline in violent juvenile crime (Snyder, 1999).

DURKHEIM, SOCIAL POSITIVISM, AND THE FUTURE

As society changes, so does the fluctuation in types and seriousness of crimes. According to Emile Durkheim's version of social positivism, crime is a part of human nature because it has existed in every age, in times of both poverty and prosperity. Even if "real" crimes were eliminated, Durkheim believes that human differences will exist and continue as an inevitable part of the future. He argues that crime is healthy for society because it provides a doorway for social change.

On the other hand, if crime did not exist, we could assume that people are like creatures behaving in the same manner. People, therefore, would totally agree on what is right and wrong, making society rigid and not subject to change. Another problem for a society that is free of crime and has like belief systems is it would lack creativity and independent thinking (Siegel, 1998). In Durkheim's social positivistic view, crime also is beneficial because it calls attention to social ills. A rising crime rate can signal the need for social change and promote a variety of programs designed to relieve the human suffering that may have caused crime in the first place (p.11).

With all of this in mind, it is critical to produce quality research concerning juvenile crime in the twenty-first century. The manipulation of data or unethical research practices will have little to contribute to society when the United States needs it the most. If Durkheim is correct in that crime is a cue for the need to change, society should adapt to the ever-dynamic elements of life and actively seek solutions to social ills.

THE AMERICAN WAY

The American way of life was built on freedom, the Bill of Rights, and the Constitution of the United States. The sad fact about crime in this democratic society is that no amount of tinkering, no amount of prison construction or amendments to penal codes will solve the crime problem. This is so for a number of reasons. In the first place, the United States cannot and will not adopt truly savage, draconian measures. As a hypothetical example, the death penalty might be a deterrent if used as Hitler or Stalin did, with utter ruthlessness and speed. If America were to routinely cut off the hands of thieves, this might stop thievery (Friedman, 1993).

Obviously, these methods of punishment are inconceivable in modern-day America. Cutting off hands is out of the question, and as far as the death penalty is concerned, it takes years to move an individual from court to death row to appellate court to execution.

THE PRICE OF DEMOCRACY

The United States has always taken pride in its status as a free society. Americans are able to elect public officials and monitor their progress and, if not satisfied with their performance, vote them out in the next election. Americans have the freedom of speech and religion and all the other rights and privileges protected by the Bill of Rights. In countries such as China and other dictator-led countries, crime is fairly low. Citizens of these countries fear reprisal for unlawful actions, and when caught stepping outside of the strict law of the land, they are punished harshly. Is it possible that a byproduct of a free society is crime?

The United States has been a society that traditionally has accepted the differences in people, their beliefs, and lifestyles. As a result of this freedom, and freedom of choice, crimes at all levels of seriousness have plagued society. Over the years, the government has attempted to regain some control of the population it governs and maintain a sense of order. As a result, gun control, drug laws, and juvenile violent crime legislation have been at the forefront of much legislation in the recent past.

The future of government intervention, as in the past, probably will be driven by societal tragedies such as the string of the school shootings in the 1990s. Crime in the twenty-first century and beyond is inevitable. Stopping crime entirely is unrealistic. Although it cannot be "cured," the problem of crime can be controlled. The history of American society paints a picture that includes violence and lawlessness, and the new millennium will be no different. As a result, the shift from a cure for crime to crime control is a realistic goal of intervention.

WHAT ABOUT THE FAMILY?

To assist schools in dealing with students who have anger and conflict problems there will be a need for more parent-involvement programs in the future. The Educational

Research Service (1999) believes parent involvement can consist of "parent-teacher conferences, parent-friendly support, family education, and parent workshops. Parent involvement is a critical component of a schoolwide effort to help students constructively manage anger and conflict (p. 10)." To be successful, parent-teacher conferences have to be friendly and open. Parent-friendly support can be improved by orientation programs that encourage parent involvement. Family education teaches parents about school support systems that are available to them, as well as ways to nurture a child's learning at home. Parent workshops might cover topics such as discipline, communication skills, self-esteem, and substance abuse.

Since 1966, the Center for the Study and Prevention of Violence (CSPV) at the University of Colorado at Boulder has been identifying juvenile violence-prevention programs that have been effective. Some of these programs are discussed in *OJJDP Fact Sheet* "Blueprints: A Violence Prevention Initiative" (Office of Juvenile Justice and Delinquency Prevention, 1999). Some of the unique programs are:

- The *Life Skills Training program* is a 3-year primary prevention with a goal of preventing junior high and middle school students from getting involved with the use of cigarettes, alcohol, and marijuana.

- The *Functional Family Therapy* (FFT) program is designed to motivate youths and families to change their communication, interaction, and problem-solving patterns. This technique has been successful even with youths with serious criminal offenses such as theft or aggravated assault.

- The *Bullying Prevention Program* is a special school-based program with a goal of restructuring the school environment to reduce opportunities and rewards for bullying behavior by elementary and secondary school children.

- The *Prenatal and Infancy Nurse Home Visitation Program* sends nurses into the homes of at-risk pregnant women bearing their first child. The goal is to ensure the health of the mother and child. Parents also learn useful parenting skills for the prenatal period to 2 years after the child's birth.

- *Quantum Opportunities* assists disadvantaged teens from poor families. The program provides educational, developmental, and service activities. The goal is to help these kids graduate from high school and attend college by improving their basic academic skills.

GOVERNMENT INTERVENTION

Another fundamental question for the future is what role government is to play. Many want the government, at all levels, to increase spending on programs to prevent violence at the community level as well as the school level.

Additional funds could be used to establish more after-school programs to include tutoring and character education. If more money is available to school districts, classroom size might be reduced and students can receive more individualized attention. Extra funds also could establish additional Youth Corps programs.

Some citizens who believe more funds are needed to increase the prosecution of violent youths. They promote get-tough laws as the way to curb the tide of violence. Others think parents who abuse their children should be prosecuted more harshly.

Recent school shootings also have increased the cry for more funding for school security. This might include hiring additional deputies and purchasing more metal detectors to screen individuals for weapons.

Some scientists believe the behavior of teenagers can be explained by brain development and urge more funding for research in this area. According to Brownless (1999), recent research has showed that most young teenagers don't yet have all the brain power they need to make good judgments (p. 48) and "the vast majority of kids will make it through adolescence with few permanent scars" (p. 54).

INDIVIDUAL RESPONSIBILITY

Some citizens believe the answers cannot be found by throwing money at youth problems. They say the answer lies in the accepting individual responsibility. Parents should strive to instill individual responsibility in their children and teach them right from wrong. Schools should not have to assume the duties of parents.

Another important influence is that of the church. Churches are seen as developers of morals for teens. Church leaders are urged to sponsor activities for youth in their community, such as scouting and athletic events. Youths also should be given the opportunity to give back to their communities. One example of a good project for youths is repairing homes for the elderly who cannot afford to make these improvements. Also, the feeling is that youths who associate with church-going peers will be less likely to get involved in gang activities.

COMBINATION APPROACHES

Maybe the final solution will be found in a combination of government intervention and individual responsibility, resulting in secure schools with students who accept individual responsibility. Schools that have too few teachers and inadequate facilities will not succeed. Schools that serve children whose parents do not care about them will not succeed. But schools that have teachers and administrators who care and parents and students who care will not fail.

JUVENILE JUSTICE IN THE FUTURE

A final factor that must be considered in the context of juvenile violence is the continued need in the United States for a separate juvenile justice system. The increase in juvenile violence in schools and on the streets has caused the juvenile system to shift closer and closer to the adult system. The line separating the two court systems is blurred in many states and more and more juveniles are being tried as adults (Pope, 1995).

The twenty-first century probably will continue to see a separate juvenile justice system. The major reason is not related to the need or effectiveness of a juvenile system but rather, the tradition of having this system in place and the problems in having to dismantle the system. The juvenile court of the next decade probably will be different from what was functioning in the 1990s, though. The court of the future probably will be more punitive as a reaction to public demands for get-tough policies. This may result in more and more juveniles being waived to adult courts, and thus receiving adult punishments (Pope, 1995).

If present trends continue, the juvenile court of the future will see more minorities placed in secure public facilities while Whites will more often be placed in diversion programs in private facilities. Demographics will play some role, as present trends show the White birthrate decreasing, while the minority birthrate is drastically increasing (Pope, 1995).

Social and school disturbances have been shown to relate to lower socioeconomic status. In the contemporary school setting, these young people usually are considered at risk. Economics will continue to influence at-risk populations. The past decade has seen the erosion of many industrial jobs and entry-level positions. The United States has seen a large service-based economy with lower wages and unskilled labor. These changes have placed the underclass in a relatively disadvantaged position. This isolation probably will continue to produce children who experience different outcomes and behaviors. Living in this fashion often produces children who have to be more concerned with survival than education and self-improvement. Many of these children will become clients of the juvenile justice system (Pope, 1995).

In the twenty-first century, there probably will be a continued interest in developing a fair and equitable juvenile justice system. But many of the problems of juvenile delinquency cannot be solved by this system. Solutions have to be developed before a child enters the juvenile justice system. This was true in the 1990s and will continue to be so in the future. Only by attending to social and economic problems that force children into the system can the United States hope to have an impact on this problem (Pope, 1995).

RECOMMENDATIONS FOR THE FUTURE

Possible recommendations for future efforts can be divided into four categories: (1) recommendations for the larger society, (2) recommendations for parents, (3) recommendations for schools, and (4) recommendations for further research and investigation.

Recommendations for the Larger Society

The recommendations for society center on informed decision-making and involvement with youths.

1. Concrete research on juvenile violence, especially school disturbance, is lacking. Research and factual information will result in informed concern rather than the overexaggeration that sometimes has been accompanied by panic and fear.

2. Individuals can make a difference in the lives of juveniles by becoming involved in their local schools. These people go beyond parents to concerned citizens in all walks of life.

3. Social institutions must continue to generate meaningful activities for youths, as most experts agree that there would be less violence in schools and society if there were more positive things for young people to do.

Recommendations for Parents

A second category of research recommendations is that of parental responsibilities and opportunities.

1. Parents need to become more involved in their child's lives. To succeed, students must feel that they have support from their families.

2. Parents need to know what their children are involved in—school activities, peers, and neighborhood associates.

Recommendations for Schools

A third area for research recommendations is in the schools themselves.

1. Teachers need to be more accessible to students. Students must feel comfortable in talking with school personnel about their school-related and personal problems.

2. Schools must target certain groups for special juvenile delinquency prevention efforts: students who have been victims of violence, are minorities, or of lower socioeconomic status.

3. Students must not be treated like numbers. They must be given as much individual attention as possible.

4. Students must understand the impact of violence and the long-lasting consequences it can have on their lives and the lives of others.

5. Schools should strive to increase students' success. Students who do not achieve in school (getting mostly C's, D's, and F's) and those who have been victims of violent incidents sometime in their school life are more frequently involved in confrontation.

6. Schools must offer a disciplined environment. Because tracking leads to discipline problems for students in low-ability groups, eliminating this practice might help to dispel the problem. Other helpful measures include smaller schools, self-contained classes, and teacher involvement beyond the classroom.

7. Alternative schools are a good option in some cases, especially in communicating a caring attitude and more individual attention.

8. Student suspension does not seem to be a successful disciplinary measure; in-school alternatives seem to offer a better solution for less serious offenders.

9. School principals who focus on instructional leadership and interpersonal relationships, and involve teachers in planning, are more successful in reducing discipline problems, in addition to increasing the level of student achievement.

Recommendations for Further Research and Investigation

A fourth area consists of recommendations for scholarly research and investigation into the problem of juvenile violence, as follows:

1. Study of the relationship between drug use and juvenile violence should be continued.

2. The effect of improved curriculum and instruction on school disturbance should be studied.

3. The effect of school atmosphere and teacher attitudes upon school disturbance and juvenile violence is another prime topic for study.

4. Research should continue to determine what efforts the society can make to assist families, communities, and schools in being more effective.

5. Study should be directed to procedures by which schools and communities inform the larger society of juvenile violence problems and soliciting support in counteracting them.

6. Ways to improve communication among teachers, students, and parents require continued study.

Experts such as Peter C. Kratcosk (2000) believes that "the treatment counselor, in addition to having training in various treatment techniques, is called upon to act as a service broker, that is the person who discovers and links those in need of specific services with the exact agency in the community that can provide services most efficiently and effectively" (p. 668).

CONCLUSION

As Americans strive to deal with juvenile violence in the future, research will be needed to provide more insight into the causes of violence afflicting so many of America's young people, and the means of preventing them. Although the roots of these ills may be deeply imbedded in society, families, schools, and communities can be well positioned to reduce the type and extent of juvenile violence. Armed with an understanding of the complex linkage among the factors that put children at risk, focusing on the related protective factors that may shelter children from these risks, and drawing on strong family and community involvement, the United States can offer healthy environments that will be the strongest defense against juvenile violence.

ABOUT THE AUTHORS

Dr. Gordon A. Crews is an Associate Professor and Department Head of Criminal Justice at Jacksonville State University, Jacksonville, Alabama. He serves on the Board of Directors for the Southern Criminal Justice Association and speaks nationally on issues surrounding school violence and juvenile delinquency. He earned a Ph.D. in Education/Criminal Justice, a Graduate Certificate in Alcohol and Drug Studies, and a Bachelor of Science and Masters degrees in Criminal Justice from the University of South Carolina.

Prior to teaching, Dr. Crews worked in law enforcement as a bloodhound officer and trainer, field-training officer, and criminal investigator; in corrections as a training and accreditation manager; and in insurance fraud as an investigator.

His publications include journal articles dealing with school violence, occult and Satanic involvement by youths, and various law enforcement issues. Books he has authored include *Faces of Violence in America* (Simon & Schuster), *The Evolution of School Disturbance in America: Colonial Times to Modern Day* (Praeger), and *A History of Correctional Violence: An Examination of Reported Causes of Riots and Disturbances* (American Correctional Association). Dr. Crews lives with his wife, Pamela, and their two children, Garrison and Samantha, in Jacksonville, Alabama.

Dr. Reid H. Montgomery, Jr. is an Associate Professor and Graduate Director in the College of Criminal Justice, University of South Carolina. He joined the University after service as a federal probation officer with the U.S. District Court in Washington, DC, under Chief Judge John J. Sirica. Prior to graduate study, he served on active duty with the Third Infantry (Old Guard) at Ft. Myer, Virginia. He earned the Bachelor of Science, Master of Education, and Ph.D. from the University of South Carolina, where his dissertation analyzed attitudes leading to prison riots.

In 1984, Dr. Montgomery was named as Educator of the Year by the Southern Association of Criminal Justice Educators. He has pursued postdoctoral study at George Washington University in Washington, DC. He also has co-authored six books: *Federal Probation in Practice, Probation and Parole in Practice* (two editions), *Prison Violence in America* (two editions), and *A History of Correctional Violence: An Examination of Reported Causes of Riots and Disturbances.*

CONTRIBUTING WRITERS

Dr. Steven Dillingham, Ph.D., LL.M., serves as Special Counsel to the U.S. House of Representatives, Subcommittee on Criminal Justice, Drug Policy and Human Resources. He also has served as Special Counsel for Criminal Law for the U.S. Senate Judiciary Committee. Dr. Dillingham has held senior legal, policy, and management positions in several federal agencies, including the U.S. Department of Justice. While at the Department of Justice, he was appointed by the President to the position of Director of the Bureau of Justice Statistics. He also has served as a legal advisor and manager for a major corporation.

Dr. Dillingham served on the faculty of the University of South Carolina and has taught law and policy courses at George Mason University. He has authored and contributed to numerous criminal justice articles and books. He received his Juris Doctorate Ph.D. from the University of South Carolina, and the LL.M. from Georgetown University.

Jeffrey Allen Tipton, MCJ, is currently employed with the South Carolina Department of Public Safety in the Office of Justice Programs as a Juvenile Justice Program Coordinator. His educational accomplishments include: Who's Who Among Students in American Junior Colleges, National Dean's List, Golden Key National Honor Society, and Alpha Phi Sigma, the national criminal justice honors organization. Prior to teaching, Mr. Tipton was enlisted in the military as a Reservist and worked as a Juvenile Correctional Officer in Virginia prior to pursuing graduate study. His current research interests include youth gangs, causes of juvenile delinquency, cult and Satanic groups, school violence, and ethics in criminal justice and juvenile corrections.

REFERENCES

Abadinsky, H. (1997). Probation and Parole Theory and Practice. Upper Saddle River, NJ: Prentice Hall.

Advocate Seeks End to Violence in Youth Prisons. (2000). *The State* (Columbia, SC), Jan. 20.

Agnew, R. (1994). The Techniques of Neutralization and Violence. *Criminology*, 32(4), pp. 555–568.

Albanese, J. S. (1996). *Dealing with Delinquency: The Future of Juvenile Justice*. Chicago: Nelson Hall Publishers.

Allen, H. A., Splittgerber, F. L., & Manning, M. L. (1993). *Teaching and Learning in the Middle Level School*. New York: Macmillan.

"Alternatives to Incarceration." (1999). National Juvenile Justice Conference. Washington, DC.

Altman, J., & Ziporyn, M. (1967). *Born to Raise Hell*. New York: Grove Press.

Anti-Defamation League. (1998). *Report Cites Neo-Nazi National Alliance as Most Dangerous Organized Hate Group in America*. Washington, DC: Author. http://www.adl.org

Applebome, P. (1995). For the Ultimate Safe School, Eyes Turn to Dallas. *New York Times*, Feb. 20, B11.

Arciaga, M. (1999). *Gothic Gang Update*. Salt Lake City: Salt Lake Area Gang Project.

Association of California School Administrators. (1995). *Preventing Chaos in Times of Crisis*. Sacramento, CA: Author.

Baldwin, J., & Garry, E. M. (1997, April). *Mentoring: A Proven Delinquency Prevention Strategy (Juvenile Justice Bulletin)*. Washington, DC: Office of Juvenile Justice and Delinquency Prevention.

Ballard, C. (1999) Violence Prevention in Georgia's Rural Public School Systems: Perceptions of School Superintendents. *Southern Rural Sociology*, 14, pp. 91–109.

Bandura, A., & Walters, R. H. (1963). *Social Learning and Personality Development*. New York: Holt, Rinehart and Winston.

Barnes, H. E. (1972). *The Story of Punishment* (2d ed.). Montclair, NJ: Patterson Smith.

Barton, B. (1990). *The Secret Life of a Satanist: The Authorized Biography of Anton LaVey*. Los Angeles: Feral House.

Bastian, L., & Taylor, B. (1991). *School Crime: A National Crime Victimization Survey Report*. Washington, DC: Bureau of Justice Statistics.

Batton, S. R., Hill, K. G., Abbott, R. D., Catalano, R. F., & Hawkins, J. D. (1998). The Contribution of Gang Membership to Delinquency Beyond Delinquent Friends. *Criminology*, 32(4), pp. 102–132.

Benedetto, R. (1999). Blame is Placed on Parents, Media. *USA Today*, April 22, p. 3A.

Berger, K. S. (1994). *The Developing Person Through the Lifespan*. New York: Holt, Rinehart and Winston.

Bromley, D. G. (1991, May/June). The Satanic Cult Scare. *Society Transaction*, pp. 55–66.

Brooks, B. D. (1993). *School Safety*. Rockville, MD: National Institute of Justice.

Browning, K., & Huzinga, D. (1999, April). *Highlights of Findings from the Denver Youth Survey*. Washington, DC: Office of Juvenile Justice and Delinquency Prevention.

Brownless, S. (1999). Inside the Teen Brain. *U.S. News and World Report*, Aug. 4, pp. 44–54.

Buckland, R. (1990). *Buckland's Complete Book of Witchcraft*. St. Paul, MN: Llewellyn Publications

Bumpass, L. (1990). What's Happening to the American Family? *Interactions Between Demographic and Institutional Change. Demography*, 27, pp. 483–493.

Bureau of the Census. (1992). *Statistical Abstracts of the United States*. Washington, DC: U.S. Department of Commerce.

Bureau of Justice Statistics. (1991). *Special Report: Women in Prison*. Washington, DC: U.S. Department of Justice.

Bureau of Justice Statistics. (1993). *Special Analysis*. Washington, DC: U.S. Department of Justice.

Bureau of Justice Statistics. (1994). *Murder in Families*. Washington, DC: U.S. Department of Justice.

Bureau of Justice Statistics. (1994, Aug.). *Partnerships to Prevent Youth Violence*. Washington, DC: U.S. Department of Justice.

Burgan, L., & Rubel, R. (1980). Public School Security: Yesterday, Today and Tomorrow. *Contemporary Education*, 52, pp. 34–39.

Butterfield, F. (1995). *All God's Children, the Boskey Family and the American Tradition of Violence*. New York: Avon Books.

Buttress, P. (February, 1999). "Finding God's Love—Weekend Retreat Helps Juvenile Detainees Overcome Difficult Times in Their Lives." *The State*. Columbia, SC.

Butts, R. F., & Cremin, L. A. (1953). *History of Education in American Culture*. New York: Holt, Rinehart and Winston.

Carnegie Council on Adolescent Development. (1994). *Turning Points, Preparing American Youth for the 21st Century*. New York: Carnegie.

Carnegie Council on Adolescent Development. (1992). *A Matter of Time: Risk and Opportunity in the Nonschool Hours* (Report of Task Force on Youth Development and Community Programs). New York: Carnegie.

Carper, J. (1995). *School and the Social Order*. Unpublished manuscript, University of South Carolina: Columbia, South Carolina.

Chambliss, W., & Ryther, T. (1975). *Sociology: The Discipline and Its Direction*. New York: McGraw-Hill.

Charlier, T., & Downing, S. (1988). *Justice Abused: A 1980s Witch-Hunt*. Memphis, TN: Commercial Appeal.

The Charters and General laws of the Colony and Province of Massachusetts Bay. (1814). Boston: Massachusetts legislature.

Children of Divorce. *Methodist Health Care System Quarterly Magazine*. http://www.methodisthealth.com/health/family/chldivrc.htm

Chua-Eoan, H. (1999). Escaping from the Darkness. *Time Magazine*, 153(21), pp. 44–49.

Church of the Antichrist. www.the600club.com/sastanic-search

Church of Satan Homepage. http://www.churchofsatan.com/

Ciabattari, J. (1999). Teen Drinking on the Rise, *Parade Magazine*, Dec. 1999.

Clique of Gothics; Conflict Fueled Talk of Killings (1999). www.geocities.com/bourbon-street/2672/wisconsingothl.html

Cloud, J. (1999). Just a Routine School Shooting. *Time Magazine*, 153(21), pp. 44–49.

CNN Gallup Poll. (1994). 1993 Survey of 400 Parents. *USA Today*, Oct. 2, p. A1.

CNN Gallup Poll. (1999). *Poll: One-Third Teens Fear Copycat School Shootings*, April 30.

Cochran, F. (1999). CNN Live: Are Hate Groups Becoming More Violent? Aug. 13. (TV appearance).

Cohen, A., Lindesmith, A., & Schuessler, K. (Eds.). (1956). *The Sutherland Papers*. Bloomington: University of Indiana Press.

Collins, J. (1972). Jury Trial by a Jury of Teen Peers. *Insight*, 38, pp. 14–16.

Colorado Closes Down Juvenile Facility, Citing a Pattern of Violence. (1998). *Washington Post*, April 22.

Coordinating Council on Juvenile Justice and Delinquency Prevention. (1966). *Combating Violence and Delinquency: The National Juvenile Justice Action Plan*. Washington, DC: U.S. Government Printing Office.

Cremin, L. A. (1970). *American Education: The Colonial Experience 1607–1783*. New York: Harper & Row.

Crews, G. A., & Counts, M. R. (1997). *The Evolution of School Disturbance in America: Colonial Times to Modern Day*. Westport, CT: Praeger.

Crews, G. A., Montgomery, R. H., & Garris, W. R. (1996). *Faces of Violence in America*. Needham Heights, MA: Simon & Schuster.

Crossen-Tower, C. (1999). *Understanding Child Abuse and Neglect* (4th ed.). Needham Heights, MA: Allyn & Bacon.

Crowe, T. D. (1991). Safer Schools by Design. *Security Management*, 35, pp. 81–86.

Curcio, J. L., & First, P. F. (1993). *Violence in the Schools: How to Proactively Prevent and Defuse It*. Newbury Park, CA: Sage Publications.

Czajkoski, E. H. (1992, Sept.). Criminalizing Hate: An Empirical Assessment. *Federal Probation*, 56(3), pp. 36–40.

Donmoyer, R., & Kos, R. (Eds. (1993). *At-risk Students: Portraits, Policies, Programs, and Practices*. New York: State University of New York.

Douglass, A. A. (1940). *The American School System: A Survey of the Principles and Practices of Education*. New York: Farrar and Rinehart.

Driver, G. R., & Miles, J. C. (1968). *The Babylonian Laws*. Oxford, England: Clareondon Press.

Drowns, R., & Hess, K. (1990). *Juvenile Justice*. New York: West Publishing.

Druidism Guide Page. www.uoguelph.ca/~bmyers/druid/

Dwyer, K. (1999). Troubled Students Lack Easy Access to Adults and Psychologists. *USA Today*, June 30, p. 15A.

Elias, M. J., Lantieri, L., & Patti, J. (1999). Violence Is Preventable. *Education Week*, 18(36), May 19.

Elkind, D. (1984). *All Grown Up and No Place To Go: Teenagers in Crisis*. Reading, MA: Addison Wesley.

Fagan, J. (1990). Social Processes of Delinquency and Drug Use Among Urban Gangs. Gangs. *Gangs in America* (C. Ronald Huff, Ed.). Newbury Park, CA: Sage Publications, pp. 183–219.

Fagan, J., & Forst, M. (1996, March). Risks, Fixers, and Zeal: Implementing Experimental Treatments for Violent Juvenile Offenders. *Prison Journal, 76*(1), pp. 22–59.

Fegelman, A. (1996). School Gun Check Upheld. *Chicago Tribune*, Feb. 27, p. 1.

Fields, G. (1999). Administration Releases Plan to Cut Drug Use in Half. *USA Today*, Feb. 9, p. 7A.

Finding God's Love—Weekend Retreat Helps Juvenile Detainees Overcome Difficult Times in Their Lives. (1999). *The State* (Columbia, SC), Feb. 26.

Fine, G. A., & Victor, F. (1994). *Desegregation in American Schools: Comparative Intervention Strategies*. New York: Praeger Publishing.

Fitts, W., & Hammer, W. T. (1969). The Self-Concept and Delinquency. Nashville, TN: Counselor and Recording Tests.

Flach, T., & Robinson, B. (1999). School Requires Clear Backpacks. *The State* (Columbia, SC), July 15, A-1.

Foley, D. (1990, May). Danger: School Zone. *Teacher Magazine*, pp. 57–63.

Friedman, L. M. (1993). *Crime and Punishment in American History*. New York: Basic Books.

GA Teens Face Charges Over Gang-Related Web Site. (1999). *The State* (Columbia, SC), March 22, p. A4.

Garrin, L., & Furman, W., (1989). Age Differences in Adolescents' Perception of Their Peer Group. *Developmental Psychology, 25*, pp. 825–834.

Glass, A. J. (1999). New Tools Coming to Help Parents Protect Kids on Internet. *The State* (Columbia, SC), May 6, p. A3.

Glasser, W. (1978). Disorders in Our Schools: Causes and remedies. *Phi Delta Kappan, 59*, pp. 331–333.

Glick, B., & Goldstein, A. P. (1995). Juvenile Delinquency in America. New York: Allyn & Bacon.

Goals 2000: Educate America Act. (1993). Washington, DC: U.S. Government Printing Office.

Goldstein, A., Apter, B., & Harootunian (1984). *School Violence*. Englewood Cliffs, NJ: Prentice Hall.

Goleman, D. (1997). *Emotional Intelligence*. New York: Bantam Books.

Gore Announces $18 Billion Strategy for Controlling Drugs, *The State* (Columbia, SC), Feb. 9, 1999, p. A12.

Goth Primer. (1999). lexicon.psy.tufts.edu/gothic/primer.html

Greenbaum, T., Gonzales, R., & Ackley, J. (1989). *Student Views*. Sacramento, CA: State Department of Education.

Greenwood, P. W. (1999, Feb.). Costs and Benefits of Early Childhood Intervention. *OJJDP Fact Sheet*. Washington, DC: Office of Juvenile Justice and Delinquency Prevention.

Grossman, J. B., & Gary, E. M. (April, 1997). "Mentoring—A Proven Delinquency Prevention Strategy." *Juvenile Justice Bulletin*. Washington, DC: Office of Juvenile Justice and Delinquency Prevention: U.S. Department of Justice.

Haan, A. (1961). *Elementary School Curriculum: Theory and Research*. Boston: Allyn & Bacon.

Hamilton, S. F. (1990). *Apprenticeship for Adulthood*. New York: Free Press.

Hanson, J. O. (January, 2000). "From Birth On, Drugs Play Major Role in Children's Deaths." *The State*, p. A-19. Columbia, SC.

Harris, L. (1995). Metropolitan Life Survey of the American Teacher, 1993–1995: Violence in America's Public Schools. New York: author.

Hatfield, L. D. (1997). Anton LaVey, Church of Satan Founder. *San Francisco Examiner*, Nov. 7, B–3.

Haven, P. (1999). Teens Are Targeted in New State Laws. *USA Today*, June 28, p. 11A.

Helping Students Deal with Conflict and Anger (1999). Educational Research Service: Arlington, VA.

Hirischi, T. (1969). *Causes of Delinquency*. Berkeley: University of California Press.

Hirischi, T., & Hindelang, M. (1977). Intelligence and Delinquency: A Revisionist Review. *American Sociological Review*, 42, pp. 571–586.

Hodgkinson, H., (1990). *South Carolina: The State and its Educational System*. Columbia, SC: Institute for Educational Leadership, Center for Demographic Policy.

Holleman, J. (1999). School Psychologists Seek "Warning Signs" of Violence. *The State* (Columbia, SC), May 22.

Hotchkin, S. 2000. Violence Against Women Is Health Issue, Study Says. *The State* (Columbia, SC), Jan. 21, p. A–1.

Howell, W. (1999). Philadelphia's Adopt-a-School Partnership to Prevent Delinquency. *Corrections Today*, June, Vol. 3.

Hyman, L. A., & Lally, D. M. (1980. Corporal Punishment in American Education: A Historical and Contemporary Dilemma. In J. R. Cryan (Ed.), *Corporal Punishment in the Schools: Its Use Is Abuse*. New York: Harper & Row.

Ianni, F. A., & Ianni, E. (1999). What Can Schools Do About Violence? *Today's Education*. Washington, DC: National Education Association.

Illich, I. (1971). *De-schooling Society*. New York: Harper & Row.

Ingersoll, S., & LeBoeuf, D. (1997). *Reaching Out to Youth Out of the Education Mainstream*. Washington, DC: Office of Juvenile Justice and Delinquency Prevention.

Jeffery, C. R. *Crime Prevention Through Environmental Design*. Beverly Hills, CA: Sage Publications.

Johnsen, D. P. (1992). *Educational Law Enforcement: Community-oriented Policing in the Public Schools*. New York: Harper & Row.

Jones, C. (1999). ACLU Says Students' Rights Violated in Wake of Littleton. *USA Today*, May 21.

Jones, J. E., & Pfeiffer, J. W. (1975). Co-facilitating. *The 1974 Annual Handbook for Group Facilitators*. LaJolla, CA: University Associates Publishers.

Jones, V. M. (1999, Jan.). *Youth Crime Watch of America*. Washington, DC: Office of Juvenile Justice and Delinquency Prevention.

Kaestle, C. F. (1983). *Pillars of the Republic: Common School and American Society, 1780–1860*. New York: Hill and Wang.

Kaplan, H. B., Martin, S. S., & Johnson, R. J. (1986). Self-rejection and the Explanation of Deviance: Specification of the Structure of Latent Constructs. *American Journal of Sociology*, 92, pp. 384–411.

Keller, B. (1999). Blame Is Placed on Parents, Media. *USA Today*, April 22, p. 3A.

Kellogg, A. M. (1893). *School Management: A Practical Guide for the Teacher in the Schoolroom*. New York: E.L. Kellogg & Co.

Kelman, H. C. (1963). The Role of the Group in the Induction of Therapeutic Change. *International Journal of Group Psychotherapy*, 13, pp. 299–432.

Kennedy, D., Piehl, A., & Braga, A. (1996). "Youth Violence in Boston: Gun Markets, Serious Youth Offenders and a Use-Reduction Strategy." *Law and Contemporary Problems, 59*(1), pp. 147–196.

Kobetz, R., (1971). *The Police Role and Juvenile Delinquency*. Gaithersburg: International Association of Chiefs of Police.

Kracke, K. (1996). *YES: Youth Environmental Service Initiative*. Washington, DC: Office of Juvenile Justice and Delinquency Prevention.

Kratcoski, P. C. (2000). *Correctional Counseling and Treatment* (4th ed.). Prospect Heights, IL: Waveland Press.

Kuder, G. F. (1965). *Kuder General Interest Survey*. Chicago: Science Research Associates.

Lab, S. P., & Whitehead, J. T. (1990). *Juvenile Justice*, Cincinnati, OH: Anderson Publishing.

Lacayo, R. (1994). When Kids Go Bad, *Time Magazine*, Sept. 19.

Larson, B. (1989). *Satansim: The Seduction of America's Youth. Nashville*, TN: Thomas Nelson Publishers.

LaVey, A. (1969). *The Satanic Bible*. New York: Avon Books.

LaVey, A. (1972). *The Satanic Rituals*. New York: Avon Books.

LaVey, A. (1989). *The Satanic Witch*. Los Angeles: Feral House.

Lazerson, M. (Ed.). (1987). *American Education in the Twentieth Century: A Documentary History*. New York: Teachers College Press.

Leavitt, P. (December, 1999). "Teen Worries." *USA Today*, p. 17a.

Lemert, E. M. (1951). *Human Deviance, Social Problems and Social Control*. Englewood Cliffs, NJ: Prentice Hall.

Lester, W. (1999). Troubled Students Lack Easy Access to Adults and Psychologists, Not Nation. *The State* (Columbia, SC), July 6.

Leuner, H. (1969). Guided Affective Imagery (GAI): A Method of Intensive Psychotherapy. *American Journal of Psychotherapy*, 23, pp. 4–22.

L.H. Research (1993). A Survey of Experiences, Perceptions, and Apprehensions about Guns Among Young People in America. Cambridge, MA: Harvard University, School of Public Health.

Lingren, H. G. (1995). *Adolescence and Peer Pressure*. Lincoln: University of Nebraska.

Loeber, R., & Dishion, T. J. Early Predictors of Male Delinquency: A Review. *Psychological Bulletin*, 94(1), pp. 68–99.

Loeber, R., & Stouthamer-Loeber, M. (1986). Family Factors as Correlates and Predictors of Juvenile Conduct Problems and Delinquency. *Crime and Justice: An Annual Review of Research* (Vol. 7, pp. 29–149). Chicago: University of Chicago Press.

Lore, D. (1999). Can We Stop the Violence? *Atlanta Journal-Constitution*, June 13, pp. A1, A8.

Lund, N. L., & Salary, H. M. (1980). Measured Self-Concept in Adjudicated Juveniles. *Adolescence*, 25, pp. 65–74.

Majority Staff of the Senate Judiciary Committee. (1994, April). *Catalogue of Hope: Crime Prevention Programs for At-risk Children*. Washington, DC: Author.

Man Held in "Satanic" Deaths. (1997). *The State (Columbia*, SC), Dec. 30.

Matza, D. (1964). *Delinquency and Drift*. New York: John Wiley and Sons.

McTeer, J. E. (1976). *Fifty Years As a Lowcountry Witch Doctor*. Columbia, SC: R. L. Bryan.

Merton, R. (1938). Social Structure and Anomie. American. *Sociological Review*, 3, pp. 574–576.

Moles, O. (1987). *Trends in Student Misconduct: The 70's and 80's*. Washington, DC: National Institute of Justice.

Moore, J. (1991). Addressing a Hidden Problem, Kansas Youth Center Treats Sexually Abused Female Offenders. *Corrections Today*, 53(1).

Morrison, S. L. (1989). *The Modern Witches Spellbook*. New York: Carol Publishing Group.

Moskowitz, J., & Jones, R. (1988). Alcohol and Drug Problems in the Schools: Results of a National Survey of School Administrators. *Journal of Studies on Alcohol*, 49(4), pp. 299–305.

Natalucci-Persichetti, G. (1996). Youth Violence: A Learned Behavior (Ch. 8, p. 55), in *Juvenile Justice Programs and Trends*. Lanham, MD: American Correctional Association.

National Alliance Homepage. http://www.natall.com/what-is-na/nal.htm

National Center for Education Statistics. (1974). *Safe Schools Study*. Washington, DC: U.S. Department of Education.

National Center for Education Statistics. (1997). *Principal/School Disciplinarian Survey on School Violence*. Washington, DC: U.S. Department of Education.

National Association of School Psychologists Statistics. (1993). *Safe Schools Study*. Washington, DC: Author.

National Center for Education Statistics, 1991 Statistics, Washington, DC.

National Center for Education Statistics, 1994 Statistics, Washington, DC.

National Crime Victimization Survey. (1993). *National Crime Victim Survey for 1991* (NCJ-131545). Washington, DC: U.S. Government Printing Office.

National Institute of Justice. (1994). *D.A.R.E. Program: A Review of Prevalence, User Satisfaction, and Effectiveness*. Washington, DC: U.S. Department of Justice.

National Juvenile Justice Conference. (1999). *Alternatives to Incarceration*. Las Vegas, Nevada, August 15, 1999.

National School Safety Center (1999, May). School-Associated Violent Deaths Count. *School Safety Update*. Malibu, CA: Author.

National School Safety Center. (1992). *Working on a Game Plan for Safety (School Safety Update)*. Malibu, CA: Pepperdine University.

National School Safety Center. (1995). *School Bullying and Victimization*. Malibu, CA: Pepperdine University.

Neill, P. (1996, June). Mass Testing for "Delinquency" Gene. http://www.parascope.com/mx/genel.htm

New Jersey Juvenile Delinquency Commission. (1972). Programmed for Social Class: Tracking in High School. In K. Polk & W. Schafer (Eds.), *School and Delinquency* (p. 110). Englewood Cliffs, NJ: Prentice Hall.

Nilsen, A., & Donelson, K. (1993). *Literature for Today's Young Adults* (4th ed.). New York: HarperCollins College Publishers.

Norwood, G. (1999). *Maslow's Hierarchy of Needs*. http://www.connect.net/georgen/maslow.htm

Office of Juvenile Justice and Delinquency Prevention (1991a). *National Juvenile Custody Trends: 1978–1989*. Washington, DC: National Institute of Justice.

Office of Juvenile Justice and Delinquency Prevention. (1991b). *OJJDP Update on Statistics*. Washington, DC: U.S. Department of Justice.

Office of Juvenile Justice and Delinquency Prevention. (1994). *Gang Suppression and Intervention: Problem and Response. Research Summary*. Washington, DC: U.S. Department of Justice.

Office of Juvenile Justice and Delinquency Prevention. (1995). *Family Life, Delinquency, and Crime: A Policymaker's Guide*. Washington, DC: National Institute of Justice.

Office of Juvenile Justice and Delinquency Prevention. (1995). *Prevention Works*. Washington, DC: National Institute of Justice.

Office of Juvenile Justice and Delinquency Prevention. (1996). *State Responses to Serious and Violent Juvenile Crime*. Washington, DC: National Center for Juvenile Justice.

Office of Juvenile Justice and Delinquency Prevention. (1996, April). *Curfew: An Answer to Juvenile Delinquency and Victimization?* Washington, DC: National Institute of Justice.

Office of Juvenile Justice and Delinquency Prevention. (1996, June). *Juvenile Offenders and Victims: A National Report*. Washington, DC: U.S. Department of Justice.

Office of Juvenile Justice and Delinquency Prevention. (1998, Feb.). *OJJDP Fact Sheet*. Washington, DC: U.S. Department of Justice.

Office of Juvenile Justice and Delinquency Prevention. (1998, April). *Juvenile Justice Bulletin*. Washington, DC: U.S. Department of Justice.

Office of Juvenile Justice and Delinquency Prevention. (1998, May). *Serious and Violent Juvenile Offenders*. (Juvenile Justice Bulletin). Washington, DC: U.S. Department of Justice.

Office of Juvenile Justice and Delinquency Prevention. (1999). *Blueprint: A Violence Prevention Initiative* (OJJDP Fact Sheet 110). U.S. Department of Justice.

Office of National Drug Control Policy. (1998). *National Drug Control Strategy*. Washington, DC: U.S. Government Printing Office.

Officials Glossed Over Brawl at Youth Prison. (1999). *Arizona Star*, Jan 11, Metro/Region section.

Order of the Nefarious Mass. (1999). www.the600club.com/satanic-search

Order of the Nine Angels. (1999). www.the600club.com/satanic-search

Paganism Guide Page. www.uoguelph.ca/!bmyers/pagan/

Parent, D. (1993, April). *Conditions of Confinement: A Study to Evaluate Conditions in Juvenile Detention and Corrections Facilities*. Washington, DC: Office of Juvenile Justice and Delinquency Prevention.

Parker, L., & Kasindorf. M. (1999). Schools Taking Security to Heart. *USA Today*, May 21.

"Partnerships to Prevent Youth Violence." (August, 1994). Bureau of Justice Assistance: Washington, DC.

Pertman, A. (1996). Clinton Touts School Uniforms. *Boston Globe*, Feb. 25, p. 25.

Pope, C. (1995). Juvenile Justice in the Next Millennium. In J. Klofas & S. Stojkovic (Eds.), *Crime and Justice in the Year 2120* (pp. 100–120). New York: Wadsworth Publishing.

Problems at Juvenile Centers Said to Persist. (1999). *Richmond [Virginia] Times Dispatch*, Dec. 16.

Rafael, T., & Pion-Berlin, L. (1999, April). *Parents Anonymous Strengthening Families. Juvenile Justice Bulletin*. Washington, DC: Office of Juvenile Justice and Delinquency Prevention.

Rankin, J. (1997). The 90s—The Gothic Decade. *Dallas Morning News*, Oct. 12.

Ray, M. (1999). Gang Affiliation History. http://www.magforce.org/gp.htm

Reece, Mark L., & Moran, Hans S. (1997). "Goths" Say Culture Isn't to Blame for Death, *Deseret News*, April 6.

Regoli, R. M., & Hewitt, J. D. (1994, 1997). *Delinquency in Society: A Child-Centered Approach*. New York: McGraw Hill.

Religious Tolerance. (1999). *Satanism*. Religious Tolerance Web page, http://www.religious tolerance.org/satanism.htm

Richard, A. (March, 1999). "Hidden Dropouts—Schools Pattern Dropout Solutions to the Fabric of Their Communities." *The State*, p. A6, Columbia, SC.

Richardson, J. T., Best, J., & Bromley, D. G. (1991). *The Satanism Scare*. Los Angeles: Aldine De Gruyter Publications.

Riley, R. (1994). Celebrate Goals 1000! *Teaching K–8*, May 12.

Rosen, L. E. (1994). We Need a Positive Perspective and Leadership. *High School Magazine*, 2(1), pp. 24–26.

Rothman, D. J. (1971). *The Discovery of the Asylum*. Boston, Little, Brown.

Roy, J. C. (1999). When Depression Strikes Children, Parents, Teachers Play a Critical Role. *The State* (Columbia, SC), June l, p. D2.

Rubel, R. J. (1977). *The Unruly School*. Lexington, MA: D.C. Health and Co.

Sadler. W. (1988). Vandalism in Our Schools: A Study Concerning Children Who Destroy Property and What To Do About It. *Education*, 108(4), pp. 556–560.

Safe Schools Coalition. (1994). *School Intervention Report*, 7(4).

Satcher, D. (2000). Mental Health Gets Noticed. *Psychology Today*, 33(1), p. 32.

Schmitze, W. T. (1993). *Law Enforcement in California Public Schools by the Year 2002*. Sacramento: California Commission on Peace Officer Standards and Training.

Scolaro, J. A., (1998). Taking a Look Inside the Goth World. *Journal Times* (Racine, WI), Nov. 18.

Sefton, D. (1999). Teasing, Bullying Can Make Life Miserable for Some School Students. *The State* (Columbia, SC), May 6, p. A3.

Sernau, S. (1997). *Critical Choices, Applying Sociological Insight in Your Life, Family, and Community*. Los Angeles: Roxbury Publishing.

Sexon, P. (1961). *Education and Income*. New York: Viking Press.

Shaw, C. R., & McKay, H. (1969). *Juvenile Delinquency and Urban Areas*. Chicago: University of Chicago Press.

Sheely, J., & Wright, J. (1995). In the Line of Fire: Youth, Guns, and Violence in Urban America. New York: Aldine de Gruyter.

Sheley, J. F., McGee, Z. T., & Wright, J. D. (1995). Gun-related Violence In and Around Inner-City Schools. *American Journal of Diseases of Children*, 146(6), pp. 677–682.

Shepherd, R. E. (1998). *Doing Justice to Juvenile Justice*. http://www.ncjfcj.unr.edu/home-page/da.html

Shepherd, G. D., & Ragan, W. B., (1993). *Modern Elementary Curriculum* (7th Ed.). New York: Harcourt Brace Jovanovich.

Siegel, L. J. (1998). *Criminology: Theories, Patterns, and Typologies* (6th ed.). Belmont, CA: Wadsworth Publishing.

Siegel, L. J., & Senna, J. J. (1994). Youth Gangs: Continuity and Change. In Michael Tonry and Norval Morris (Eds.), *Crime and Justice* (Vol. 12). Chicago: University of Chicago Press, 1990, pp. 171–275.

Sivard, R. L. (1989). *World Military and Social Expenditures 1989*. Washington, DC: World Priorities.

Six Juveniles Placed in State's Custody After Riot. 1998. *Baton Rouge Advocate*, Sept. 23.

Slawson, J. (1926). *The Delinquent Boys*. Boston: Budget Press.

Snyder, H. (1993). *Arrests of Youth in 1991*. Washington, DC: Office of Juvenile Justice and Delinquency Prevention.

Snyder, H. (1999, April). Violent Juvenile Crime: The Number of Violent Juvenile Offenders Declines. *Corrections Today*, 61(2).

Snyder, J., & Patterson, G. (1987). *Family Interaction and Delinquent Behavior*. Washington, DC: Office of Juvenile Justice and Delinquency Prevention.

South Carolina Department of Alcohol and Other Drug Abuse Services. 1996–1997. *Annual Report*. Columbia, SC: Author.

South Carolina Department of Alcohol and Other Drug Abuse Services. (1999). *The Bridge Program—Successful Transitions for Adolescents*. Columbia: Author.

South Carolina Department of Alcohol and Other Drug Abuse Services. Annual Report 1996–1997 (1999). Columbia: Richland County Juvenile Drug Court.

South Carolina Department of Education. (1993, May). School Crime Incidents in S.C. Public Schools, June 1991 through May 1992. Columbia: Education Information Services Report Series.

Southeastern Regional Vision in Education (1993, March). *Reducing School Violence*. Atlanta, GA: Author.

Spaid, E. (1996) Flying Bullets Put School Up Against a Wall. *Christian Science Monitor*, Jan. 24, p. 1.

Spergel, I. A. (1995). *The Youth Gang Problem: A Community Approach*. New York: Oxford University Press.

Spring, J. (1989). *American Education: An Introduction to Social and Political Aspects*. New York: Longman.

Spring, J. (1994). The American School: 1642–1993 (3rd ed.). New York: McGraw-Hill.

State Responses to Serious and Violent Crime (1996). National Center for Juvenile Justice; Office of Juvenile Justice and Delinquency Prevention. Washington, DC.

Spring, J. (1994). *The American School: 1642–1993* (3d ed.). New York: McGraw-Hill.

Stephen, C. A., & Stephen, W. G. (1990). *Two Social Psychologies*. Belmont, CA: Wadsworth.

Stephens, G. (1997). *Saving the World's Most Precious Resource: Youth at Risk*. Bethesda, MD: Futurist.

Stephens, G. (1998). Saving the Nation's Most Precious Resources: Our Children, *USA Today*, May.

Stouffer, G. A. (1952). Behavior Problems of Children as Viewed by Teachers and Mental Hygienists, A Study of Present Attitudes as Compared with Those Reported by E.K. Wickman. *Mental Hygiene*, 36, pp. 271–285.

Student Nazis. (1999). *Gamecock (University of South Carolina)*, 91(70), April 7.

Subcommittee to Investigate Juvenile Delinquency. (1977). *Challenge for the Third Century: Education in a Safe Environment—Final Report on the Nature and Prevention of School Violence and Vandalism*. Washington, DC: U.S. Government Printing Office.

Summer Jobs Give Youths More Than Pay. (1998). *The State* (Columbia, SC), Aug. 18, p. A8.

Taba, H. (1962). *Curriculum Development: Theory and Practice*. New York: Harcourt, Brace & World.

Teachers, ETV Offer School Safety Programs. (2000). *The State* (Columbia, SC), Jan. 21, p. B-3.

Teague, M. (1999). The Aryan Nations Homepage, http://:www.nidlink.com/ aryanvic/ youthcorps.html

Teen Inmates in Custody After Standoff. (1998). *The Columbian*, July 16, Clark County/Region section.

Teen Worries. (1999). *USA Today*, Dec. 7, p. 17a.

Temple of Set. (1999). www.the600club.com/satanic-search.

The Monsters Next Door, A Special Report on the Colorado School Massacre. (1999). *Time Magazine*, 153(17), May 3.

They're Turning in Their Guns. (1998). *Parade Magazine*, May 3, p. 10.

This Fabulous Century, 1920–1930. (1988). New York: Time-Life Books.

This Fabulous Century, 1940–1950. (1988). New York: Time-Life Books.

This Fabulous Century, 1950–1960. (1988). New York: Time-Life Books.

This Fabulous Century, 1960–1970. (1988). New York: Time-Life Books.

Thomas, K., & Weise, E. (1999). Hate Groups Share Youths with Web Games. *USA Today*, July 8, p. D1.

Thornberry, T. P., Krohn, M. D., Lizotte, A. J., & Wierschem, D. D. (1993). The Role of Juvenile Gangs in Facilitating Delinquent Behavior. *Journal of Research in Crime and Delinquency*, 30, pp. 55–87.

Thrasher, F. (1936). *The Gang*. Chicago: University of Chicago Press.

Torbet, P., & Szymanski, L. (1998). *State Legislative Responses to Violent Juvenile Crime. 1997–1997 Update* (Juvenile Justice Bulletin). Washington, DC: Office of Juvenile Justice and Delinquency Prevention.

Toufexis, A. (1992). When Kids Kill Abusive Parents. *Time Magazine*, Nov. 23.

Trump, K. S. (1993). Effective School-Safety and Security Programs. *Updating School Board Policies*, 24(4), pp. 11–13.

Tursman, C. (1989). Safeguarding Schools Against Gang Warfare. *School Administrator*, 46(5), pp. 8–15.

Two Teens Stab Dad, Cops Report Satanic Ties Seen in Lakewood Attack. (1998). *Denver Post*, Aug. 15.

U.S. Department of the Army. (1978). *Religious Requirements and Practices of Certain Selected Groups*. Washington, DC: Author.

U.S. Department of Education. (1998, Aug.). *Early Warning Timely Response: A Guide to Safe Schools*. Washington, DC: U. S. Government Printing Office.

U.S. Department of Health, Education and Welfare. (1997). *Violent Schools, Safe Schools*. Washington, DC: U.S. Government Printing Office.

U.S. Department of Justice. (1998). *Guideline for Drug Courts on Screening and Assessment*. Washington, DC: U.S. Government Printing Office.

U.S. Department of Justice (1998, June). *Juvenile and Family Drug Courts: An Overview*. Washington, DC: U.S. Government Printing Office.

U.S. House of Representatives. (1975). *Safety and Violence in Elementary and Secondary Schools*. Washington, DC: U.S. Government Printing Office. (Hearings Before a Subcommittee of the House Committee on Elementary, Secondary, and Vocational Education).

U.S. Prison Population Has Doubled in 12 Years. (1999). *The State* (Columbia, SC), March 15.

Vampire Exchange Network (1999). http://www.vampexchange.com

Viadero, D. (1999). Class-Size Study Finds Long-term Benefits. *Education Week*, 17(34), May 5, p. 5.

Violence in Schools. *U.S. News & World Report*, Nov. 8, pp. 31–35.

Vold, G. B. (1968). *Theoretical Criminology*. New York: Harcourt, Brace and World.

Walters, G., & White, T. (1989). Heredity and Crime: Bad Genes or Bad Research? *Criminology*, 27(3), pp. 455–485.

Weapon-Carrying Among High School Students: United States. (1991). *Morbidity and Mortality Weekly Report*, 40, pp. 681–684.

Wedge. T. W., & Powers, R. L. (1988). *The Satan Hunter*. Canton, OH: Daring Books.

Weil, J. L. (1992). Early Deprivation of Empathic Care (Ch. 8, pp. 152–155). Madison, CT: International Universities Press.

Werewolf Order. (1999). www.the600club.com/satanic-search

What Can the Schools Do? (1999). *Time Magazine*, May 3, p. 38.

What Is a Gang? Are Gothics a Gang? http://www.Gothics.org/subculture/gang-definition.html

White Order of Thule. (1999). www.the600club.com/satanic-search

Williams, J. W. (1992, July). Understanding How Youth Gangs Operate. *Corrections Today*, 54(5).

Wilson, J. Q., & Hernstein, R. (1985). *Crime and Human Nature*. New York: Simon & Schuster.

Wilson, J. Q. & Kelling, G. L. (1989). Making Neighborhoods Safe. *The Atlantic Monthly*, 263(2), pp. 46–52.

Winik, Lyric Wallwork. (2000). He Has a Better Way. *Parade Magazine*, Jan. 16.

Wooden, W. S. (1995). *Renegade Kids, Suburban Outlaws*. New York: Wadsworth Publishing.

Woodham Testifies He Was Involved in Satanism. (1998). *USA Today*, June 11.

Young Inmates Riot, Hold Guards Hostage. (1999). *Cincinnati Enquirer*, Feb. 24.

INDEX